Ireland and Early Europe

*Essays and Occasional Writings
on Art and Culture*

Liam de Paor

FOUR COURTS PRESS

Set in 10.5 on 12 point Ehrhardt
by Carrigboy Typesetting Services for
FOUR COURTS PRESS
55 Prussia Street, Dublin 7
e-mail: fcp@indigo.ie
and in North America for
FOUR COURTS PRESS
c/o ISBS, 5804 N.E. Hassalo Street, Portland, OR 97213.

A catalogue record for this title
is available from the British Library.

ISBN 1-85182-297-6 hbk
1-85182-298-4 pbk

This book is printed on an acid-free paper.

Printed in Ireland
by ColourBooks Ltd.

Contents

For Deirdre

Preface

Most of the pieces printed here have been published before, although there are some exceptions. Some of the shorter essays appeared in the 'Roots' column which I wrote for the *Irish Times* between 1970 and 1977, and a few slightly longer pieces appeared later in *Irish Times* series. It was Dónal Foley who (in 1970) first had me write for the paper, where I dealt also with Brian Fallon and the then editor Douglas Gageby. Later, Conor Brady encouraged me to continue the connection. Of all of them I have the fondest recollection: the *Irish Times* has been for me a paper of friendship.

The longer items included here consist mostly of lectures delivered on various occasions and of a few academic papers. In reprinting these I have, for the present purpose, omitted footnotes and endnotes, trying however, in re-editing some of the texts, to build in sufficient information so that the reader can readily go to the sources.

There is a common theme in this selection. It is the theme that has commanded my attention and my interest for many years of study of the past: acculturation; the impact of cultures one upon another. Ireland, the centre from which by force of birth and circumstance I must look out to the wider world, is an island; islands, however, are not necessarily 'insular' or 'isolationist.' For most of history the seas were highways, facilitating intercourse, not cutting it off. The topics touched on here mostly – but not quite all – concern Ireland's dealings with the outside world; and the outside world, in the period covered (up to the late Middle Ages) was chiefly Europe: the islands of Great Britain, the Continental main, and the farflung world of the Vikings.

For purposes of this collection, of writings from the past thirty and more years, minor editing was necessary, so that they might conform to a common style of spelling, punctuation, and similar conventions of presentation. On the whole, however, the essays have been left as they were written. A very few topical references, virtually meaningless now, have been omitted, and in one instance a brief revision has been appended (to a lecture on the Book of Durrow), which is however clearly distinguished from the original text.

A great deal of work has been done on the study of early Ireland in the past thirty years, the period in which most of these pieces were written. Our understanding of that history has been both enlarged and changed. In the middle years of this century, largely in reaction against nationalistic or ethnicist fantasies about the past, we were diffident about the work of our ancestors of more than a thousand years before our time, and slow to realise how remarkable was their achievement. The crowding in of new evidence has shown us an ancient society much more sophisticated, much more in mastery of its world, than we had ventured to imagine. My occasional writings of two or three decades ago partake more of the diffidence than of the new knowledge; but they are a testimony of their own time and a record of sorts of one pilgrim's quest for understanding of what went before us.

Michael Adams, the publisher of this book, encouraged me to publish the collection. Deirdre Glenn gave much editorial and other help in putting it together.

An Intimate History

Europeans and Asians inhabit the same landmass, and between them there extends no unduly formidable barrier, so that throughout history communications have been open. Indeed, linguists have long made us familiar with the term 'Indo-European', which has broader cultural and protohistorical as well as linguistic meaning. The late Professor Myles Dillon liked to search out instances of the well-known phenomenon of 'peripheral survival' by finding, in details of the society portrayed in ancient Sanskrit religious literature, matches for culture-traits manifest in the earliest Irish literature. Even today, counting up to ten in Nepali sounds quite like a Cumberland shepherd reckoning his sheep. It is important, I think, if we are surveying great stretches of time, to be aware of certain underlying strata which have survived the accumulations and the erosions of history.

But in the landmass inhabited by Europeans and Asians, the populous areas lie at the extremes, and between the two ends of the great Eurasian continent there are differences rooted deep in historical consciousness.

The European end of the landmass is by far the smaller, and its present-day physical shape is extremely complex. This is one of the keys to its historical character. It may be regarded as a peninsula of Eurasia, one which is itself made up of smaller peninsulas, archipelagos and inland seas. In its broad physical character, it may be divided into three zones, north to south. In the north, there is a zone of islands, enclosed seas and mountainous peninsulas. The centre has a broad corridor of plains and lowlands, watered by great rivers and communicating with the vaster spaces of Asia. In the south, there is again a complexity of mountainous peninsulas, inland seas and islands.

The divides between these are not unduly formidable. All have been crossed and re-crossed by many millions of people throughout history. Nevertheless they remain, and they assert themselves. Some of them take the form of gentle

---

This essay was read as the opening paper at a seminar arranged in Trinity College, Dublin, in September 1988 by the combined inspectorates of the Department of Education, Dublin, the Department of Education, Northern Ireland, and the Department of Education and Science, London, on *The Place of the Irish in British and European History*. The proceedings were published under that title in 1990. The paper has been edited and slightly modified for printing here.

gradients, so that, as one travels eastward across Europe, for example, cultural and landscape changes are gradual. But the change to the south, to the *midi*, often comes suddenly. Characteristically, the traveller enters a tunnel and emerges at the other end into a new world, a landscape of shallow-pitched pantile roofs, olive groves, and the sun. It corresponds, very roughly, to an old stadium in the moving divide between the two different kinds of culture that have principally formed Europe.

One of these has long impressed its values on our education and our minds and has traced the very history of Europe itself through the diffusion of its values from the Mediterranean northward and westward. The line of descent, by this genealogy, was from Greece and Rome to modern Europe, with the intervening Christian centuries from the fall of Rome to the revival of learning providing a somewhat dubious 'Middle Age'. The 'Dark Ages' and the 'Gothic' period – as they were pejoratively called – represent an interlude in which there was too much of the barbarian, non-Mediterranean, tradition for the taste of either the Renaissance or the Enlightenment. These, to simplify their view, saw modern Europe as the culture achieved by reviving that of the ancient Mediterranean.

There is more to modern Europe than that. In its barbarian as in its urbanely civilized areas ancient Europe provided the foundations on which modern Europe – together with a good part of the modern Americas – was built.

A generation ago, we were still being taught, in European prehistory, '*Ex oriente lux*'. The light diffused westward, from the Near East, Egypt and the Aegean. Like the rays of the midwinter sunrise creeping along the passage at Newgrange to illumine the carvings of the end-chamber, it gradually traversed Europe, to reach ultimately what Donatus of Fiesole described in his ninth-century poem: '*Finibus occiduis*' – the western edge of the world, Ireland.

In the course of the past thirty or forty years, however, as the details of what was happening in the various parts of Europe before the Roman conquest have been filled in, a revolutionary change has occurred. Radiocarbon and other scientifically objective dating methods have forced a radical review of our presuppositions about the processes of civilization. A great many of the developments previously thought of as part of these processes are now known to have happened *earlier* in the more westerly and northerly parts than in the Mediterranean and eastern regions. Newgrange, for example, used to be thought of as an Early Bronze Age monument, remarkable indeed, but a crude barbaric version of chambered tombs in the East Mediterranean. Now it is known to be at least as old as, and probably older than, the Great Pyramid. The work of Lord Renfrew, Barry Cunliffe and many other archaeologists has forced the most drastic reassessment of the relationship between the regions of Europe in antiquity. We have been shaken out of several prejudices which we were not aware of as prejudices but took as data. For example, the very notion of cultural diffusion has had to be seriously questioned, and we must now, it seems, accept the idea of separate inventions of different kinds of civilizations; of independent developments of agriculture in different parts of the world (the so-called 'Neolithic revolution' or 'agricultural revolution' was not a single but a multiple event). A kind of pluralism has been introduced into the study of pre-history and old models have had to be discarded in favour of new.

For, in the study of history and prehistory, we employ thought-models, and the model we use governs our interpretation of what we observe.

Let us take a look at Western Europe as it was, say about the year 100 BC An indentifiable and reasonably coherent polity dominated that extensive part of Europe that was watered by the Thames, the Rhine, the upper Danube, the Po, the Rhône, the Minho, the Loire and the Seine. Celtic Europe, in its expansion, very roughly approximated to the extent of the European Community lands in the 1970s.

In 100 BC, what Lord Salisbury was to refer to disparagingly as 'the Celtic Fringe' was probably a 'pre-Celtic fringe', a survival area for older cultural patterns, a reservoir of what was then antiquity, of the remnants of the civilizations that had produced the great chambered megalithic tombs with their mysterious art, the highly sophisticated work in gold and other metals of the Bronze Age, the complexes of open-air temples in the form of henges, alignments and stone circles (including Stonehenge) that were also largely works of the Late Neolithic and Bronze ages. But by the time Claudius and his legions invaded Britain, that island was largely if not wholly Celtic in its language and dominant institutions (there is some uncertainty about the northern Picts), and Ireland, to judge from place-names, was dominated, at least, by a Celtic language.

At this point we may begin to look at Europe from the standpoint of Britain and Ireland. These form one of the major archipelagos of Europe's northern zone, with one of the enclosed seas: the Irish Sea has been described by geographers as 'the inland sea of Britain', a description slightly lacking in political tact, perhaps, but an attempt to define an important fact about these islands. Two axes mark the spatial relations of the islands, and each has played a significant part in their history. The north-east/south-west Caledonian system shows its strike clearly on the map in the line of the Great Glen in Scotland, which is taken up on the east in the fjords and mountains of western Norway, and on the west is continued, to fade into the ocean in the fjord known as Killary Harbour in Connemara. This axis corresponds to the corridor of the Atlantic seaway, by which peoples have moved freely throughout history, a corridor that provided rapid communication between Europe's three zones: Norway, Scotland and the Isles; Ireland, Brittany, northern Spain and Portugal; North Africa and the entrance to the Mediterranean. This is the corridor along which the Western Neolithic peoples moved – including some of the megalith builders – and along which came at least some of the bearers of Celtic speech and, later, the Vikings.

The other axis is marked or defined by the Armorican folds, which run east-west, from the Harz mountains in Germany through southern Britain, to end

in the long fingers of the Kerry and Cork peninsulas with the fjord-like bays
between them. It is, as it were, a marker of the connection formed by the North
European Plain, Europe's centre zone, the zone of land communication, with
only the interruption of the Straits of Dover, from Poland through Germany,
the Low Countries and Northern France, into south-eastern England. Following
Mackinder, Sir Cyril Fox long ago expounded the significance of this corridor
in his book, *The Personality of Britain*. This 'Lowland Zone', in its extension
into Britain, marked the 'area of easy settlement', open to new peoples, cultures
and ideas. It contrasted with the 'Highland Zone' of western and northern
Britain, the 'area of difficult settlement', the refuge of older peoples, cultures
and ideas.

If we look at this Highland Zone, which corresponds roughly to the 'Celtic
Fringe', we find that both in prehistory and in history it has been an area of
some common experience. I would agree with Professor Woodman that, in
genetic terms, the basic Irish stock was probably formed as far back as the
end of Mesolithic times; that, although of course many significant additions
have been made to it down the millenia with the arrival of various groups of
new settlers, there was probably a sufficient population in Ireland by the beginning of Neolithic times to absorb the comparatively small increments involved in later settlements; and that, by the end of the Neolithic period, there
was a sizeable population in the island. But to refer to the late-Mesolithic
population-groups as 'the Irish' is to beg too many questions. For one thing,
they were almost certainly much the same as the people who were in northern
and western Britain at the time. It is possible, indeed likely, that even as early
as then there was a good deal of intercourse between the two islands – certainly among the small islands of the archipelago which links, and always has
linked, Ireland and Scotland at the head of the North Channel.

If we move on to Neolithic times, say from about 4000 BC onwards for
roughly two thousand years, we find what appears to be a drift of settlers into
both Britain and Ireland, and a slow process of acculturation and accommodation with the earlier Mesolithic inhabitants. There is some evidence to
suggest that both of our salient axes were involved in the Neolithic movements: settlement from the North European Plain, mainly affecting, therefore,
Lowland Britain (chiefly eastern and southern England), and settlement coming by the Atlantic seaway, mainly from the direction of Iberia and France,
which chiefly affected Ireland and the Highland Zone of Britain. In material
culture there are close similarities betwen the Western Neolithic of Ireland and
that of western and northern Britain. Again there is no reason to believe that
there were significant differences between the peoples on the two sides of the
Irish Sea. In particular, we can observe what was virtually the same culture
extending across the northern half of Ireland into Scotland.

Bronze Age distribution patterns are more complicated. The clusterings of
Early Bronze Age stone circles, for example, which are persuasively interpreted as tribal assembly centres, are quite discontinuous; but they occur in

Ireland, western Britain and Brittany, with similar artefacts, suggesting the settlement or formation of culturally very similar tribal groups, again in various parts of Ireland and the Highland Zone. In the Late Bronze Age, Ireland is still dominated by the Atlantic, or north-east/south-west axis, with connections extending to Scandinavia and Iberia. These developments occurred in centuries when there were in the Highland Zone centres of the advanced technology of the age; and we have also abundant evidence of long-distance trade, with some Irish products probably going as far as the Aegean.

The 'political geography', so to speak, of the Bronze Age, is not the political geography of today: when we speak of the 'British Bronze Age' or the 'Irish Bronze Age' or the 'French Bronze Age' we are imposing modern categories somewhat arbitrarily on the past. Such observer-imposed categories can be the bane even of the study of documented periods. There is a good deal of evidence, over very long prehistoric periods, of community, at least in the sense of common culture, between groups in all parts of Ireland and in many parts of western and northern Britain. The community extends much less perfectly – sometimes not at all – into south-eastern Britain. By later prehistoric times – by the Early Iron Age – a discontinuity, or at least a gradient, is established, with the line of division running diagonally across Britain, roughly from the Severn mouth to the Humber mouth. That line is probably as significant today as it was in 100 BC.

Even for the Neolithic and Bronze Ages, the uniformities in Ireland and western Britain have been oversimplified in this sketchy argument. The Early Iron Age, which remains a more obscure period, shows much greater discontinuities, within Ireland as within Britain. There was for a while a brilliant La Tène art style whose centre was the Irish Sea, but its products were confined to limited areas on either side of the Channel.

This is a time when technical advances in agricultural equipment, notably ploughs, were making lowland areas much more productive than they had been. People were moving down into the previously impenetrable valleys. From now on the Lowland Zone becomes steadily more productive than the Highland Zone. Early metallurgy as a source of wealth and trade gives way to agriculture. Ireland appears to regress for some centuries, economically and culturally (between roughly 200 BC and AD 200). Lowland Britain is steadily penetrated by new influences from the central European zone. This is intensified not long before Caesar's two raids on the island, with new, more sophisticated, warfare methods (marked by the creation of multivallate hill-forts in the south, designed for defence against missiles) and extensive Belgic settlement in southern Britain. There was probably warfare of one kind of Celt against another kind of Celt.

The slowly accumulating evidence about the Roman occupation of Britain from the mid-first century AD to the early fifth shows that it was never wholly successful. There was hardly a decade when the country was quite stable, and, although the initial thrust of conquest brought the Romans to the far north to defeat the chariot-driving Caledonians, or Picts; although they held the waist of Scotland from the Clyde to the Forth for a while and marked it with the Antonine Wall, and established a semi-Romanized area south of that wall, yet they soon fell back to the defended frontier established by Hadrian, running approximately along the present English-Scottish border. They reconnoitred Ireland but didn't attempt an invasion; and Ireland thereafter became a much more distinct entity, its island integrity however being compromised at the north-east: the North Channel, as always, was a connection rather than a divide, and relations with Pictland were close and intimate.

Ireland traded with the Roman Empire, probably mainly with Roman Britain, although there was a wine importation from Gaul and further afield. But Roman artefacts found in Ireland indicate a much less intensive export business than was conducted into Germany beyond the frontiers – a business which sustained whole industries on the Rhine and Danube. Ireland, in other words, appears to have been more isolated in Iron Age and early Imperial Roman times than it was for much of earlier prehistory. And in this, as in other periods of comparative isolation or withdrawal, we see signs of cultural impoverishment and decline.

New stimulus came with the change in the Roman situation that followed the restoration of order after the great Germanic raids of the mid-third century. Before these, as Alföldi showed in his *Spät-Römische Kunstindustrie* for the Danube, and Paule Spitaels, Siegfried de Laet and others for the Rhine, much of the production of the barbarians was carried out by Romanized Celts, carrying on, in a very modified form, La Tène traditions in craftsmanship. In the later Empire, however, the frontier production was largely in the hands of Germanic settlers inside the *limes*. But we find a sudden adoption of Roman forms of dress, dress-fastening and other products in the west, in Ireland and in the British Highland Zone. This coincides, roughly, with the beginning of the profitable raiding of the Roman provinces by the Irish, Picts and others, which created both the economy of an heroic age and a militarized aristocratic barbarian society. Similarly, an heroic age and a militarized society were created among the Germans beyond the frontiers.

Roman Britain succumbed to its own internal instability, and to the pressures and assaults from the Irish in the west, the Picts in the north, and the Angles, Saxons and other Germans in the east. Britain remained British as the Roman legions departed; that is to say, Celtic, or Romano-Celtic. The Britons had not been as fully assimilated as the Gauls; their primary language was not Latin but British, from which Welsh, Cornish and Breton were to be derived. At this stage the British and Irish languages may have been close enough to be mutually comprehensible. The Irish established settlements along the coasts of western Britain, in Wales, the Isle of Man and Scotland. Of these, the permanent lodgment was that made in Scotland, which established the Irish language there. The kingdom of Dál Riada continued to expand, and ultimately was to be united with the Pictish kingdom under a single ruler. A Gaelic cultural unity – at the level of literature and learning at least – was established, which was to last until the early modern period. The Britons appear to have summoned German aid from across the North Sea in their efforts to resist the attacks on them from north and west; but the Germans after a period decided to settle in Britain on their own behalf, and a long period of bitter warfare ensued in which the Germans – the Anglo-Saxons – were first checked along a line confining their settlements to parts of the east and south; then they pushed forward again, ultimately reducing the northern British kingdoms and forcing the southern British more or less to the line of the present Welsh border. The Irish, meantime, were reduced by the British in west Wales. By the eighth century, the Highland-Lowland division in Britain had asserted itself again, and the south-east of Britain was now occupied by Germans, naturalized as 'the English'. This settlement was an expropriation which caused great displacement of people and led to an intense bitterness of feeling between English and British. The thoroughness of the displacement can be seen in the virtual disappearance of Celtic place-names from south-eastern England. The bitterness probably contributed to the new community, or at least sense of common understanding, established between the Highland Zone and Ireland.

This was most clearly shown in the distinctive character of what has often been termed (understandably but misleadingly) the 'Celtic Church', which developed a common ecclesiastical culture in Ireland, Scotland, Wales and Brittany (Brittany had been settled by a large-scale British migration from south-western England in the fifth century). The British, however, appear to have made little if any attempt to convert the pagan English. This was left to the Irish and to missions from Rome. The Irish and Roman missions came into conflict in the seventh century, and the Irish withdrew from England, leaving a reinforced division between the Celtic-speaking and the Germanic-speaking nations. But the period of close ecclesiastical intercourse was highly fruitful, and there is no doubt that the intimate connections then formed with Picts, Britons and English contributed great stimulus to Ireland's brilliant 'Golden Age' of its early Christian period.

Important historical developments were occurring in Ireland round about AD 700. The distinctive monastic organization of the church was being fully developed, and monastic 'cities' were already in being. A vernacular literature was established. The process of state formation – with the collaboration of the Church – was in train. A most self-confident high culture was being created, and in great metropolitan centres like Iona, in touch with developments in the Byzantine Empire as well as those in its own family of monasteries in Ireland, England and Scotland, history, art and literature were being cultivated. Irish monks on the Continent were setting an example of learning and of integrity, which, down to the present day, has been remembered in France, Belgium, Germany, Italy, Switzerland and Austria. They also set an example of stubborn independence of mind, which was not always agreeable either to the rulers or to some of the ecclesiastics with whom they came in contact. But

this was one of the periods when the Irish (as we may now, without any com-
punction, call them) were functioning on the east-west axis and making their
mark in Central Europe. They were also active on the western seaway – their
monastic system functioned largely through water-borne communications systems – and we have clear evidence of trade and other contacts with the eastern
Mediterranean, probably by way of southern France. Irish hermits were establishing their cells on the islands of the ocean, and were settled in Iceland before
the first Vikings arrived there.

The Vikings who appeared in Ireland a century later, initially as raiders and
explorers, were to have a great impact on the island's external relations. Having
failed in the ninth century to obtain large tracts of Irish land for settlement
on the lines of the Scandinavian settlements in France and England, in the early
tenth century they established trading towns, including Dublin, Waterford,
Limerick, Cork and Wexford. Dublin, the most important, became a way-
station on the long sea-route between Scandinavia and North Africa. It also
conducted a considerable trade with England. The staples of long-distance
Viking trade, to oversimplify a complex matter, were slaves from Europe and
silver from North Africa and Spain. The cross-Channel trade was to some
extent in those commodities: Bristol shipped Anglo-Saxon slaves to Ireland,
most of them probably being transhipped southward. The Scandinavian towns
in Ireland also developed close relations with the hinterland, including trade
relations, and became themselves, to an extent, manufacturing centres for the
hinterland's supply. In the much-studied history of the regrowth of towns in
Europe from the eleventh century onward, the early importance of Dublin
and Waterford has now become clear. For Ireland, the significance of these
developments was twofold: the political centre of gravity was shifted to the east
coast and to the new urban and trading society; and south-eastern Ireland
entered into new and closer relations with the outside world, but especially
with Britain. The Norman Conquest of England had considerable repercussions
throughout the Highland Zone, and Irish rulers took an active interest in the
Norman penetration of Wales. The fleets of Irish Viking towns were active in
the affairs of western Britain throughout the twelfth century, and Diarmaid
MacMurrough's bringing in of Norman allies to his Irish quarrels was well
prepared for. We find, with the Viking and Norman developments – apart from
their other internal effects on Ireland – that there was a re-orientation of the
south-eastern half of the island towards the outside world, while the north-
western half looked more inward and backward to the past.

The division was intensified after the climatic optimum of the thirteenth
century, when Norman settlement in Ireland approached its limit. With climatic
deterioration added to other causes of settlement failure in the fourteenth and
fifteenth centuries, further fissures manifested themselves.

Religious division is important throughout Irish history. The traditions of
the early Irish Church by no means died away with the reforms of the eleventh
and twelfth centuries, and, although there was notionally one church in Ireland

in the Middle Ages, there were in everyday practice two churches, or, as Jack Watt put it in the title of his book a number of years ago, *The Two Nations in the Medieval Irish Church.* The English colony in Ireland didn't take kindly to Irish ecclesiastical ways, and this complicated further what had already become a very complicated Anglo-Irish relationship in the Irish lordship that had been established by Henry II.

The conquest of Ireland, carried out under the Tudors, was a part of the process of early-modern state-formation, involving the subduing and suppression of more or less autonomous feudal and semi-feudal lords, and the extension of central authority through the lands subject to the monarch. It was a process which affected more than Ireland, involving as it did a modernizing conquest of the Highland Zone from the wealthier and more powerful Lowland Zone. As part of the process of establishing his own independent empire in his realms, Henry VIII declared ecclesiastical independence from Rome, and assumed the title 'King of Ireland' in place of that of 'Lord of Ireland'. This change was to lead to other major changes. His action caused no great immediate problem in Ireland, but the confusion and instability which soon set in, to last for more than a century in English affairs, had extremely destabilizing effects on the country. The rapid changes in religious policy after Henry spread alarm and unease among the (Catholic) English colony. After the abrupt reversals of the reigns of Edward VI and Mary Tudor, in the long reign of Elizabeth England leaned towards the Reformation, but in a somewhat compromising way, while most of Scotland, but particularly the Lowlands, embraced the Reformation wholly.

The religious conflicts that ensued were to affect the whole future course of Irish history. Among the immediate effects was a considerable re-orientation – politically at least – of most of Ireland towards the Catholic powers of Europe. At the very moment when the Tudor conquest was being completed, the expanding British nation-state (a multi-ethnic state) was crucially divided. And the old Irish-Scottish community was compromised. The common difference between Ireland and the British Highland Zone, on the one hand, and the Lowland Zone, on the other, remained; but there was now an invidious division between Ireland and the Highland Zone. Ireland, that is, Gaelic Ireland, was now aligned, in general sympathy and sometimes in politics, with the Catholic powers. Into the calculation of these powers – mainly Spain, and, later, France – Ireland on the whole only entered marginally. But the new alignment gave a firm basis to what was to be England's chief interest in the neighbouring island for the next several centuries – a strategic interest. The impact on Europe was to be, in due course, not inconsiderable. The number of Irish who served the French King as Jacobite soldiers in the course of the eighteenth century – that alone was very large.

Within the early modern period the great Irish migrations began. Initially very large numbers travelled to the Continent. But already by the seventeenth century numerous Irish were travelling across the Atlantic, many of them

involuntarily. By the eighteenth century they were already moving in some
numbers into Britain.

Although Ireland in theory was integrated into the United Kingdom in
1801, it remained distinct, and was seen as distinct in Europe and around
the world. This must be because, as to the great majority of the people of the
island, it was Roman Catholic. Surely this is the chief reason that Ireland, unlike Scotland or Wales, didn't settle down to be a member of the expanded
British nation-state. It was the glaring exception in an English-speaking world
whose ethos was (and still is, to an extent) Protestant. One of the unexpected
experiences for someone brought up as an Irish Catholic, on a first visit to the
Continent, is to find that in an imperial and metropolitan power like France, a
large part of one's ethos is not marginal but central. Ireland, to Catholic (even
if secularized) Western Europe, is the friend within the white Anglo-Saxon
Protestant-thinking camp.

This is tremendously reinforced by the extraordinarily out-of-proportion
contribution Irish writers have made to modern literature in English – partly
because many of these writers are or were themselves of Protestant background.
In recent times it is in cultural matters that the Irish have played by far their
biggest part.

This brings us back to the questions of marginality and centrality implicit
in the geography discussed here at the beginning. That geography asserts itself
in spite of changes in the technology of travel and communcations. By the
Armorican reckoning we are on the margin of things, beyond the last headlands of the European main. By the Caledonian reckoning, we are in the middle
of things, half way between New York and Moscow, half way between Oslo
and Seville. And from this centre people have always gone out: it is an island
after all, and its inhabitants have been peregrines throughout most of history.
Ireland's impact on the political and social history of Britain and America in
modern times has been considerable; its impact on the political and social history of Continental Europe slight. But the people who have gone out from
here include many who have played a substantial part in that other history,
the history of high culture, of thought, expression and art.

2

Cultural Relations

In periods of isolation, Irish culture has stagnated; in periods of fairly active intercourse with the outside world it has often been stimulated. The stimulus, by a seeming paradox, has not been merely to imitation, but, quite rapidly, to originality. Originality comes not from consciously attempting to be different but rather from persistent efforts to improve on foreign models and adapt them to the needs, tastes and resources of the country.

Many examples of this are provided by the art of the so-called 'Golden Age' of the seventh and eighth centuries AD. This was a time when a vast amount of what was originally foreign was fully assimilated. Christianity had come, already moulded by its development over the first few centuries within the rigid and elaborate forms of Roman Imperial civilization and administration. Its structures and hierarchies were Roman; its thought, language and outlook, in the West, were Roman, with an extensive Greek background. All this could not be absorbed immediately. There is evidence to suggest that for quite some time the Christian communities in Ireland were distinct from their pagan neighbours not only in faith but in many other attributes of culture. By the seventh century, however, the process of adaptation was well advanced: the Irish language had received the respectability of a written form (and writing a vernacular was already an innovation in itself); members of leading Irish families had begun to enter and patronize the Church; and the steady supplementing of an episcopal by a monastic organization marked the progressive Gaelicization of the Roman import.

Similarly, secular influences from the Roman world had been absorbed, perhaps from an even earlier date. The agricultural methods, dress, personal ornaments and, to some extent, the political structures of the Roman world had been imitated and adapted. Copies of the works of Roman writers (Virgil, Horace and others) had begun to circulate in Ireland. There was some knowledge of the principles of Roman law, some dim acknowledgment of the special position of the Roman emperors as 'Kings of the World'.

To these were added in the seventh century the influence, very significant in art, of the Germanic peoples, whose wanderings, in war-bands and migrations

This appeared in the 'Roots' column in the *Irish Times*, 30 November 1976.

made up of alliances of tribes and petty nations, had brought them so far west as to be neighbours of the Irish in Britain and Gaul. In particular the Anglo-Saxon immigration into Great Britain had brought Irish artists and craftsmen into contact with a new world of imagination and technique. The pilgrimage or mission of Irish monks overseas made the contacts close and significant; for both the Anglo-Saxons and the Franks were pagans when they arrived in the West, unlike the majority of German tribes (who were mostly Arian Christians when they crossed the frontiers and began to settle down inside the Empire): they soon became the objects of evangelizing activity.

The showy polychrome jewellery and other metalwork of the Anglo-Saxons plainly made an impression on the Irish. The Germanic peoples had long been fond of making ornaments of animal forms, the animals being stylized, stretched out into ribbon-like shapes and often arranged in intertwined patterns, or depicted with one beast biting or entangled with another, sometimes to form a continuous range or register in which it is only at second or third glance that one can tease out the interlace and identify heads, tails and claws. The evolving animals styles have been classified by scholars, notably by the German, Salin. Salin's 'Style Two', exemplified on Anglo-Saxon belt-buckles and other objects of display, suddenly appears in an almost pure form, without Irish predecessors, filling a whole page of the Book of Durrow. Manuscript illumination is obviously secondary to the work of the jeweller. Patterns and designs are copied from the metalwork by the book painters. They are not such patterns as would ever have been invented by scribes; and we don't find scribal devices imitated by the metalworkers.

The Irish craftsmen in the medium of metal had derived from their predecessors remarkable skills in the casting and working of bronze, the craft of enamelling in red, and certain ornamental forms mainly based on whirling, swelling and diminishing spirals. They had long applied this knowledge in the manufacture of brooches and other objects derived from types worn and made in the Roman Empire. With the coming of Christianity they had begun – again in imitation of Roman prototypes – to make little reliquary caskets in the form of miniature houses, churches or tombs. These in turn were adorned with jewels or gaudy coloured work in which techniques and also patterns borrowed from the craftsmen of Gaul began to appear. To this Roman repertoire the Irish smiths in the seventh century began to add motifs, techniques, or imitated effects, from Germanic metalworking.

The Germans, including the Anglo-Saxons, were not enamellers. They achieved their polychrome effects by inlaying minutely cut tablets or sheets of coloured semi-precious materials in tiny cloisons, to offset the sheen of gold, silver and bronze. Meerschaum, for whiteness, or garnet, for redness, were among the commonest of such materials, and, apart from a consummate skill in the cutting and inlaying of these substances, the craftsmen had many tricks for improving brilliance and colour. It is fascinating to see how the Irish workers attempted to achieve closely similar effects while using different materials and methods. Garnet will be replaced by red enamel, other substances by yellow or blue enamel or by coloured glass insets. Much of the glitter of Anglo-Saxon jewellery comes from the skilful use of beaded wire filigree, soldered on to represent animal forms or other patterns. We find that the Irish artists who produced such splendid objects as the Tara Brooch and the Ardagh Chalice learned to copy very faithfully this Anglo-Saxon technique, although their animal and other forms of ornament had already assumed a distinctive Irish character by this time.

Each borrowing, whether of technique or of style, was merely the starting point for the elaboration and development of a local variant which came to form one of the elements in a quite distinctively Irish synthesis, giving in due course (by about the end of the seventh century) a unified style and art. This gave visual expression to a culture that was already unified through its literature, customs and laws. The powerful sense of a self-conscious and immensely self-confident identity which we receive from the Ireland of the eighth century, in every aspect of its life and thought, embodies this paradox. It has an organic unity like a good mosaic, but when we examine it closely, we find it to be made up of numerous tesserae, most of them borrowed from the work of other cultures and now put to new service.

Yet there is great originality. There is much to be known about the Ireland of that time, much more than about the earlier 'Golden Age' in the Bronze Age, for example. Eighth-century Ireland had a literate civilization. It possessed to the full the necessary basis for originality: the sense that it was unique, whole and good; that it did not need to be anything other than it was or to feel in any way inferior to other cultures. It borrowed from them freely, not fearing that its own independence of mind and of values would be diminished by such borrowing, any more than the eighteenth- and nineteenth-century English felt in danger of being swamped by Indian culture when they freely borrowed words and ideas from the sub-continent – bungalows, verandahs, punch, polo and frequent baths and many more. Oddly enough, it is xenophilia, not xenophobia, that strengthens one's own identity.

3

The Elgin Marbles or
the Parthenon Frieze

Byron was something of a Norman Mailer among poets. Besides having an eye to see beneath the surface of things, as a poet by definition should, he was good on the surface too. He was an excellent journalist.

His 'Childe Harold's Pilgrimage' was published on 28 February 1812. As it appeared in print, the last of the ships bearing many tons of pale honey-coloured marbles from the Parthenon in Athens was beating its way round the capes of Europe from Greece to England. But the poem already comments on this event:

> But who, of all the plunderers of yon fane
> On high, where Pallas linger'd, loth to flee
> The latest relic of her ancient reign;
> The last, the worst, dull spoiler, who was he?
> Blush, Caledonia! such thy son could be!
> England! I joy no child was he of thine:
> Thy free-born men should spare what once was free;
> Yet they could violate each saddening shrine,
> And bear these altars o'er the long-reluctant brine.
> But most the modern Pict's ignoble boast
> To rive what Goth, and Turk, and Time hath spared:
> Cold as the crags upon his native coast,
> His mind as barren and his heart as hard,
> Is he whose head conceived, whose hand prepared,
> Aught to displace Athena's poor remains;
> Yet felt some portion of their mother's pains,
> And never knew, till then, the weight of Despot's chains.

This was written in 1983, intended originally for a newspaper article. However, the subject seemed to require more length than would suit that purpose, and it was just put aside. The Greek suit for the return of the sculptures is still active as I write this in 1996, and I have slightly revised the essay to take account of that.

Byron here engages in a debate which was fierce then and has been renewed. When Greece, in recent years, claimed back the sculptures, the convoluted legal processes of the European Community, now the European Union, became involved. But if, in 1812, Athena's sons were 'too weak a sacred shrine to guard', it was, appropriately enough, a daughter, Melina Mercouri, who brought a Byronic passion to Athena's cause.

Byron's genius went straight to the heart of things. His protest is against sacrilege and rape. The marbles were 'altars', The maternal shrines were violated.

And yet ... They have been safely housed for the best part of two centuries. They form the solid foundation of that cornerstone of Western civilization, the British Museum, although that institution was already six decades old when they arrived. Its Director in the 1980s, Sir David Wilson, therefore had good reason for asking Melina Mercouri, in a heated exchange, if she wanted to ruin the Museum by claiming the sculptures back for Greece.

And yet again ... What is the British Museum? What is any museum? A temple of the muses, as the name would suggest? Only partly. This expression may apply to libraries (therefore to that large part of the British Museum which is now the British Library) and to some kinds of art galleries, but less appropriately to miscellaneous collections. Something between a freak show for bank holiday entertainment and an archive of material evidence to be worked on by scholars. I think we all have ambiguous feelings about museums (and menageries). As Horace Walpole wrote to his friend Horace Mann, on 14 February 1753:

> You will scarcely guess how I employ my time; chiefly at present in the guardianship of embryos and cockleshells. Sir Hans Sloane is dead, and has made me one of the trustees of his museum ... He valued it at fourscore thousand; and so would anyone who loves hippopotamuses, sharks with one ear, and spiders as big as geese! It is a rent–charge, to keep the foetuses in spirit! You may think that *those* who think money the most valuable of all curiosities, will not be the purchasers.

He is writing jokingly about the collection – much more varied even then than his words would suggest – which formed the nucleus of the huge assemblage now housed north of Great Russell Street in London. An Irish visitor to the Museum some twelve years later, in 1765, Daniel O'Connell's uncle, 'Hunting Cap', gave his own account of the collection:

> First the British Museum exposed to view in Montague House ... You go up a Grand Hall cover'd all over Wall and Ceiling with Noble paintings by the best hands, ascend a noble staircase wth these Decorations still growing on you, and among other noble paintings you see the Sun in two opposite Corners of this Hall, shining on ye ceiling, and reflecting all down it soe naturally and strongly to ye Eye, as to cause an

Astonishing Deception. Thence you lead into a suite of rooms Most Magnificent in themselves, where you see an Innumerable fund of curiosities Antient and Modern, Two Egyptian Mummies, Two Pillars of Agate and Amber, a vast Collection of Antient Roman Curiosities, Dresses, Arms, Medals, Tools, Sacrificing Implements, Coins, Statues, Paintings and Carvings, A noble and numerous Collection of Paintings by the first Hands of Every Country; all Foreign Fishes and Fowls, insects and Animalls, Fossils and Minerals and Shells; with a variety of the forementioned rings, Arms, etc., etc., of foreign Countries, Antient and Modern; vast, Large, and Numerous Librarys in all Languages, with, in short, everything the whole World almost y^t is Rare and Curious. Whole sets of Agate and Amber Tea things and spoons, an Agate Draget Box, etc., etc., mostly collected by the Late Sir Hans Sloane at a vast expence, and reckoned among the compleatest and best assorted Museum in Europe, and purchased from his Heirs att £25,000. You have here an Indian Scalp with the Hair on. You gett in here by Tickett, and pay noe Money. The time allowed to any one company is only 3 hours.

Hunting Cap manages to convey all the joy and dismay of such collections.

Muses are uncomfortable beings to have about. The discomfort associated with museums, however, is slightly different. They provide, not merely the kinds of pleasure we can enoy in reading Catullus or Gibbon, or listening to Vivaldi, or visiting Chartres, but quite commonly something more like the pleasure elderly gentlemen derive from the death columns of newspapers – a touch of *Schadenfreude*. They are irreligious. It is not only the great gods that have ended up in them, but little household gods also – and which of *them* can retain any mana when displayed in a dusty glass case with a faded label – or even in a clean perspex case with Bauhaus-typography caption and unobtrusive burglar alarm. The moth pinned to the board is, whatever else may make it an object of interest, patently dead.

And there is a further discomfort in museums. In their way they exemplify imperialism, and we are no longer comfortable with imperialism (were people ever?). The major museums are in imperial capitals and are filled with apes and angels from the jungles and cathedrals of subject territories. They are metropolitan repositories of the plunder of provinces. The British Museum has, for example, a good deal of Irish material, although one notable collection of gold objects was wrenched from its grasp at the beginning of the century in a law case in which Edward Carson (later the Ulster Unionist leader) doughtily and successfully defended the cause of the Irish nation.

The 'Elgin Marbles' are a special case. The British Museum no longer gives them that offensive title: it is happy to yield on a point of no substance. But 'the Elgin Marbles' they were for a long time.

Thomas Bruce, Earl of Elgin, Byron's 'modern Pict', was a major-general in the British army who was appointed in 1799 to be Ambassador Extraordinary to the Ottoman Porte. Advised by an architect friend named Harrison, who designed some buildings in classical style for the old city of Chester, he decided that it would benefit up-and-coming British architects if they had good specimens of Athenian work available to them at home in England, which they could sketch and copy without going to the trouble and expense of a grand tour. (This line of thought – providing approved models for the artist and the craftsman – was to gain ground by the middle of the nineteenth century, leading to the foundation of the Victoria and Albert Museum in London, and in Ireland, through the recommendations of the Kildare Commission, to the establishment of the National Museum, the National Library and the National College of Art and Design.) Elgin employed a team of artists to make drawings and moulds of the reliefs at Athens (then, of course, under Turkish rule) and these were sent to London.

He became persuaded that the buildings in Athens were in danger from the carelessness of the Turks. Finally he concluded that the Parthenon was 'so chaste and perfect a model of Doric architecture' that he

> conceived it to be of the highest importance to the arts, to secure original specimens of each member of that edifice ... so that, not only the sculptor may be gratified by studying every specimen of his art, from the colossal statue to the basso-relievo, executed in the golden age of Pericles, by Phidias himself, or under his immediate direction; but the practical architect may examine every detail of that building ...

His first notion was to have the Parthenon carvings 'restored' before shipping them to England. He went to Rome and tried to employ Canova to do this. Canova, to his great honour and credit, declined. He regretted that the sculptures had suffered so 'much from time and barbarism' but pointed out that

> they had never been retouched; that they were the work of the ablest artists the world had ever seen; executed under the most enlightened patron of the arts, and at a period when genius enjoyed the most liberal encouragement, and had attained the highest degree of perfection; and that they had been found worthy of forming the decoration of the most admired edifice ever erected in Greece.

He concluded that 'it would be a sacrilege in him, or any man, to presume to touch them with a chisel'.

Lord Elgin, by means always available to money and power, obtained a local Turkish permission. He had a huge quantity of sculptures taken down from the Parthenon and shipped to England, but, thanks to Canova, he didn't have them 'restored'. They came in a number of shipments between 1803 and 1812. His action was criticised by many in Britain besides Byron, and he published a memorandum in his own defence. In 1816 a Parliamentary Commission recommended the purchase of the marbles, for £35,000 – much less than it cost Lord Elgin to provide them.

This important episode was one of many in the process by which Western Europe researched the ancient world while at the same time it discovered the non-European contemporary world. The two processes went together. In late-fifteenth-century Italy, Lorenzo di Pierfrancesco de' Medici was the patron of Ficino, Botticelli and Amerigo Vespucci, subsidizing, like a one-man Ministry of Culture and Science (of extraordinary perception), at once the scholarly recovery of Plato, the restatement of Greek thought in visual terms, and the European discovery of the New World.

By the late eighteenth century, the 'noble savages' of America and the Pacific, the exemplary civilization of China, and the true treasures of European antiquity had entered the consciousness of Western Europeans and were exerting a major cultural influence. The late Renaissance had already ransacked antiquity for models, digging up marble fragments in Rome and elsewhere, and forming larger and larger colletions of ancient bronzes, coins, medals and other specimens of art.

Greece was, in art-historical terms, the best documented of the ancient civilizations. The names of the major artists and the names of their works were known. But the works themselves weren't. Michelangelo never set eyes on a genuine sculpture by Phidias. What the Renaissance people knew, in this area, was the up-market end of the vast Hellenistic copying industry. And they were deceived. Even in the mid-seventeenth century, when connoisseurship was well founded, John Evelyn, for example, thought that he saw works of Phidias and Praxiteles in Rome – but he didn't.

So, the recovery by Western Europe of the art of antiquity was a prolonged labour, a combination of exploration, excavation, mensuration – and plunder. Lord Elgin had predecessors, but he introduced a drastic change of scale into the process of collecting antiquities. 'The great age of collectors', Glyn Daniel wrote, 'began with the travels of Stuart and Revett in 1751–53, and may be said to extend to the work of Lord Elgin.' Stuart and Revett arrived in Athens in 1751 and spent three years drawing and recording the antiquities. Their publication in four volumes, *The Antiquities of Athens*, appeared between 1762 and 1816. Many other volumes appeared in the same period, recording the antiquities of Greece, Asia Minor, Egypt, Syria and Palestine. Then, when Napoleon invaded Egypt, he brought in his train a whole team of draftsmen and scholars.

They founded the French Egyptian Institute in Cairo. Although the Museum of the Louvre was opened in 1801, the great amount of material collected by the French didn't arrive there. The British Museum, through the British victory over the French at the Battle of the Nile, received the French cultural loot. The Rosetta Stone, so acquired, was described by its British captor, Major-General Sir Tomkyns Hilgrove Turner, as 'a proud trophy of the arms of Britain (I could almost say *spolia opima*), not plundered from defenceless inhabitants, but honourably acquired by the fortune of war'.

As the nineteenth century wore on, and field archaeology began in earnest, a hitherto unknown ancient world was steadily revealed, and whole forgotten civilizations came to light. The process can't wholly be separated from the concept of *spolia opima*. But, besides the hunt for 'treasures' for museums, and the demand for models for artists, there were more detached scholarly interests at work.

Winckelmann, before his murder by a robber in 1768, published a *History of Art* which had introduced an imporant principle. As R.G. Collingwood wrote:

> He conceived a profoundly original idea ... a history of art itself, developing through the work of successive artists, without their conscious awareness of any such development. The artist, for this conception, is merely the unconscious vehicle of a particular stage in the development of art.

This important concept required, for its realisation, the assembly of bodies of comparative material. Albums of measured drawings and sketches served this purpose only in a very limited way. The creation of what André Malraux has famously called 'the museum without walls' wasn't really possible in the nineteenth century. So, there was a powerful drive to collect appropriate materials gathered from distant places into central repositories. When the materials assembled were sufficiently monumental in scale and splendid in design, the repositories themselves tended to become monumental and splendid, proclaiming a kind of Roman triumph.

Great imperial colonnaded buildings, housing the collections, were hardly distinguishable from other palaces of state power and occupied similar positions in the Hausmannized city centres. The most consciously designed as imperial display was probably the Naturhistorisches Museum in Vienna, built as part of the great Ringstrasse scheme, but the major museums of Berlin, Paris and other centres follow the pattern. As does the Metropolitan Museum in New York, broadly contemporary with this European development. The chief spoils of the past were displayed in idealized triumph – as witness the siting within the Louvre of both the Victory of Samothrace and the 'Venus de Milo'.

In the British Museum, the galleries which house and display the Parthenon marbles attempt (in particular in relation to the frieze) a kind of pastiche of their original setting. The galleries themselves are both monumental and a parody of the style of the work they house, compromising – not altogether unhappily – between making the sculptures visible, recreating something of their original relationships to one another, and making them secure. The lighting fixtures are obtrusive. The light they supply is for delineation and study, serving purposes other than those envisaged by the artists for the light in their original situation.

The Parthenon too, of course, was triumphalist. Athens was an imperial city and the temple of the goddess was paid for with the spoils of empire. But it celebrates the city through honouring the goddess; in this it is comparable to the great temple of the Virgin at Chartres. The pastiche in Great Russell Street is not ignoble in its purpose; but it is different: it is secular.

Each time I visit the Parthenon galleries, to enjoy, through the courtesy of the great museum, the incomparable beauty of those works, I am troubled by the persistent feeling that they are in the wrong place and *can't really be seen*. Perhaps not everyone feels this. Perhaps it is a feeling that arises from a logical confusion. For, one thing that is inescapable about any ancient work is that, whatever about place, it is in the wrong time. It has also, inevitably and inexorably, been affected by time. We can't see it as it was when it was made. All conservators of the past try to solve the insoluble. But if they can never wholly succeed, yet their work is not wasted. Something is transmitted.

Who owns such works nowadays? Does anyone? The decline, both in power and in confidence, of many imperial states has been matched by the rise of numerous jealous nationalisms. Countries all round the world pass laws to protect 'their heritage', and to prevent antiquities and works of art from passing beyond their frontiers. There are many ironies. Agitations are now raised to protect Britain's heritage from the cheque-books of Americans and Japanese. Sometimes the 'heritage' consists of works collected from other parts of the world when Britain's was the fattest cheque-book, backed by the strongest arm. Or, if the heritage is genuinely and indigenously British, then the British Museum itself, although filled with the tribute of the world, is an agency primarily responsible for preventing the export of British antiquities, whose right place is assumed to be the land of their origin.

Travel is easier nowadays than it was two centuries ago; means of communication, of exact illustration, of the transmission of accurate images, are vastly better. The case that was made round the beginning of the nineteenth century for forming collections like that of the British Museum is weakened. But so, perhaps, is the case for dispersing collections already in existence. What they contain can be regarded as the inheritance of humankind, and the chief criterion should be, not who 'owns' them by national right, but how and where, now, can they be best looked after. There are many problems. For example, the uniquely important ethnographic collection made by Captain Cook on his second voyage ended up partly in Dublin, Ireland, partly in Berne, Switzerland. Where should it be as a whole; should it, a collection gathered from many places but at one time, be as a whole?

And there are other considerations: Byron reminds us of some of them. The case of the Parthenon marbles is very special, if not unique. Here we have, not just any old bit of humanity's heritage, but one which is both supremely and inextricably associated with the unique meaning of Athens within that heritage. There is a violation; although the British Museum is in almost every way a beneficent institution.

Among the most moving of the carvings are those grievously afflicted by time and the accidents of weathering (and weathering can occur within a museum). In some this has gone so far that the grain of the stratified stone all but masters the sculptor's modelling: faint hints of horses' ghostly muzzles, and mummy masks of their riders forming an almost abstract pattern. There is an infinite pathos about the death of this stone on the walls of a museum. The worthy principles of Winckelmann don't apply here. Phidias (if indeed it was he who was the master carver involved) was not 'the unconscious vehicle of a particular stage'. This work is the manifestation of a glory that shines very rarely through: should it not die in Athens?

4

The Art of the Celtic Peoples

For the purpose of this discussion I take 'the Celtic peoples' to mean those peoples who, at one time or another in the past, were speakers of languages of the Celtic group. This is a tall order in several respects. For one thing, we have inadequate knowledge of the early history of the Indo-European languages and don't know how to recognise, with reasonable confidence, by archaeology or otherwise, the speakers of original Celtic. Informed guesses on the subject vary widely. Essentially, we depend on early accounts by non-Celtic reporters, such as Herodotus, to give us our bearings. These sources supply the word 'Keltoi' – 'Celts' – itself a term which has been extended by modern scholars and others to apply to peoples who never heard of Celts and had no idea that they might be classified with the other cultures in the group now called 'Celtic'.

But even if we set our limits conservatively, we are still left with an enormous range of time and place: from the second millennium BC to the present day; from Ireland to Asia Minor. The Celtic peoples today, by a strict definition, consist of some of the people of Brittany, some of the people of Wales, and a handful of people scattered in tiny isolated communities along parts of the west coasts of Ireland and Scotland. Even within this reduced remnant we are dealing with several cultures. Apart from language-type, what they have in common that we might distinguish as 'Celtic' is largely artificial and the result of romantic or nationalist revivalism of the past two or three centuries. There is a highly self-conscious Celticism, for example, in the popular music of Alan Stivell and the groups known as Horselips and Lindisfarne which gives them something of a common character, but this is contrived rather than derived from the musical traditions to which they all refer.

The Celts of later prehistory, the peoples of Central Europe about whom the Greek and Latin writers first inform us, remained on the margins of the expanding world of Mediterranean urban civilization. Other groups of the Indo-Europeans were drawn into that world – the Hittites, the Greeks, the Iranians, for example – or, like the Aryans, moved into areas of non-Mediterranean urban

This paper was read in Toronto in February 1978 at a conference on 'Canada and the Celtic Consciousness'. The proceedings, edited by the late Robert O'Driscoll, were published in Toronto in 1981 under the title, *The Celtic Consciousness*. The paper has been slightly modified for publication here.

culture. Some Indo–European groups remained separated at one or two removes from the urban world; for example, the Germanic and Slavic peoples. The Italic and Celtic peoples were ultimately more or less absorbed by Mediterranean culture; but the Celts in particular developed their characteristic institutions, myth, and perception of the cosmos as a high barbarian culture exposed to the great tensions and instability characteristic of systems straddling the divide between the desert and the sown.

It is important to remember in this respect that analogies between the ancient urban civilizations and modern urban culture cannot usefully be pushed too far. When we compare ancient and modern urbanisms, in respect of their contrast with external barbarian cultures, we find a vast difference in the technology gradient. Modern empires have imposed themselves on the whole world by superior rational organization (including in particular the manipulation of money) combined with greatly superior technology which provided good communications and weapons. The urban civilization of the ancient Mediterranean had a social organization that was more complex than those of the cultures north of the Alps and was literate and numerate. But in many respects the barbarians were the superior in technology; in agricultural methods, for example, and in the metallurgy of iron. The old tag, *ex oriente lux*, which in the early twentieth century could be applied to the diffusion of crafts and knowledge as well as arts and letters from the eastern Mediterranean to prehistoric Europe, has had to be discarded because the coercive evidence of radiocarbon dating has forced us to concede that very often the innovative and doctoral system was that of the northern or western barbarians. Newgrange and Gav'rinis, both in lands which came to be occupied later by Celtic-speaking peoples, are as old as the pyramids. The German excavations at Numantia, in Spain, where Scipio Africanus, the victor of the Punic Wars, carried out extensive siege operations, recovered large numbers of iron weapons. From these and other finds it seems that the weapons of the Republic, with which Rome was to conquer the Mediterranean world, were largely based on Celtic prototypes. It was neither technology nor innate superiority – for Rome's soldiers came to be drawn from the barbarian world – but organization that gave the Romans the edge.

Each side of the divide admired and looked down on the other. The barbarians admired and envied the stability, wealth, order and elegance of the civilizations south of the Alps. But they feared and disliked the organization which made those civilizations possible. They resented the concept of an order externally imposed on them, and the speeches which Mediterranean historians put into the mouths of Celtic leaders very frequently touch on the topic of freedom. Freedom, of course, was not for the populace at large, but for the warriors, whose required behaviour was recklessness, vainglory, valour beyond reason: the story of the hero taking his weapons to fight the sea is widespread. The Celts who were met by a general of Alexander the Great somewhere in Dalmatia and asked what they feared most in the world, instead of answering diplomatically that what they feared most was Alexander himself, replied that they feared *nothing* – except that the sky might fall on them. This may be a reference to the oaths which Celtic people swore by the elements, or by sky, wind or sun, calling on these natural forces to avenge the forsworn oath. Leaders of tribal alliances took megalomaniacal titles – Dumnorix, Vercingetorix, etc. An excess characterized them, which was envied, admired, feared and despised by the careful methodical Romans – but also by the earlier Etruscans and Greeks. The relationship between the Roman and the Celt was something like the relationship between the British colonist and the Afghan, or the early-twentieth-century relationship between Englishmen and Arabs, with similar overtones of homosexuality, militarism, retarded adolescence, and uneasy comradeship in loyalty or enmity against wily Bengalis, Greeks, Phoenicians or other clever people who lacked the military virtues and were unsound in politics. The Celt was a decent chap, a worthy foe, only occasionally given to regrettable excesses.

The frontier zone, with its military background, is where the acculturation took place which is the background of the art of the Celtic peoples. Two stereotypes offer us the contrast between the view from the Hellenistic or Roman side of the frontier and the view of the Celts themselves. The 'dying Gaul', a favourite Hellenistic theme, shows us the idealized noble savage, caught in the pathos of beauty and nobility inevitably broken and overcome by the majesty of empire. Observation is frozen into a stylized view. A few distinctive points are noted and sketched: the spikiness of limewashed hair; the heavy metal torque, sacred and ornamental; the warrior's nakedness, which scorns protective covering but, more aggressively, implies womanliness in the foe; the drooping moustache which both certified the barbarian and distinguished his ethnic species. It is a type, the marble somehow suggesting the blue-eyed blondness which is what Mediterranean observers perceived in the warrior peoples from north of the Alps.

The head – it might well be of the same warrior – from Mšecké Žerovice shows the type again, with torque, limed hair and heavy moustache, but quite differently observed. There is no pathos here, of the wild thing tamed by civilization and death; but rather the deincarnation or apotheosis of the warrior. This is a head: the Celtic artist's synecdoche, eschewing the mere mechanics of representation, found in the human (or divine) head a sufficient focus for meaning and, in rendering its features, used a notation quite different from that of the classical artist. Psychology, like the body, is omitted. What we have instead is a concentrated expression of meaning, the godhead of warriordom, where the features are stylized, as if the mere accidents of human shape were irrelevant, in favour of an energetic pattern. The large staring ovoid eyes are a durable cipher, and this prehistoric head from Bohemia can be matched over a thousand years later in metal and stone from Ireland.

The famous coin series – a typology of devolution – in which the Parisii and other Gaulish tribes can be seen imitating and adapting the stater of Philip II of Macedon until both the head of the king on the obverse and the two-horse chariot on the reverse become abstract or geometric patterns, shows us the direction of the process by which Celtic artists adapted classical motifs. They made patterns out of images. But this particular series is an hypertrophy; for generally the Celt stopped short of the full reduction to abstract patterns, and retained, in however stylized and distorted a way, something of the original natural form. Indeed, he regularly complemented the process, finding in abstract patterns suggestions of natural forms, or in foliage the shapes of animals, in animals' limbs and crests the shapes of leaves. A dynamic balance, one form or mode on the point of passing into another, is characteristic of Celtic design.

For this reason the balanced ambiguity of masks and disguises is especially attractive to the Celtic artist. Men were disguised, or half-disguised, as animals, by wearing horned or crested helmets which made them taller, distorted their shapes and suggested tribal totems or divine avatars. Such disguises are, of course, found everywhere, among warrior peoples from the South Pacific to the forests of Africa or the plains of North America; in Greek hoplites and Roman legionaries, and on the Horse-guards' Parade in Whitehall. Celtic artists added a subtlety which is almost a further disguise. Not content with the gross shape of horns or boar-crest which could strike unease into the foe, they added to the warrior's display fine and subtle patterns and techniques which, if they served the same purpose, must have done so in the manner of secret spells written in an arcane language. Beautifully but finely wrought patterns, cast, chased or beaten in sheet bronze, shallowly and subtly engraved, touched with delicate and minute chequers of polychrome enamel, ornament the warrior's equipment. They could not be read across a battlefield, but they must have added greatly to the value of weapons and military harness, and perhaps they conveyed the same message as the warrior's own nakedness: a scorn to bring into the hazard of war anything except what was most fine and valuable: a boast as loud as a warcry. If we look, for example, at British objects like the Waterloo helmet, the Battersea shield, or the Stanwick horse-mask, we find in the lavishing of delicate craftsmanship on equipment that must encounter sling-shot, spear-thrust and sword-cut, an extravagance, not merely of material wealth, but of spirit, which is echoed in the Irish sagas, and in *their* echoes:

> A great man in his pride
> Confronting murderous men
> Casts derision upon
> Supersession of breath;
> He knows death to the bone –
> Man has created death.

This is to say, perhaps, no more than that the world of early Celtic art, the chief patrons of which were warrior aristocrats, was the world of an heroic age. But the extravagance, the scorn for the contingent, endures. The 'white martyrdom' of the Christian monks who stormed the pinnacles of Skellig or Slieve League, or put out on the Atlantic 'to seek a solitude in the pathless sea', found its counterpart in some aspects of the art of the Christian period. The most dedicated and superb craftsmanship of the Tara Brooch is in the ornamentation of the reverse, which would have lain against the wool of the wearer's cloak; the richest metalwork and settings of the Ardagh Chalice are on the underside of the foot: there is a conspicuous absence of bourgeois calculation in this art.

The prehistoric Celts were a Central European people, transmitting to the West impulses from the East, most notably the knowledge and use of iron. Their art initially reflected some of the forms developed by nomads and seminomads from the vast reaches of the Eurasian steppe, which extended to the remote East from the Celtic lands. Scythians, Cimmerians, Thracians, Illyrians, passed on both skills and motifs, and the Eurasian animal style found its way into Central Europe. Bird and animal protoms abound in early Celtic metalwork, and birds and animals figure largely in the religious cults of the early Celts. Other impulses came from the south: the wine trade, which came to be of great importance, brought Greek and Etruscan vessels and equipment north of the Alps, as we see for example in the rich grave-goods from the Mediterranean buried with a Celtic princess at Vix, in France. The elaborately decorated wine vessels – great kraters, bronze jugs and other equipment – exercised such an influence on the recipients that J.M. de Navarro, for one, wrote forthrightly in 1928 that Celtic art is a product of Celtic thirst. We can see the absorption of classical motifs beginning in such objects as the wine-jug (*oinochoe*) of Celtic manufacture from Basse-Jutz on the Moselle, now in the British Museum. Acanthus and vine-scrolls and similar foliate forms gave rise in course of time to the subtle and extraordinarily dynamic curvilinear patterns of developed La Tène art. This sometimes has a baroque richness, as in the Waldalgesheim style, named from the exquisitely wrought gold personal ornaments found at a place so called in Germany; sometimes, as in the engraved ornament of the Lisnacrogher sword-scabbards from north-eastern Ireland, or the Birdlip bronze mirror from south-western England, the curves flow into over-all linear patterns – almost wholly abstract in their feeling – with contrasting textures of hatched and unhtached bronze. But whether in chunky repoussé or in chased line-patterns, we find a continuing and very widespread preference for sinuous and coiling forms, for near-abstraction, and for a tense balance which always avoids exact symmetry.

Over much of Europe the originality and liveliness of mature La Tène art gives way to the deadening effects of mass production and uniformity associated with the Roman conquests. Under Roman rule a late Celtic industry in small ornamental bronzes catered for the military frontiers from Hadrian's Wall to the mouths of the Danube, and beyond, producing a multitude of cast openwork pieces and small polychrome enamels; but these lack life compared with earlier work. Some of the finest productions in the late La Tène style come from workshops on or near the Irish Sea – they include superb chased and relief bronzes like the chamfrain from Torrs, as well as fine work in lathe-spun bronze – and after the Roman conquests of most of the lands of the West, the La Tène tradition lived on beyond the frontiers, in Scotland and Ireland.

These countries, however, came under powerful Roman influence. It seems that, from the third century AD (if not even earlier) the Irish chieftains began to imitate Roman, or at least Mediterranean, costume and personal ornaments. Cranked pins and penannular pins came into fashion, and the Germanicized styles of the late Imperial frontier – belt-buckles and strap-tags, kerbschnitt brooches, and, finally, animal patterns, began to be adopted and adapted in Britain and Ireland. The period of the *Völkerwanderung*, and then of the abandonment of Britain by the legions and of the migration into the Western provinces of many different groups of barbarians, provided a remarkable variety of stimulus for changes of style. In the old Celtic heartland there was now a Germanic overlay on the Roman conquest, and this extended to parts of Britain. Beyond, in northern and western Britain and in Ireland, Germanic and traditional Celtic motifs competed for the fancy of the artists and craftsmen and their patrons. The steady spread of the Romanizing Christian faith added to the complexity of the process. In Pictish Scotland, whirls of prehistoric serpents competed and mingled with strange symbols derived from Roman icons or from native traditions of animal ornament. In Ireland, the varied curvilinear forms of the Iron Age gave way to a fashion for elegant spinning patterns of 'trumpet spirals' winding in and out of one another with increasingly colourful touches of enamel. Interlacings, biting animals, polychrome frets and keys, were rapidly added to the patterns in bronzework – soon metamorphosed into enamel-like manuscript pages – in an eclectic style that, far from being swamped by the new borrowings, contrived to retain both the spirit and the basic organization of prehistoric Celtic art. Iron Age society absorbed Christianity without Roman conquest, and the culture remained both firmly integrated and remarkably self-confident. The carapace of Imperial order in which Christianity reached the far West was dissolved, to be replaced by an order that was neither rigid nor wholly organic: the obsessive reiterations that are characterized by the serpentine writhings and coilings of Celtic visual forms.

The order comes from within: this is the key to what is 'Celtic' in Irish art of the early Christian period. It cannot be imposed by T-square and set-square, or marked off by numbers like the layout of a Roman legionary camp; nor even guided by a development of harmonic modules like a Greek entablature: it spirals out from the heart of the design; it expresses neither essence nor being but constant becoming, and the artist must have been as fully engaged in every veering of a line as in the planning of his overall design. A fair comparison is the calligraphy of the Far East. The master calligrapher can charge and poise his brush, stare at and absorb the blank page, and then swiftly place the right shape in the right balance in the right place. This the early Irish artist could do – with the Chi-Rho Monogram of Christ, for example, on an unsquared slab of stone, as in the Inis Cealtra grave-marker, or with the simple incised cross on an early grave-slab at Assylin, near Boyle. This is why modern imitations of 'Celtic' (i.e. early Irish) manuscript pages, which depend on elaborate, imposed, setting-out patterns of squares, rectangles, triangles and compass-drawn curves (although the early artists did all this – but didn't depend on it) are as dead as doornails.

The Book of Kells is rightly famous as a supreme product of the final phase of this art. There is little 'Celtic' about it, except its spirit. As difficult, and in some ways as alienating to the modern consciousness, as *Finnegans Wake*, it repels and fascinates because its order, barely controlling an explosive anarchy, allows us to glimpse the chaos at the heart of the universe which our own Romanized culture is at pains to conceal.

From the ninth century onwards the Celtic spirit, in so far as it survived from prehistory, was in retreat before the advance of Romanesque Europe. It becomes increasingly difficult to trace continuities, at least in the visual arts. Literature, oral or written, is a different matter. There is some evidence for the transmission of a conspiratorial culture, like that of the European Jews or the Japanese Christians, by which some tenuous threads link the Celtic past to communities in modern Scotland, Wales or Ireland; the occasional oath or spell, or reference to a forgotten saga:

> ... in rustic speech a phrase,
> As in wild earth a Grecian vase.

5

The Celtic Woman

At the beginning of the year a book appeared on *Boadicea*, by J.M. Scott. More recently a translation from the French of a work on *Women of the Celts*, by J. Markale, has been issued. The account of Boadicea is a slight, popular, work. Professor Markale's, which includes a number of references to that Queen of the Iceni, is an attempt to relate contemporary ideas on women's liberation to the hints – which he discerns in the literatures of several Celtic languages – of an ancient matriarchal order.

Most of the women discussed by Professor Markale belong to myth or legend rather than history. Boadicea, however, was a person who really existed, even if very little can now be found out about her. Her name is most familiar in the Latinized form, in which it appears in the earliest accounts of her, written by Roman writers. It should more properly be something like 'Boudicca', from a British word meaning 'victory'. She was the wife of Prasutagus, king of the Iceni, a British tribe in East Anglia (as it later became) at the time of the Roman conquest of England. He died in AD 59, leaving half his fortune to the Emperor Nero and the other half to his two daughters. However, the Roman tax-gatherers decided to take all for the Emperor, and in the course of making this exaction in Icenian territory, they, or the soldiers with them, flogged the queen and raped her two daughters.

This happened at a time when the governor of Britain, with the main Roman military force, was campaigning in distant Wales. Boudicca raised an allied force of the Iceni and a number of neighbouring British tribes and conducted a destructive and bloody campaign against the Romans before the governor, Suetonius Paulinus, could reach south-eastern England and defeat her.

Roman fury at being opposed – for a time successfully – by a woman seems to have embittered the whole episode, and the final destruction of the Iceni was merciless. The Roman accounts of the affair were hostile to her and, as Mr Scott points out in his introductory chapter, later renderings of the story, beginning with the ecclesiastical writer Gildas, tended to be not very sympathetic to Boudicca, or to play down her part, gratuitously introducing male generals into the story to explain her initial successes. She was a natural candidate for

This appeared in the 'Roots' column in the *Irish Times* on 24 September 1975.

modern romanticization; all the more so as the Roman descriptions of her personal appearance fitted her well for the character of Brittania: huge of frame, terrifying of aspect, with a harsh voice, with bright red hair streaming down to her knees, a golden chain, a large brooch fastening her outer mantle, and a multicoloured dress.

A bronze group, 'Boadicea and her Daughters', stands in Westminster, in the shadow of the Houses of Parliament, the work of Thomas Thorneycroft, who spent fifteen years on it. 'The group', wrote the art critic of *The Times* in 1871,

> is nearly twice the size of life, for the figure of Boadicea measures 10 ft. A car, the body of which is wicker-work and the wheels thick circles of solid wood, is drawn at speed by two unbidled horses rudely belted to the heavy pole. They plunge asunder as they sniff battle in the wind; one would dart forward and the other attempts to hold back. In the car, naked to the waist, crouch the Queen's two daughters, and strain their gaze towards the Roman host ... Her face and her attitude are instinct with commanding grandeur; she orders the extinction of her foes; she appeals to her people not in frenzy and tears, in tones heartstirring and eloquent no doubt, but with more pride than rage in them, and her haughty spirit does not dream of defeat.

Unfortunately, the Roman descriptions of Boudicca are likely to be based as little on observation and as much on a received stereotype of the barbarian (especially the Celtic) woman as are Thorneycroft's statuary and the art critic's description of it. 'The Gallic women are not only equal to their husbands in stature, but they rival with them in strength as well', according to Diodorus Siculus.

In the stereotype there must have been some element of truth, derived mainly from earlier Greek observations of the Celts rather than the partial and propagandist writings of the Romans. For Celtic literature itself bears out some details in these accounts, and the caricature of Boudicca presented by Tacitus and Dio finds some echoes in the portrait of Queen Medb in *Táin Bó Cuailgne*. There was something about the status of women in Gaulish, British and early Irish society that struck the Romans in particular, as well as the Greeks, as strange and outlandish. It is on this difference, or pecularity, that Professor Markale has seized in prsenting the main argument of his *Women of the Celts*. This is that:

> Celtic law gave women a position that they did not hold in contemporary societies. They were able to play some part in political and religious life; they could own property, even when they married (though certain conditions were attached to ownership); they could govern; they could choose freely when it came to marriage; they could divorce; and, if they were deserted or molested, they had the right to claim considerable damages.

Such a thesis deserves examination. It is supported in his book by generalizations drawing on much too wide a variety of sources from too many periods and cultures, and often from evidence (such as myth) which is of dubious value for this purpose. There is a large element again of romanticization, of creating the image of the heroic 'Celtic' woman, the Boadicea or Maeve of late-Victorian fancy. It yields too much to the temptation to support a vision of the future with a vision of the past as a golden age. Yet there is something in it.

Most studies of the development of the theme of romantic love in European literature trace it back through the medieval theme of courtly (which is adulterous) love. And this has its roots deep in the literatures of the Celtic languages. Markale singles out the act of choice, the woman choosing the man, and relates this to the more independent status of the 'Celtic' woman, which in turn he relates rather tenuously to the tradition derived from an ancient matriarchy (for which the evidence, it must be said, is very thin indeed). The idea is worth pursuing.

What can be said fairly confidently is that there is something very un-Roman about the position of women in the *literature* of the Celtic languages. Déirdre and Gráinne belong to a very un-Roman world, a world in which women had souls and men were often the sex-objects. Perhaps Markale is right to see Boudicca's rebellion against the Romans as a symbol of women's liberation. But that massive group of imperious and imperial bronzes in Westminster would suggest that the symbol needs careful handling.

6

Central Europeans, Ancient and Modern

On the Heiligenberg, the forested moutain which looks down across the Neckar on to the red roofs of Heidelberg, there are historic monuments of various periods. The most recent is a great open-air auditorium, massively constructed of concrete and stone, tier after tier of stepped seats rising up from an elaborate stage area, with heavy-base supports for great flagstaffs, one or two of which still remain. The whole architectural structure is grass-grown and weed-grown, and large cast-iron fragments from its flag-mounts and other fittings lie scattered among the tree-trunks down the steep hill-slopes. Some very crudely painted lettering on a broken black door announces (in English) an 'open-air concert' to be held in October 1971. The concert was obviously not an official one, and the advertisement probably recalls the passage this way of some youthful Americans (for traditionalist American vistors, Heidelberg is in Germany the equivalent of Killarney in Ireland) who decided it was a good place to entertain themselves.

The hilltop auditorium was not however built for such concerts. It is a Nazi monument, built in the 1930s, when the Depression unemployment was solved by the recruitment of military-style labour corps, and it was intended for the holding of rallies and other celebrations of the revived Germanic spirit, which could be given extra point by a hilltop setting among a green sea of forest, to set off the waving banners and the flaming torches. A chorus of manly voices, rising above the dark forest, would re-enact the war-chant of those ancient Germans who had destroyed the three legions of Varrus.

One of a number of cast-iron reliefs on the site, lettered in the Gothic script favoured under the Nazis, draws attention to the hill-fort within whose ramparts of stone and earth the later monument is set; and says that this was erected by the Celts about the year 100 BC as a defence against the south-westward advance of the Germans.

This precision in fact goes beyond the evidence. When the open-air theatre was being built, the workers unearthed many potsherds and other archaeological objects. These, which were not very scientifically excavated, were of various periods, including the Roman, but a large proportion of them came

---

This was written in Frankfurt am Main and appeared in the 'Roots' column in the *Irish Times* on 20 November 1973.

from the culture which bears the archaeological label 'La Tène'. However, there was earlier material as well, and it seems that the mountain may have been occupied as early as the Neolithic period – some two thousand years before – and that the fort whose ramparts are slung like a necklace around the upper slopes may be rather older than La Tène. Nonetheless, the iron notice, if somewhat inaccurate in its precision, conveys information which roughly corresponds to historical fact.

The Continental La Tène culture, fully formed by about 500 BC, had quite a wide extension, from northern Spain, France and Britain and Ireland in the west, to Austria and Bohemia in the east, with a patchy distribution much further afield. Over that area the material remains, of the last centuries before the Roman presence was established in Central Europe, show an instantly recognisable unity of style. There is no doubt that this culture corresponds in time and place to the great barbarian nation which the Greeks and the Romans described as that of the Celts. The correspondence may not be quite exact, because the culture for a time was dominant to such an extent that its material may have been acquired or copied by neighbouring peoples. To establish the frontier between the Celts and the Germans in particular is difficult at any given time, although we have the testimony of classical writers, as well as other evidence, for the Germanic advances from the north-east which tended to push back the eastern borders of the later Celtic lands.

The La Tène culture in turn derived from an earlier culture, named archaeologically after the salt-mining site of Hallstatt in western Austria. It is generally inferred therefore that the Hallstatt people, or at least those of the western part of the Hallstatt region (which in general had a centre of gravity a good deal to the south-east of that of the La Tène culture) were also Celts, or 'proto-Celts'. There is no break which would indicate a population change in the transition from Hallstatt to La Tène; rather a fairly rapid transformation of the material content of the culture under the influence of newly expanded traffic with the ancient Mediterranean world. This appears to have coincided with a westward shift of the main centres of political power among the Celts, from southern Germany to the Middle Rhine region – around Heidelberg – and from Burgundy to the Marne in France. All the evidence goes to indicate that Celtic society was one which sustained a rich warrior aristocracy, and that it had a tribal organization, each tribe, at least in the later phases of Celtic history, tending to have its own territory and its tribal centre – often a hill-fort.

Some of these centres were the equivalent both in size and in population of the towns of the Mediterranean lands. Others were perhaps not much more than ceremonial assembly- and defence-places of essentially rural tribes. The hill-forts were already a feature of Halstatt culture; they were not a La Tène innovation. The change shows itself rather in a transformation of the equipment used by the society. The richly furnished princely graves, one of the forms of display and measures of prestige of the aristocracy, change in character. Four-wheeled waggons are replaced by two-wheeled cars, or chariots, with a concentration of the rich graves in the newly important Middle Rhine and Marne areas.

There is also, however, a scatter of chariot-burials outside these areas, including an interesting group, more or less of Marnian type, in northern England. From the graves, from other archaeological evidence, and very fully from written sources, we can discern that one of the agencies bringing about cultural transformation was the wine trade, which became very important in La Tène times. Both Greeks and Etruscans were engaged in supplying the Celts with wine. The Greeks had founded a colony actually on the coast of Celtic territory, at Massilia, now Marseille, from which they trafficked with the Celtic interior up the Rhône valley, while the Etruscans operated a trans-Alpine trade. The great demand for wine and the high price offered by the Celtic lords fascinated the Mediterranean people, who also remarked more than once on the barbarous Celtic habit of drinking their wine without the admixture of water or any other liquid or substance.

We also learn that the Celts were tall, blond and blue-eyed; that they were fond of boasting; that they lime-washed their hair; that they went naked into battle; and that their women were, if anything, more formidable than the men. Much of this information is borne out independently, either by the archaeological evidence or by the fragments of old sagas which have survived in Celtic literature (mainly Irish) and which correspond in many details with the classical writers' observations, although these were referring to earlier people in Central Europe.

The contacts with the Mediterranean were important. With the wine went some of the elaborate equipment which was used for preparing, straining, storing and drinking it, in the form of elaborately ornamented bronze and silver vessels of various kinds made in Mediterranean workshops and shipped into the heart of the Continent. The Celts had their own skilled bronzesmiths and goldsmiths, and they copied and modified the forms of these vessels and, taking the numerous decorative motifs with which they were adorned, transformed these virtually out of recognition. The palmettes and acanthus leaves of the Greeks, stylized in bronze with a careful preservation of the natural forms of the vegetation, became the basis for flowing curvilinear forms of dazzling ingenuity, which also drew freely on the fantastic animal-art of the East European steppe peoples, to produce the extraordinarily sophisticated art-style which is the major monument of La Tène culture.

The culture expanded in a series of migrations and raids, spilling over the Alps in the great invasions of the early fourth century BC, which led to the capture of the still relatively unimportant city of Rome and to the Celtic settlement of northern Italy. In the following century Celtic bands drove down through the Balkans to Greece and Asia Minor. But the Romans, aided by the Germanic pressure from the east, tackled the Celtic peoples and put an end to their dominance of Central Europe.

Ireland was not included by the ancient writers in the Celtic lands, nor is there any early Irish tradition linking them with the Continental Celts. Yet some links there must have been, since the Irish in early historic times spoke a language closely related to that of the Gauls and Britons, and since their institutions were similar to those of the Celts. In archaeological terms, the La Tène culture is only peripherally represented in Ireland, confined in its main distribution to limited areas in the island.

Ireland has come to be thought of as a typically 'Celtic' country only by the accident of long survival of an Iron-Age social system. The last couple of centuries of Romantic ancestor-worhip in Europe, which produced such oddities as the Heiligenberg Nazi monument, have tended to obscure rather than to illuminate; yet there is something in the past of places like the Heiligenberg which connects at some point with our island past.

7

The Painted People

The Picts were a people or peoples who inhabited early Scotland. Like the Irish (*Scotti* at that time) they took part in the raiding of Roman Britain in the fourth and fifth centuries AD. Although there is a *Pictish Chroinicle*, consisting largely of the names of real or mythical kings, the Picts are known chiefly from the reports of non-Pictish neighbours.

Since these reports are generally confused or confusing (their neighbours were probably not very well informed about them) the whole subject, like that of the Druids, abounds in mystery and lends itself to speculation. Were they one people or two? For a distinction is made between 'northern Picts' and 'southern Picts'. And had they one language or two? When were the southern Picts converted to Christianity, and by whom? The northern Picts, or many of them, it seems were probably converted by the Irish monks of the Irish-founded monastery of Iona. Were the people who built the brochs (elaborate prehistoric circular defensive and dwelling structures of stone) Picts? What is the meaning of the strange symbols and stylized animals found carved on many natural boulders or stone cross-slabs in the Pictish area? These and many other questions have been asked; few have been answered to the satisfaction of all.

The Irish, or Scots, of Antrim established a colonial kingdom in western Scotland – Scottish Dál Riada – and in due course this became joined to the Pictish kingdom under a single (Scottish) ruler. The Irish, or Gaelic, language spread to many parts of Scotland, and the Pictish language, or languages, disappeared, adding considerably to the mystery. But the Picts (the Latin name simple means 'painted people') undoubtedly contributed much to the make-up of the medieval kingdom of Scotland, forming probably the bulk of its population.

Such a problem has a very strong appeal to a certain kind of speculation and to the urge to reconstruct full pictures from scattered fragments. There is scope in particular for Romantic hypothesis. The kind of mind which likes to search for clues to the history of the lost tribes of Israel, or to follow Sir Thomas Browne and Robert Graves in the enquiry as to 'what song the Sirens sang, and what name Achilles assumed when he hid himself among the women'

This appeared in the 'Roots' column in the *Irish Times* on 15 July 1975.

can find among the remains of vanished Pictland the lineaments of such Eden as seems appropriate – just as Romance created Avalon from similar fragments and hints at the other end of Dark Age Britain.

The Picts have an Irish dimension. The name which is applied to them in early Irish records is also applied to certain Irish population groups, especially in the north-east. It has more than once been suggested therefore that there were Picts in Ireland, or even that the pre-Goidelic inhabitants of Ireland were Picts. The name, *Cruthin*, has also been equated with that from which Britain and Ireland were named when they were known (to the Mediterranean peoples at least) as the 'Pretanic Isles'.

The whole subject abounds in the pitfalls and difficulties which cannot be separated from the names people give to alien groups; sometimes disparaging; often indifferent to the distinctions the aliens may make among themselves. All Chinese, or Blacks, or Italians look alike to those who have not taken the trouble to know them, and the historian of the distant future would have a difficult task in trying to discover, from a few scattered surviving references and descriptions, who in the twentieth century were the Wogs, or the Honkies.

The Irish dimension of the Picts has given them a significance in relation to the search for identity which is going on at an increasing pace among the loyalists of Northern Ireland. The 'Ulster Scots' (as many of them thought of themselves) resisted Home Rule; the 'Scotch-Irish' (as they became known in America) played a part both in the colonization of North America and in the achievement of the independence of the United States. The recollection of the bond, especially strong between the Presbyterians of Scotland and the Presbyterians of Ulster, but also existing between other sectors of the population on the two sides of the North Channel, served well to provide Ulster unionism with a sense of identity. As the British political connection now weakens, as the Ulster loyalists feel increasingly isolated, so the need for this sense of identity grows.

This shows clearly in a recent book which appears to be selling well in Belfast. It is *Cruthin: The Ancient Kindred*, by Dr Ian Adamson, who dates his prologue from Watson Street, Linfield Road, Sandy Row, Belfast (as loyalist an address as could be imagined). The work is an interesting exercise in myth-making; which is not to say that it is wholly without validity. Dr Adamson has used his authorities uncritically, and displays more enthusiasm than dexterity in presenting his case. But he makes a good point about the way the Gaelic aspect of the past dominated Irish historical studies, and about the way an orthodox myth developed from the nationalist manipulation of the past.

He accepts, and applies to such nationalist myth-making the warnings of scholars about the confusion of linguistic criteria with those of race, and about the concept of race itself within the context of the tangled history of European population-movements in the past. But the warnings are forgotten as he develops his theme of the 'pre-Celtic' Cruthin, their importance as 'the ancient kindred', the early pre-Gaelic population of Ireland, and their special significance for Ulster as an ethnic group which has moved backwards and forwards across the North Channel. The migration into Antrim and Down in the sixteenth, seventeenth and eighteenth centuries, which is so important for the modern history of Ulster, becomes the 'return of the Cruthin'. The Ulster loyalists are provided with roots in the soil of Ulster which are at once ancient, spreading to Scotland, and exclusive of Gaeldom.

This is most interesting, because it is by such process of shaping history to ideological requirements that nations have been identified and defined in the modern world. There is a great deal of truth in Dr Adamson's thesis. There is an Ulster-Scottish connection and there are features common to Ulster and Scotland, culturally and perhaps genetically, which neither shares with either England or the other Irish provinces – although Ulster probably shares more with the other Irish provinces than with Scotland. The Picts, or 'Cruthin', may, remotely, have something to do with the common Ulster-Scottish characteristics, although they are too distant in time, and too much has happened since their time, for them to be taken very seriously into the reckoning. It is more important that people should feel the need to put forward such a thesis.

It is important that the search for identity should find so old-fashioned an expression. Recent loyalist songs and ballads are frequently parodies or inversions of nationalist ballads. Loyalist paramilitary organizations ape the IRA to the extent of emulating their bogeyman fancy-dress. Loyalist phrases echo nationalist phrases in the current reaction against the British Government (the Ulstermen on the Somme, according to the current issue of *Orange Cross*, were sent to slaughter by British generals because they had in 1912 'defied the might of the British Empire' – just like the men of Easter, 1916, in so many nationalist renderings). Loyalist early Irish history is parodying the case that was made, for example, by MacNeill against Orpen in the early years of the century. And MacNeill himself (as Ulster as he was nationalist) is quoted with approval by Adamson. *Briseann an dúchas tré shúilibh an chait.*

8

Hillforts from the Air

Photography from the air continues to enlarge our archaeological knowledge of Ireland. When viewed through the vertical air photographer's lenses, by far the most spectacular of the monuments (whose scale we are just beginning to appreciate) are hillforts; but perhaps the most important thing about the new additions to our knowledge is that these form just parts of sets of a variety of structures. They appear in themselves to be complex, with works of different periods, alterations, modifications, and so on, and hint at activities extending over many centuries. Among them none is more remarkable than the complex at and near Baltinglass, Co. Wicklow, which has recently been described by Tom Condit of the Sites and Monuments Records Office. Here we have evidence of the activities, extending it would seem over a period of some centuries at least in later prehistory, of a sizeable population who built on a grand scale. Mr Condit made his discovery after examining thousands of aerial photographs for the Office of Public Works. 'It is extraordinary that something of such great size had escaped notice for so many centuries', he said.

The photograph of the monument known as Brusselstown Ring shows a complex hillfort enclosing 320 acres, the largest prehistoric site in the country, indeed one of the largest of its type anywhere. Three miles of defensive walls surround the 2,700-year-old town. The stone ramparts extend over such a vast area that previous field work had failed to identify them. The enclosure is on the summit of the 1,300-foot-high Spinnans Hill, near Baltinglass. It consists of a central citadel and a large enclosed area with three entrances through a double rampart, each wall of which was ten feet thick and at least seven feet high. The inner citadel was well populated and the remains of at least twenty-five stone huts have been identified. But much of the acreage may have been used to shelter cattle – and people – in times of war, or for markets and festivals in peacetime.

It is estimated that the citadel and outer ramparts consisted of 700,000 cubic feet of stone, and that it would have taken over 200,000 man-hours to build. Nevertheless archaeologists suspect that only a few hundred people may actually have lived in the town.

This appeared in the *Irish Times* on 30 January 1993.

The site is also unique for the fact that it forms part of an unprecedented concentration of hilltop defended sites. Within an area of six square miles, there are, including Spinans Hill, a total of five separate fortified settlements. Their precise age is not known, but excavations suggest a date in perhaps the eighth or seventh century BC – the Late Bronze Age.

The reason for the unparalleled scale of the fortified complex remains a mystery, although there is some speculation that the area was the centre of tribal power. There is some evidence that mineral wealth, industry and trade may have lain behind that power: earlier excavations revealed 4,000 bronze-casting clay mould fragments – the largest concentration of evidence for bronze manufacture found in Ireland. And one of the complex's hilltop sites, Tinoranhill, was also of great religious importance, being connected with the Celtic god Lugh, a sun-god associated with metal-working.

Work on, and in, the ground is necessary to sharpen our understanding of the monuments; but in the present state of knowledge we can at least attempt interpretation. They show us something which has parallels elsewhere not only in Ireland but also in Britain and on the Continent. 'Hillfort' is the term applied by archaeologists to a large hilltop enclosure with defensive features. The walls, or ramparts, which bound the enclosure will often follow a contour line around the hill. The main outer rampart of the Brusselstown Ring, for example, runs – not perfectly regularly – around the hillside at roughly 1,100 feet above sea-level. There are, however, many types of hillforts; some with simple ramparts; some with multiple closely spaced ramparts; some with multiple widely spaced ramparts. They are common in western and west-central Europe, where they have been most commonly associated with the Early Iron Age; that is, with the latest phases of prehistory – the 'Hallstatt' and La Tène cultures of this region – just before the Roman conquests brought the peoples of the West fully into the light of documented history.

Indeed, Celtic hillforts played a part in some of the Roman campaigns of conquest, being defended against the legions both in Gaul and in Britain. British archaeologists before the Second World War became very interested in hillforts – which are numerous and fairly well recorded in Britain. They could show, for example, that some of the complex multivallate hillforts in Britain were fortresses (at least in their final years) of the Belgae, the Celtic people who had occupied southern England (displacing or subordinating other Celtic peoples) not long before the Roman conquest. In a prewar study of the hillforts in northern France, Sir Mortimer Wheeler showed that some at least were tribal 'capitals', whose locations could be matched with the locations and names of Gaulish tribes mentioned in Caesar's *Gallic* War.

Post-war work has gradually revealed a much more complicated picture, and a great variety of hillforts, from Portuguese *castros* (hilltop settlements with widely-spaced stone enclosing walls, and frequently a dense settlement within, in stone huts or houses) to German *oppida* (sometimes very large fortified hilltop settlements, often commanding important trade routes), some of which in their earlier phases appear to have come under the influence of Greek acropolis builders, and perhaps even to have employed Greek engineers. Further, a quite long period of time is involved in the evolution of these many types of spectacular mountain fortification.

Hillforts in Ireland seemed to be comparatively few, and often aberrant in type; but they were sufficiently interesting to attract attention since the early days of archaeology. Round the turn of the century that great field-worker T.J. Westropp strove to record as many as possible, in association with his work on raths and other earthworks and monuments. More than half a century later, Dr Barry Raftery, in a comprehensive study, located about fifty-nine in the country, but predicted that air photograhy would reveal many more. This has indeed happened, and it may be that in time the number known will nearly double.

For a long time attention was focussed on the 'royal sites' reputed in early Irish writings to have been centres of ancient kingdoms – such as Tara, Eamhain Mhacha (Navan Fort, near Armagh) and Dún Ailinne (Knockaulin, Co. Kildare). All of these, as well as a number of other Irish hilltop sites, have peculiar features. At the southern end of the ridge of Tara there is a large, univallate, fairly regular hillfort (not much visited) known as 'Maeve's rath'. But the main central enclosure, known in Tara's Romantic nomenclature as 'the Rath of the Kings', is surrounded by a rampart which has a ditch on the *inside* – so that it is impossible as a fortification. The same is true of enclosures at Knockaulin and Navan.

Why should an apparent fortification be turned inside-out? Well, we might speculate that the force against which it provided defences was within, not without: a sacred or magical force. Such a monument is not a fortification but an enclosure containing some other-worldly power. Excavation at a number of these places has suggested that this was indeed so. Some at least of them had structures which appeared to be for ritual or religious purposes, although habitation was also involved. And it appears that a high proportion of the hilltop sites have histories going back well beyond the Iron Age, histories which may have involved considerable changes of usage down the centuries.

This brings us back to the question of complexity. A great many of the Irish hillforts are associated with, or enclose, early prehistoric burial mounds. At Tara, for example, within the 'Rath of the Kings' is 'the Mound of the Hostages', a Neolithic passage tomb. And the air photographs of the monuments of the Baltinglass complex clearly show a number of early mounds. An incomplete double-ramparted hillfort on Baltinglass Hill itself surrounds a Neolithic passage tomb. But the evidence for the enclosures themselves increasingly shows that many of them originated in the Bronze Age.

The Brusselstown Ring complex looks quite like a Portuguese *castro* – but it also has parallels closer to home, in Britain, and some resemblances to a great *oppidum* like the Heuneberg in Bavaria. The new knowledge coming from the air photographs, like all good new knowledge, tells us how much we don't know. Vertical aerial photography, as used in military intelligence surveys, is the tool for precise mapping, and this is now employed by the Ordnance Survey, the Army and the Air Corps, and the Archaeological Survey. For the past few years the Sites and Monuments Record Office of the Office of Public Works has been examining the archaeological record engraved on the face of Ireland (through the binocular lenses of a stereoscope in Hatch Street, Dublin). This is enriching and is drastically revising our understanding of our past, both prehistoric and historic.

Early field archaeologists saw the landscapes of long-settled countries like Ireland and Britain as palimpsests, on which generation after generation of our forebears had left documents in the form of field patterns, enclosures, house sites, roads, frontier defences and other features. Successive generations erased, but could not wholly obliterate, the traces of the predecessors' work. In interpreting these documents, the archaeologists made use of the accurate large-scale maps which are such a significant product of the modern age in our part of the world; then they were quick to see the possibilities of photography from the air.

Years ago, in the 1950s, I had the fortune to accompany O.G.S. Crawford on a trip from Konstanz in Germany to St Gallen in Switzerland, and to spend a couple of days in his company listening to tales of his early days in archaeological field work. He was then at the end of his career, but had spent most of his life in the British Archaeological Survey and had been the great pioneer of air photography, although he had some predecessors, such as Sir Henry Wellcome, who took vertical air photographs of his excavations in the Sudan from a box kite in 1913. Even before he had ever seen an air photograph, Crawford realised how valuable such a tool could be to the field archaeologist, and he made efforts after the Great War to get hold of some, finally succeeding in seeing vertical photographs of hundreds of acres of Hampshire taken by the RAF. 'What I saw surpassed my wildest dreams', he afterwards wrote, 'and I felt as much the same excitement as, according to the poet, did stout Cortez on a memorable occasion.' This led to much fieldwork on the ground and to his paper to the Royal Geographical Society, published in 1924: *Air Survey and Archaeology*.

The information revealed by the air photographs and by subsequent investigation on the ground in Baltinglass has been summarized by Mr Condit in the autumn 1992 issue of *Archaeology Ireland*. The whole area on the western slope of the Wicklow Hills is shown to have been one of intense activity, partly at least of a religious or ceremonial nature, throughout a long period that brings us close to the dawn of written history. It is the area where the rulers of the Lagin – the Leinster kingdoms – had the centre of their power just at the beginning of our records.

But we should be slow to extrapolate back from historical legends to understand the meaning of the monuments. We should not even think in terms of Celts – because thinking we know what we don't know is sure to lead us astray.

This is a local complex, which may or may not be associated in its meaning with other complexes in the same area. For example, the rings of standing stones which we call 'stone circles' (generally taken to have been something like open-air temples of prehistoric peoples) are not evenly distributed over the country, but tend to occur in clusters (just as Richard Warner and others have observed that hillforts do). There are concentrations of them in Tyrone, in Kerry and West Cork, and in other areas – including the western slope of the Wicklow Hills. They too in their time (which for most of them was in the Bronze Age) were probably ceremonial places of tribal assembly. If the stone circles were a real part of the complex of monuments in the area, we may be looking in the air photographs at evidence for a very long history, perhaps of a local tribal nation which will not fit very easily into the backward extrapolations we make from the stereotypes of the recorded past.

Mr Condit has completed a preliminary report on a new area of knowledge which is rapidly opening up but will take a long time to mature. It promises revisions, which may turn out to be quite drastic, of our understanding of the Irish past and of the people who came long before us – people who will, I suspect, turn out to be extremely interesting in all kinds of unexpected ways.

9

Tara

One of the most interesting examples of the interaction between history and myth is provided by the old royal site of Tara, in Co. Meath. It is interesting because the site is in itself unimpressive, and has been so probably for fourteen or fifteen hundred years. Tara is a low and inconspicuous hill. It is quite easy to pass it on the road from Dublin to Navan without noticing it. Not only is the hill itself inconspicuous, but it has no obviously spectacular monuments of the past. It is only after the visitor has walked about on its grassy slopes for some time that he begins to realise just how extensive a complex of earthworks is there. But to those who are not especially interested in such matters earthworks signify little.

Yet this is the place which became, in post-medieval times at least, the symbol of Irish nationality:

> The harp that once through Tara's halls
> The soul of music shed
> Now hangs as mute on Tara's walls
> As if that soul were dead.

Tom Moore used Tara as the pre-eminent symbol of Ireland's conquered and vanished glories. There is probably hardly anyone nowadays who thinks of Tara in anything like this way – Romantic nationalism has finally run its course in Ireland – but it is not so very long since a small political party which, in the nineteen-forties, had hopes for a while of making an impression on Irish politics, adorned its headquarters with plans for a new Irish capital on the Hill of Tara.

All this is in a sense a tribute to the success of learned propagandists of the eleventh century. These were men of their time, who realised that the right thing to have, in terms of the best eleventh-century European practice, was a national monarchy. So they persuaded, themselves perhaps, and certainly the interested public for generations to come, that this is just what Ireland had long had. They propagated the idea of the ancient high-kingship of Ireland,

---

This appeared in the 'Roots' column in the *Irish Times* on 23 October 1973. The statue of St Patrick mentioned has since disintegrated and been removed.

centred on Tara, drawing on every idle boast that an Irish king had made for centuries previously, to support this thesis. Their version of the past became the received one, and for hundreds of years subsequently, scholars working in the Irish tradition accepted it; so that the high-kingship became almost a symbol of the pre-conquest Irish nation.

The nation undoubtedly existed, but without, it would seem, the kind of political centralization, even of the vaguest kind, that is implied in the concept of the high-kingship. Yet there was a kingship of Tara, and an important one. Some of the pagan kings of very early historic times may even have lived there.

It was here, at any rate, that the *féis*, or inauguration ceremony, was performed. The very first elaboration of the Patrick legend, written in the seventh century, brings the saint to Tara at the beginning of his mission, to confront paganism in the person of King Loegaire and his druids. This is a saga of which Patrick is the wonder-working hero: the story could have been located in any of a number of places; but the selection of Tara indicates that it was regarded, in the seventh century, as an outstanding symbol of the old order. The early monastic legendary tradition embodies another story – given a sixth-century setting – in which a confrontation takes place between paganism and Christianity. This is the story of the cursing of Tara and of the conflict between St Ruadhán of Lorrha and King Diarmait, in which the saint wins a fasting contest by means of a trick (all may be fair in love and war, but in this hagiographical tradition, anything goes in religion), and is given maledictory power over the king. After this, Tara is said to have been abandoned.

But its possession was still necessary, for centuries to come, as a warrant of true kingship. It was here, for example, on what had already been for hundreds of years a grass-grown hill, that Maelshechlainn II yielded his sovereignty in 1002 to the great Munster usurper Brian Bóroimhe. The sovereignty of what? Well, Tara had been the royal centre of the most powerful among the kings of the northern half of Ireland, the Uí Néill, drawn from a group of widely dispersed dynasties. With the appearance there of Brian, from the southern half, the semblance at least of a national monarchy came into being. At any rate Tara very soon was accepted as the certification of this, and so it passed into the medieval, and later, Gaelic tradition: the symbol of vanished glory:

Tá Teamhair ina féar, agus féach an Traoi mar atá,
A's na Sasanaigh féin, b'fhéidir go bhfaghaidís bás.
[Tara is grass; behold the state of Troy;
And the English themselves; perhaps they might die.]

In more recent times, the pikemen of the surrounding areas assembled on Tara in the 1798 uprising, and a little under half a century later, Daniel O'Connell, again in a shamrock-wreathed gesture of symbolism, held one of the greatest of his mass meetings there.

The place itself is a low ridge extending north and south, with earthworks distributed over more than a mile of its length. These are generally known by the names given to them in a medieval text, the *Dindsenchus*, which gathers together the lore of important places and to which, in this context, far too much attention has been paid. At the time the text was compiled the authors had less information available on the sites (as grass-grown then as they are now) than we have today.

Near the crest of the ridge there is a large earthwork, a hilltop enclosure resembling a 'hillfort', in part all but obliterated and barely distinguishable on the ground. This is known as *Ráith na Rígh*. It had a deep rock-cut ditch with a palisaded outer bank.

It was more likely ritual than defensive in purpose. Within this, on the crest of the hill, is a round mound known (again from *Dindsenchus*) as the Mound of the Hostages, which was excavated by Professor Seán P. Ó Ríordáin and his successor Professor Ruaidhrí de Valéra in 1955–59. This was found to cover a small Neolithic passage-grave. The cairn of stones which covered the megalithic structure itself had been covered by a metre-thick mantle of clay, and this, as well as the passage, had been re-used as a Bronze Age cemetery for cremated and inhumed burials.

There are other earthworks within Ráith na Rígh, which have not been excavated. They have features which suggest that they may in part belong to the historic period or a little earlier; but one or two of them could well incorporate other prehistoric burial mounds. On the crest of one of these there stands an unusually repulsive statue of St Patrick, to commemorate his alleged defeat of paganism on this spot, as well as a granite standing stone reputed to be the *Lia Fáil* (the other claimant is the Stone of Scone) which played a part in the inauguration of the kings. The stone was re-erected in its present position as a monument to the men of ninety-eight.

To the north of Ráith na Rígh is the multiple-ramparted fort known as the 'Rath of the Synods', excavated in 1952–53. Earlier, it had been badly damaged in burrowings by a group known as the British Israelites, who had persuaded themselves that they would find the Ark of the Covenant there. They failed. The later work showed that the site had been used for ritual, occupation and burial, in the period from the second to the fourth century AD – a testimony to the Tara of the Kings and its pagan significance.

There are numerous other earthworks, including a second large hillfort-like enclosure known as Rath Maeve, at the extreme southern end of the ridge, and the 'fort of Loegaire', where, if *Dindsenchus* and the early Christian writer Tírechán are to be believed, King Loegaire is buried standing upright, his weapons in his hands, facing his Leinster enemies on the fringe of the Wicklow hills visible to the south.

Like several other royal sites in the country, Tara is of great interest to the archaeologist because of the extent and variety of the superficial remains. Cruachain in Connacht is somewhat similar in its scale and variety. Both appear to be sites of very ancient sanctity, frequented for many many centuries by the pre-Christian peoples of the island. They were royal sites almost certainly not in the sense that they were occupied by royal palaces, but rather in that they embodied in some way the spirit of pagan sovereignty, with all its magical attributes, and that their possession was a demonstration of legitimacy.

10

Arles and Lérins

It used to be said that the Arlésiennes were the most beautiful women in France; this was attributed to their inheritance of Greek blood, since Arles is within the enclave established by Greek colonists six centuries before our era around the mouths of the Rhône. The chief foundation was Massilia, nowadays Marseille. The colony was a beach-head on the Mediterranean shore of Celtic Europe, providing access to the heart of what was later to be known as Gaul, for the wines, oil and artefacts of the pioneering entrepreneurs from the Aegean. The founders of Massilia, around 600 BC, were Phocaeans from near Smyrna in Grecian Asia Minor. Some earlier Aegean traders had visited or settled in villages along the neighbouring Mediterranean coasts, but it was the Phocaeans of Massilia who gained a firm Greek foothold in France.

The Roman historian Justinus reports that the Gauls abandoned their barbarous ways and learned civilization from the Greeks:

> They set to tilling their fields and walling their towns. They even got used to living by law rather than force of arms, to cultivating the vine and the olive. Their progress, in manners and wealth, was so brilliant that it seemed as though Gaul had become part of Greece, rather than that Greece had colonized Gaul.

This naïve, not to say biassed, account of a complicated process, showing no great understanding of early 'Gaulish' (better 'pre-Gaulish') society, yet has a large element of truth in it. And the introduction of viticulture to France is not without direct interest to us even today. Massilia became a centre of manufacture (of pottery and other goods) as well as of trade, and its products made their way northward along the Rhône and the Saône and on into northern France and Central Europe, to influence greatly the late-Hallstatt culture. The famous great bronze krater (probably made in Sparta) buried with a Hallstatt queen at Vix, on Mt Lassois, overlooking the upper Seine, is just one of the many items traded north from the Rhône mouth.

Previously unpublished.

The small colony prospered, so attracting through the centuries the attention of predators, and in the second century BC it several times sought the help of the rising power of the Roman Republic – against Ligurian raiders, for example. When the Romans came to Massilia's aid in 125 BC, their arrival drew down on the colony the hostility of neighbouring Gaulish tribes, and this led to a series of conflicts and, after final victory, to the Roman Senate's decision to annex all of south-eastern Gaul as a province (for a time *the* province – hence 'Provence'). Massilia remained autonomous as an ally within the new province. In 118 a Roman colony was established at the city they named *Narbo Martius*, and the province became known as *Gallia Narbonensis*. Very shortly the whole area came under the threat of a vast migration of German peoples from the North Sea shore of Europe, the Cimbri and the Teutones, who were joined in the Alpine region by a Celtic tribal nation, the Tigurini. They turned westward into the new Roman province, fought several battles with Roman armies, and in 105 BC, at Arausio (Orange), disastrously defeated the Romans, killing, it is said, 80,000 of them. Under the consul Marius, the Romans fought back in a series of campaigns, and ultimately drove out the barbarians.

In the course of this war, Marius conducted, with his army, an engineering work to open the Rhône to Mediterranean shipping. The river's mouths were silted and impassable, and the Greek colonial city of Massilia had been built, not on it, but on the coast to the east of the delta. Marius cut a canal, the *Fossa Mariana*, from the place now known as Fos, to bypass the delta and give access to the main river near Arles, where there was a trading post of the Geek colony. The Province prospered in the last century of the Republic and, having been Hellenized on its southern shore, now became thoroughly Romanized. In 58–56 BC Julius Caesar conquered the whole region north and west of Provence as far as the Atlantic and the North Sea – the 'three Gauls', Aquitania, Gallia Lugdunensis and Gallia Belgica. Ten years later, in the Roman Civil War, the city of Massilia, after wavering, took the side of Pompey against Caesar – the losing side, as it turned out – and in punishment Caesar, although he left it its nominal autonomy, deprived it of most of the territory of the Greek colony. It rapidly declined. He laid out Arelate (Arles) as a Roman city. It was at the head of Marius's canal (which made it the chief port of the whole province), and at the lowest bridge over the Rhône, where the main road from Italy to Spain crossed, and it overshadowed Massilia, or Marseille, for a while.

Monumental works of the time of Augustus and later testify to the importance which Arles soon achieved. Its Augustan walls encompassed trade from Africa, the Orient, Spain and Gaul; manufactures of textiles, arms and goldsmith's work, and an Imperial mint. Its great arena was built shortly after the city's Roman foundation in 46 BC; its theatre in the time of Augustus.

History has its downs as well as ups. Arles later declined again. It is a small city today, comfortable to walk about in. It is physically (and nowadays touristically) dominated by its Roman remains but there are other reminders of its past, recent and medieval, while, of course, present-day life goes on (centred on the Boulevard des Lices), indifferent to what is no more. There is the gloriously sculptured Romanesque church of St Trophime, with its cloister, and just around the corner from it there is the Place du Forum – a small square, where the Roman forum once was, nowadays filled with the tables of several cafés surrounding a rather jaunty statue of the poet hero of Provençal nationalism, Mistral, erected, as an inscription testifies, by public subscription on 30 May 1909; re-edified in 1948.

But Arles bears the Roman stamp: its great days coincided with the Roman Empire and Late Antiquity; afterwards it suffered sacks and ravagings by a whole series of barbarian and Saracen invaders and went into long decline. The mighty ruins of walls, theatre and arena fill one end of the city with reminders of that vanished civilization; at the other end there is the large Roman cemetery, the *Alyscamps*, which was (as prescribed by Roman law) outside the walls. The place has a melancholy charm, having suffered much both from modern constructions and destruction and from earlier plunderings of its tomb sculptures to adorn rich bourgeois houses or to build monastic chapels. There is an avenue of great beeches, with a file of Roman sarcophagi lined along each side of the roadway, leading towards the fragmentary Romanesque ruins of the church of St Honoratus. There are other small buildings, some ruinous, some in repair. One illustrates the pathos of the death of a small child who has now been dust for fifteen hundred years: it contains a carved tomb which bears a Latin inscription asking for eternal peace for 'the sweetest and most innocent girl, Chrysogone' who lived, we are told, 'only three years, two months and twenty-seven days'. This was erected – in the early sixth century, judging from its style and ornament – by her parents Valerius and Chrysogone. The inscription is Christian; Arles by that date was an important centre of the Western Church, having extended its influence throughout Gaul, to reach, almost certainly, as far as Ireland.

It was disaster elsewhere that had brought ultimate prominence to Arles. By the third century AD it was already important enough, the gateway to the prosperous and most civilized Province. But the early years of that century saw a collapse, at the top, of the Roman system of government. The Imperial succession fell into the hands of the soldiers, most of whom by now were recruited not from within the Empire but from the barbarians without. The pretence that the Senate conferred the highest office was thrust aside: first the Praetorian Guard in Rome, then the armies on the frontiers began murdering Emperors and choosing successors (who would pay them a bounty on accession) from among their own ranks. For much of the century Imperial reigns averaged less than three years. Meantime, barbarians and enemies invaded the Empire, East and West. Goths appeared on and crossed the Danube frontier. On the lower Rhine, the Franks, an alliance of German tribes, made their first appearance in history. Large provinces beyond Rhine and Danube were permanently lost to Roman rule. The invasions of the West began in 233 with the assault of the Alamans on the upper Danube and the Rhine. German tribes entered Gaul and pursued their destructive way through the provinces, some of them over the Pyrenees into Spain. The breakdown of Imperial order was such, from causes both internal and external, that in several parts of the Empire, failing effective government from the centre, the local legions set up local emperors and empires – most notably, after 259, in Gaul. Towards the end of the century an Imperial recovery restored the rule of Rome. But the prolonged crisis had profound social effects. In Gaul, as to a less extent in Spain and in Rhaetia on the upper Danube, cities, which had been open and spreading into the countryside, were now fortified, and shrank within their walls, losing population. The cultivated aristocracy, who had played their full civic part within the cities, began to withdraw from urban responsibilities and live on their estates.

Ultimately order and central government were restored, within the boundary of Rhine and Danube in the West, and, under Diocletian (285–305), the system of administration and rule was reorganized. But some changes were permanent. Diocletian divided the Empire for administrative and defensive purposes into East and West, with two rulers, one senior, one junior, in each division. These rulers now camped on the frontiers, and Trier became in effect the Imperial capital of the West, with a great and permanent Imperial palace and the quarters for an army, where the rulers of the world maintained their watch on the Rhine. In southern Gaul, members of the senatorial aristocracy, many of them descendants of the great families of the Republic, others drawn from the middle classes, withdrew from taxes, inflation, devaluation, and the other ills of the late Empire, into their vast estates and lived in their *villae urbanae* as if in semi-independent principalities.

Meantime the Christian Gospel had long been preached in Gaul. The city of Lugdunum (Lyon), at the confluence of Rhône and Saône, had been the religious centre of pre-Roman Gaul, the site of a great shrine of the ubiquitous Celtic god Lug. The Romans, after Caesar's conquests, had taken this over, and established an altar of Augustus and Rome, where sacrifices were offered on what had been the festival of Lug (1 August). In AD 177 Christians were martyred in the amphitheatre on the festival day – evidence that there was a community of them in the city by that date. It appears that the first bishop's see in Gaul was here. By the mid-third century there were sees also in Vienne, Arles, Toulouse, Narbonne, Paris, Reims and Trier. It was a time – poorly recorded – not only of breakdown of the civil order, but of intermittent persecution of the Church. But in AD 313, the 'Edict of Milan', issued by the Emperor Constantine and his colleague Licinius, ended the persecutions, extended official toleration to Christianity and provided for the restoration of confiscated Church property.

Constantine, however, was prepared to make these restorations and other State grants only to those who were accepted by the Church as orthodox Catholics; but the Church was already bitterly divided on some points of doctrine and on the question whether those who had lapsed during the persecutions (particularly those who had surrendered the sacred books of the churches) should be readmitted to the Christian community. This had become a controversy between élitists who held that the Christian Church should be a community of the pure – of confessors and martyrs – rejecting and denying forgiveness to any who had sinned gravely after baptism, and those who believed that sinners, suitably repentant and penitent, should continue as members of the Church. The fierce persecution under Decius in the middle of the century posed these questions sharply. Marcian, Bishop of Arles, held extreme rigorist views. Rome was becoming the pre-eminent court of appeal in such disputes, and other Gaulish bishops asked Stephen I (who became bishop of Rome in 254) to depose Marcian, which however he was reluctant to do. After the Edict of Milan, Constantine felt it fell to him to sort out these disputes, which had continued through the persecutions of Diocletian. The rigorist party in Africa objected to Bishop Caecilian of Carthage because one of those who consecrated him had surrendered the sacred books, thereby rendering the consecration, as they held, invalid. They elected a rival bishop, Majorinus, shortly succeeded by Donatus who became leader of their cause, and they appealed to the Emperor to adjudicate. He commissioned the Bishop of Rome (now Miltiades) to meet in Rome with three Gaulish bishops on the matter: they excommunicated Donatus. On a second appeal to the Emperor, he summoned a general council of the West to meet (not under the presidency of Silvester, who had just succeeded Militiades in Rome, but under that of the Bishop of Arles, Marinus). It convened in Arles on 1 August (that significant Gaulish date again), in AD 314.

This First Council of Arles was also the first general Western Council after the end of the persecutions. Sixteen Gaulish churches were represented, twelve by their bishops; half of these were in the south-east of Provence. The church, although organized throughout Gaul, was still only thinly established; whereas Africa had already a great number of bishops' sees. The Council again found against the Donatists; it forwarded its findings to Rome to the newly elected Silvester, who had not attended personally but had been represented. Among other matters, in its third, fourth and fifth canons, it prohibited Christians from performing in the arena or the theatre – a difficult problem for the Church, since those who provided such entertainment largely did so under compulsion (acting, for example, was an hereditary trade and those who practised it were bound to it in a kind of serfdom). The text of the proceedings has been badly transmitted and is sometimes obscure. The third canon has often been interpreted as condemning soldiers who deserted *in pace* ('in peacetime' – given the rather strained interpretation, 'now that the persecutions have ended'). But its context suggests it has to do with the arena and the theatre, and the phrase *arma abjicere* ('to throw away arms' – commonly meaning 'to desert') is probably corrupt. The soldier's trade had long been condemned and it is unlikely that the assembled bishops were so cynical as to excommunicate people for refusing to do that for doing which they would have been excommunicated a year earlier – especially as another century was to pass before the Christian objections to warfare began to diminish significantly. It is more probably a condemnation of those who *practised* arms in peacetime – gladiators. Banning the entertainments of the people, however, was something that even the most fervently Christian emperors, for long after this, were reluctant to do; nothing was more disadvantageous politically. It is likely that in Arles itself the theatre and the arena continued to function with small regard for the Council's decrees. The finding against the Donatists, however, was reinforced by a further condemnation at a Tribunal of the Emperor in Milan in 316.

An even greater controversy arose in the Church on the interpretation of the doctrine of the Trinity, and Constantine summoned the ecumenical council of Nicaea in 325, which decreed that the Son was one in being with the Father, and rejected the teaching of Arius that the Son was created by the Father. Arianism, however, continued to divide the Church, and both Constantine, looking for a middle way, and his successor, Constantius II (who was anti-Nicene), banished the contentious Athanasius, bishop of Alexandria, who was the foremost and most persuasive opponent of Arianism, from his see. Constantius was co-emperor from 337 to 350 with Constans, but thereafter reigned alone until 361. He resided at Arles, and convened a church council there in 353 which, without endorsing Arianism, reiterated the condemnation of Athanasius.

Athanasius, repeatedly banished, spent three periods of exile in the Thebaid, among the monks of the Egyptian desert, and was three times in Gaul. The first time in the West, when he was exiled to Trier by Constantine in 336, he preached there the virtues of the monasticism he had encountered in the Thebaid. A coenobitic or eremitical community was founded at Trier as a result. Much later, St Augustine, telling of his own conversion in 385, describes a conversation at Milan with one Potitianus, an Imperial officer. This man told how, when he was stationed at Trier, he and some companions walked in the gardens of the palace while the Emperor was at the circus, and entered a monastic hut, where he picked up the Life of St Anthony of the Desert, written by Athanasius. The book changed his life and led him and his wife to celibacy and a penitential régime. This story brought about Augustine's final change of heart.

Monasticism, at any rate, was to spread through Gaul from Trier. St Hilary, Bishop of Poitiers, exiled to Asia, as Athanasius was to the West, for his opposition to Arianism, conferred minor orders there on a penitent cavalryman, Martin, who sought his patronage in religion and became his disciple. On their return to Poitiers in 360 Hilary encouraged him to found the monastery of Liguin at the gates of the city. Martin was later made bishop of Tours, and founded near there another monastery, Marmoutier. In 410 – the year Rome fell to the Goths – the aristocrat Honoratus arrived on the then desert island of Lérins, off the Mediterranean coast near Cannes, wishing to follow the way of the monks, and was soon joined by numerous companions. As Hilary of Arles wrote of him:

As if with outstretched hands and open arms, he invited into his embrace all who loved Christ; and everyone gathered in to him from every part. Indeed, by now, what land, what nation does not have its citizens in his monastery?

Or as Jeremiah O'Sullivan wrote, describing (in the introduction to his translation of *The Writings of Salvian, the Presbyter*) how Salvian had taught rhetoric in that monastery: 'It is quite possible that he [Salvian] knew St Patrick, who was a student at Lérins at the same time'. This may be doubted; but the monastery almost certainly was to have a considerable influence on Ireland as well as on Gaul.

Meantime, in the late fourth century, the menace on the frontiers grew again, and there was disaster on the Danube, where the Emperor Valens was defeated and killed trying to prevent a large-scale migration of Visigoths, Ostrogoths and Alans into the Balkans. More and more barbarians moved into the Empire and were then hired, initially to resist further incursions. Frankish *foederati* had long been settled north of the road passing through Bavae to Colonia Agrippina (roughly corresponding to the present road from Boulogne to Köln), but had been infiltrating south and east of it. They and the Alamans threatened the great Imperial base of Trier. The residence of the Praetorian Prefect of the Gauls was removed from there southward to the apparent comparative safety and more thoroughly Roman polity of Arles, where the title and office of Praetorian Prefect were to continue until even beyond the end of the Western Empire in 476. On 31 December 406, the Rhine froze at Mainz, and vast numbers of Alans, Vandals and Sueves irresistibly crossed the ice into Gaul and marched westward and southward, never to be dislodged. In Britain, in 407, the army threw up yet another would-be Emperor, Constantine, who crossed over to Gaul and marched south. Rome itself was taken and sacked by Alaric and his Arian Visigoths in 410, although what they most needed was food, of which the city produced none and had little, and they moved on after a few days. The fall of the eternal and inviolable City was, however, for the cultivated Roman world, an eschatological epoch: almost unimagineable.

The usurper Constantine was captured and killed at Arles in 411 by the army of the Emperor Honorius; but the Western provinces were to be repeatedly fought over and sometimes ravaged from now on. In the meantime, in 410 the last Roman legions abandoned Britain. In 412 the Visigoths who had taken Rome, now led by Alaric's successor Athaulph, retreated from Italy into Gaul, in desperate need for food for the great army. That year in Arles, the Bishop Heros, a disciple of St Martin of Tours, was expelled and replaced by Patroclus (a schemer who had ingratiated himself with Honorius's Master of the Troops, Constantius). The Visigoths moved into Spain in 415, but were for many years to continue to retain control of much of Aquitaine. In 418 the Emperor Honorius reorganized the provincial councils, of which, in the West, Arles was the centre.

In 417, Pope Zosimus made Patroclus, Bishop of Arles (who was in Rome at the time) Metropolitan of the ecclesiastical provinces of Vienne and the two Narbonnes. Vienne was the former metropolis, but there were bitter disputes among the sees of the region, in spite of the regulation of hierarchical relationships there by the Council of Turin in 398. Zosimus in effect established a Western vicariate for Arles. It was annulled by Boniface I on his accession in 419, who restored metropolitan rights to Vienne, Marseille and Narbonne; but it was not forgotten and, intermittently for more than a hundred years, Arles was to be the vicariate of the West. As the troubles of the fifth century gathered and worsened, monasticism in various forms, Eastern in origin, took root among the Christians of the West. It had been known there for a hundred years: Constantine's daughter is said to have founded a community of women above the tomb of the Roman martyr St Agnes. But it was the exiling of Athanasius to Rome and Gaul at the height of the Arian controversy in the mid-fourth century that gave a great impetus to the movement, especially, and importantly, among Christians of noble family, descendants of the old ruling classes of the Roman Republic and members of the senatorial aristocracy. Monastic rules were observed within some of the great houses, in Rome and elsewhere. Men, often of good family, went out to inhabit the islands and rocks of the Mediterranean which had been used by the Emperors as places of banishment for criminal and political offenders. This shocked the cultivated pagans of the time, like Rutilius Namatianus, who, returning across the Mediterranean to Gaul, passed the monastic island of Capraia, 'full of men who shun the light of day', and then the island of Gorgona, of which he wrote:

> ... Here a fellow-citizen was lost and descended alive into the tomb. Young and of noble descent, wealthy and married, he has lately been driven by the furies and, deserting gods and men, now lives, a credulous exile, in a foul retreat. Is not this sect, I ask, worse than the poisons of Circe? They transform the body; this the soul.

St Ambrose, St Jerome and St Augustine all favoured and sponsored the monastic movement, of which the foundation of establishments of women (sometimes within noble households) was an important part, as was the establishment of paired monasteries or dual monasteries of men and women living separately under a common rule. Rules, as in the East, varied greatly at this time. They were issued according to circumstance and to the judgment of the founders or directors of the communities, which themselves were greatly varied in size and context. The common impulse was one of ascetic withdrawal; a turning inward to the life of the spirit and a renunciation of the things of the world. That world was, visibly and terrifyingly in the fifth-century West, failed and fallen. Pagans blamed Christianity and the abandonment of the old gods and rites for the fall of Rome; Augustine's *City of God* was the Christian response; monastic withdrawal was in accord with that response.

But there was a paradox. The noble families who sponsored and took part in monasticism in the West were members of a governing class; when the barbarized and disintegrating Empire failed around them, instinct, training and tradition brought them back into the world *by way of the church* to discharge the ancient responsibilities of their breed. And often this was first by way of the monastic life. Montalambert, in the middle of the nineteenth century, in his *The Monks of the West*, summed up the first part of the process:

> ... The vast and sumptuous villas of the senators and consuls were changed into houses of retirement, almost in every point conformed to monasteries, where the descendants of the Scipios, the Gracchi, the Marelli, the Camilli, the Anicii, led in solitude a life of sacrifice and charity.

Lérins illustrates the second part of the process. Its literate and cultivated monks made the desert island bloom, so that it became, as one of its alumni, Eucherius, said, 'a paradise', and it was commonly to be referred to as *beata insula*, the 'happy island', and to be known as an island of saints and scholars. It was also, in the fifth century and later, an equivalent of the present-day *École Nationale d'Administration*. Beginning with its founder, Honoratus, who became bishop of Arles, it supplied bishops, mostly aristocratic, for Arles, Avignon, Lyon, Vienne, Troyes, Riez, Frejus, Valence, Metz, Nice, Vence, Apt, Carpentras and Saintes. It was to play some part in the initial organizing of the Church in Ireland; whence the stories told, although mistakenly, about St Patrick's sojourn in Lérins. It is certain that at a much later date (596) St Augustine of Canterbury and his forty missionary companions delayed there on their way to evangelize England; indeed it was there that they first showed the faint-heartedness that was to dog their mission. On hearing horror stories of the barbarism of the Anglo-Saxons, Augustine returned to Rome to call off the enterprise, only to be sent back again by Gregory the Great, with letters forbidding the monks to abandon their mission and calling on others, in particular the Metropolitan, Virgilius, Bishop of Arles, to stiffen their resolve and help them on their way.

Not too far away from Lérins, another great monastery, named after the martyr St Victor, was founded early in the fifth century at Marseille by John Cassian. He held to the old Eastern desert tradition that monks should stay away from women and bishops, and did not intend his community to be a resource for the Gaulish church as Lérins was; but this intention was not wholly fulfilled.

One of the refugees from Rome, who departed from the city for Africa in 409 as Alaric and the Goths were approaching, was the monk and moral reformer Pelagius who had made a reputation as a preacher denouncing the laxity of Roman Christians. He had been born in Britain and was possibly Irish by descent (if some of the insults hurled at him by St Jerome are to be taken literally). In Africa he continued preaching, insisting that people were responsible for their own souls and could not rely merely on baptism and membership of the Christian church for their salvation. He had reacted strongly against a prayer of St Augustine's to God (in his *Confessions*) – *Continentiam iubes. Da quod iubes et iubes quod vis* ('You command continence. Give what You command and command what You will'), seeing in it a denial of human free will. He had gone to Palestine and was not present, although his colleague Celestius was, when a Council at Carthage in 412 condemned their teachings. St Jerome was also in Palestine at the time, and worked successfully to have an Eastern synod convened for the condemnation of Pelagius. At Diospolis, the Metropolitan of Caesarea presided over the synod, where two bishops from Provence – both of whom had been deposed from their sees – accused Pelagius of heresy. They were Heros of Arles (the same whom Patroclus had replaced) and Lazarus of Aix. The accusation of Pelagius was based mainly on quoted teachings of Celestius. He replied:

> It is for those who say that these are the opinions of Celestius to look to it whether they really are his. I, however, have never held such views and I anathematize the man who does hold them.

On the central question of free will, in which he was accused of saying that all men are governed by their own will, he answered:

> This I stated on account of free will, which God helps when it chooses good; man, however, when he sins, is himself to blame as of free will.

The synod found in his favour on all his answers, to the great chagrin of St Augustine. However, in 416 two African Councils condemned both Pelagius and Celestius, and Pope Innocent I condemned a book by Pelagius. Pope Zosimus, however, in 417, first reversed Innocent's decision and rebuked Aurelius, Bishop of Carthage for condemning the two; but then, under Imperial pressure, reversed himself. The Emperor, at the urging of Augustine, had banished Pelagius, Celestius and their followers. Zosimus compelled the bishops of Italy to acquiesce in his condemnation and deposed eighteen who refused. There was a disputed succession to Zosimus, who died in December 418. Boniface, whose claim to the Papacy prevailed, continued the hounding of the Pelagians and persuaded the Emperor Honorius to require all bishops to sign Zosimus's condemnation. When he died in September 422, the Archdeacon of Rome, Celestine, was elected in his place – another firm anti-Pelagian. Celestine's secretary, Prosper of Aquitaine, a copious writer, and chronicler of his age, took an active part in the controversy, in support of St Augustine and against the Pelagians.

Zosimus, Boniface and Celestine, besides being rigorous in their opposition to the Pelagians, were also strenuous in asserting the primacy and prerogatives

of the see of Rome. The churches of Africa resisted, insisting on their autonomy, as did the church of Constantinople, the 'new Rome'. There was some
resistance too in Gaul, where, in the south, the movements and settlements
of great numbers of barbarians (most of whom were Arian Christians) and of
Roman armies (often barbarian or half-barbarian themselves) tended to disrupt
administrative and social order. Bishop Patroclus of Arles was murdered in
426, 'mangled by many wounds', on the secret orders, according to Prosper, of
Felix, Master of the Troops. The following year the Vandals, having secured
shipping, crossed the Mediterranean into Africa, the most populous province of
the Western Church and the source of much of the food supply of the Western
Empire.

Pelagianism continued to be of concern to the Western Church. The East
had been in general more sympathetic to Pelagius, but some years later, in 431,
the Council of Ephesus condemned his teaching. A modified version of that
teaching, to be known as 'semi-Pelagianism', had been put forward by John
Cassian, the founder of the monastery of St Victor, and was espoused by Vincent
of Lérins. This too was strongly opposed by St Augustine and his followers.
In the 420s word reached the bishops of northern Gaul that Pelagianism was
spreading in the churches of Britain (now outside the Imperial system but still
Roman in organization and culture, and still under constant barbarian threat,
like the Roman West in general). It seems that an appeal for help came to
Gaul from anti-Pelagian British bishops. This was referred to Celestine in
Rome. Prosper of Aquitaine tells us that at the instigation of 'the deacon
Palladius' the Pope decided on a mission to Britain. The seventh-century Irish
writer Muirchú says that Palladius was 'archdeacon of Pope Celestine' and
most modern writers have assumed that he was a deacon in Rome. (The
Archdeacon of Rome was Leo, later Leo I, but there were seven deacons.) He
was more likely a deacon of Auxerre, sent by Germanus, the bishop of that see
(consecrated in 418, when the diocese had just been overrun by barbarians), to
inform Celestine of the British problem. At any rate, in 429, Celestine commissioned Germanus and Bishop Lupus of Troyes (another alumnus of Lérins)
to go to Britain to combat Pelagianism. They went, and apparently were successful, and, like so many other bishops of the time, were called on to repel
barbarian attack, and are reported to have been instrumental in achieving a
British victory. Lupus many years later was to be successful in diverting the
Huns from his city of Troyes, before Pope Leo (according to more dubious
report) did likewise for Rome in 452. In 431, Celestine consecrated Palladius
and sent him to be the first bishop of 'the Irish Christians'. This occurred in
the context of the anti-Pelagian mission, and it may have been intended either
to forestall or to stamp out Pelagianism in Ireland

In 431 also, the third General Council of the Church was summoned at
Ephesus. Pelagianism was condemned, as were the views of Nestorius, Patriarch
of Constantinople on the two natures of Christ, God and Man (views stemming
from a rejection of the concept of Mary as Mother of God). Into the theological

controversies surrounding this issue there intruded the ecclesiastical-political issue of primacy. Nestorius, as Bishop of the New Rome, claimed to be Celestine's equal. Celestine asserted Rome's primacy in the West as well as the East and was concerned in particular to prevent the development of autonomous ecclesiastical government in Gaul, centred on Arles. One of his interventions illustrates the growing influence of the monastic movement on church practice in general; for he directs the clergy (through the Arles vicariate) not to wear dress that distinguished them from the laity; but to distinguish themselves rather by good conduct. This suggests that the distinctive coarse and plain dress of the monks was being adopted by the secular clergy. Leo the Great, Archdeacon of Celestine and of Celestine's successor Xistus III (432–40), was unanimously elected Bishop of Rome in 440. He was firm, resolute and explicit in maintaining the special position of Rome: that the church of Rome was the see of St Peter made it the first church in the world; Peter having been the first of the Apostles, through whom grace was communicated to them and to the Church. He quoted the nineteenth Psalm:

> There is no speech nor language where their voice is not heard.
> Their line is gone out through all the earth,
> and their words to the end of the world,

and made it clear that the speech, language and words were those of the Bishop of Rome. Citing this teaching, he issued a stern denunciation of St Hilary of Arles. He conferred the primacy in Gaul on an elderly bishop, Leontius. Hilary had been travelling in the Province, exercising an authority in which Leo saw an usurpation. He came to Rome to argue the case against a bishop, Celidonius, whom he had deposed but Leo had reinstated. Leo put him under house arrest when he arrived, but Hilary escaped and returned to Arles. When the bishops of the Arles metropolis wrote to Leo, pleading, against Vienne, for the ancient privileges of their city – *matrem omnium Galliarum* – 'mother of all the Gauls' (by which 'mother of all the churches of Gaul' is meant), Leo replied, on 5 May 450, dividing the metropolitan area, and giving Valence, Tournon, Geneva and Grenoble to Vienne, the rest to Arles. At this time Leo was engaged in the controversy, mainly in the East, on the Two Natures of Christ. He issued his *Tome*, or 'concise statement', affirming the teaching of 'Two Natures in One Person', when a Council at Ephesus in 449, ordered by the Eastern Emperor Theodosius II and the Western Emperor Valentinian III, and presided over by Dioscorus, Bishop of Alexandria, supported the Monophysite view that there had been Two Natures before the Incarnation, but only one thereafter. The Emperor Theodosius died in 450 and was succeeded in the East by Marcian who was willing to see this decision reversed. A further Council met, at Chalcedon, in 451, and did just that. Leo circulated his *Tome* in the West, and a general synod was assembled at Arles to give support to his view, the new Bishop of Arles, Ravennius, presiding. It was too late to intervene effectively at

Chalcedon, but it gave the full support of the West to Leo. This synod, summoned in a dogmatic emergency, was attended by a Bishop Palladius, who signed last: he could conceiveably be the Palladius sent to Ireland twenty years earlier by Celestine, since the Gaulish churches had assumed in some sense a responsibility for the farther West.

By this date the breakdown of the old order in the West was far advanced. Pagan Anglo-Saxons were in eastern and southeastern Britain; from the southwest of that island an orderly mass migration of Romano-Britons was proceeding across the Channel to create the colony of Brittany. The Frankish *foederati* took Tournai in 446 and established a dynasty, one of whose early members, Meroveus, joined with the Gallo-Romans to fight the Huns near Troyes. The Franks were settling among the Gallo-Romans in northern Gaul, the Visigoths in southern Gaul, the Burgundians in eastern Gaul. The Roman general Aëtius, in the middle years of the century, played off one group against another to try to prevent total takeover of Gaul; he used Hunnish forces against the Visigoths of Toulouse, and then, when the Huns under Attila invaded Gaul in 451, joined with the Visigoths and others to defeat them near Troyes. Roman culture and Roman order survived only piecemeal, chiefly in the south, becoming associated more and more with the persons of the bishops – the most clearly distinguished representatives of the old order.

It was from this milieu that the Gaulish bishops were drawn who organised the early church in Ireland. The priest Segetius, from Carpentras in the province of Vienne, who attended the Council of Orange in 441, is probably the priest Segitius mentioned by Muirchú in his late-seventh-century memoir of St Patrick. The Auxilius, also mentioned by Muirchú in this context, is probably the deacon who attended the same Council with Bishop Claudius of Vienne and who was present again with Claudius the following year at the Council of Vaison, and is probably also the same as the Bishop Auxilius who, according to the Irish annals, was sent, with the bishops Secundinus and Iserninus to help St Patrick in 439. The Irish annalistic date is almost certainly too early, and the association of Patrick rather than Palladius with these persons mistaken. But the Gaulish involvement in the beginnings of the Irish church is reasonably clear.

St Patrick was a Briton, not a Gaul, and his base was in Britain, as he indicates in his *Confessio* when he says, referring to the case that had been brought against his Irish mission, ' – before that case (which I did not initiate, nor was I present in Britain for it) ... ' His work in Ireland was probably in the second half of the century and in the more northerly and westerly parts of the country. He has two references to Gaul in his writings. In the *Confessio*, he tells how he is bound to his mission in Ireland:

> That is why, even if I wished to leave them so that I could visit Britain (and with all my heart I was ready and anxious for my homeland and my parents – not only that, but to go on to Gaul and visit the brethren and be in the present of the Lord's saints – God knows how much I

longed for it), I am bound by the Spirit, whose testimony is that if I do this He will afterwards find me guilty.

That does not necessarily indicate firsthand knowledge of Gaul. But in his *Letter against the Soldiers of Coroticus*, he refers to what was probably his own observation, in the north of that country:

> This is the custom of the Christian Roman Gauls: they send worthy holy men to the Franks and other heathens with as many thousand *solidi* as are needed for the redemption of baptized captives.

The story that Patrick studied at Lérins is speculation founded on speculation, and Ludwig Bieler has justly said of it:

> Since a sojourn of St Parick on Lérins has so often been maintained as if it were an ascertained fact, it seems necessary to insist on the truth that our sources know nothing about it.

It derives from a scrap of tradition cited by Bishop Tírechán at the beginning of his account, put together in the late seventh century, of St Patrick's journeys:

> ... It was in his twenty-second year that he was able to abandon the service of druids. For seven further years he walked and travelled by water, through Gaul and all of Italy, and in the islands of the Tyrrhenian Sea, as he himself said in describing his work. Bishop Ultán has told me that he spent thirty years on one of these islands, which is called Aralensis.

'The temptation,' as Bieler says, 'to correct *Aralensis* to *Lerinensis* is indeed great'. However, the little saying about the journey through Gaul and Italy, attributed to Patrick, looks most unlike his words. Lérins, as it happens (although oddly enough this has not been pointed out) is not in or even very near *Mare Tyrrhenum*, but rather in the western part of *Mare Ligusticum*. The known monastic islands which could – barely – be described as being in the Tyrrhenian Sea are those of Capraia and Gorgona. Tírechán, or his mentor Ultán, had probably got some scrap of a narrative by or about someone who had visited them. Tírechán's method – as he indicates to us himself – is to assume that whatever belonged to the primitive church in Ireland comes from Patrick. Ultán's amplification referring to the visit to '*Aralensis*' (the thirty-year stay is no more than the stuff of storytelling) must remain obscure. He may have had Arles (*Arelate*) in mind, although the city, of course, is not an island. But we don't know how much, in the seventh century, when communications with that region were difficult at best, he knew about the Mediterranean coast of France.

The breakdown of the Western Imperial system was completed in the later fifth century. James Kenney, in his *Sources for the Early History of Ireland*, cites an extract, surviving in a Leyden manuscript, from an account of these events that was written in Gaul in the sixth or seventh century, in which the collapse is attributed chiefly to the Huns:

> From them the devastation of the whole empire took its beginning, and it was completed by Huns and Vandals, Goths and Alans, at whose devastation all the learned men on this side of the sea took flight, and in transmarine parts, namely in Ireland and wherever they betook themselves, brought about a very great increase of learning to the inhabitants of those regions.

Yet at the end of the century Arles had a last recovery and resumed its position as the vicariate of the West. St Caesarius, elected bishop there in 503, had been, like St Honoratus and St Hilary, his predecessors in the see, a monk of Lérins. In 513, Pope Symmachus recognised the primacy of Arles in Gaul again. Caesarius was bishop for forty years, and presided over four councils. He was working on the construction of a great monastery for women in 508 when Arles was besieged by Franks and Burgundians who plundered the half-built buildings for stone for fortifications. He resumed and completed the work when the siege was raised, and his sister Caesaria, as abbess, ruled for thirty years, ultimately over two hundred nuns. He drew up their rule, which required them all to learn to read and write and gave them the sole right to choose their abbess. Caesarius was exiled by Alaric, King of the Visigoths, and imprisoned by Theoderic, King of the Ostrogoths, but succeeded in maintaining some sort of Roman continuity. The great nunnery he founded, exempt by decree of Pope Hormisdas from episcopal jurisdiction, must be considered as a possible model for Kildare. But by the time of Caesarius's death, Roman Gaul was no more, and Arles's decline had begun. On his deathbed, he blessed the nuns, and Arles and the monastic island of Lérins, whose civilizing mission he emphasized:

> *Beata et felix insula Lyrinensis ... quos accipit filios reddit patres ... quos velut tirones excipit, reges facit ... praeclara mater, et unica et singularis bonorum nutrix.*
>
> Blessed and happy island of Lérins; those it receives as sons it returns as fathers; those it accepts as novices it turns into kings ... The noble and distinguished mother and the nurturer of good and remarkable men.

11

The Cursing of Tara

The story is dramatic in detail. The king of Tara, Diarmait mac Cerbhaill, had a steward, Baclám, who insisted on displaying the king's power by entering the forts of subordinate kings with his spear held athwart, so that a breach had to be made in the walls to admit him. When he entered the fort of Áed Guaire, king of Uí Maine in this way, Áed killed him. Áed then sought refuge with St Ruadán of Lothra (Lorrha, in north Tipperary), but the king, Diarmait, in breach of sanctuary, took him from Ruadán's protection and carried him off to Tara.

Ruadán sought the help of his neighbour, St Brendan of Birr, and the two followed Diarmait to Tara and camped outside the ramparts, fasting and ringing their bells. Twelve royal fosterlings died in one night within Tara as a result, but, on the entreaty of their parents and foster-parents, Ruadán and Brendan raised them again from the dead.

Ruadán and Brendan then fasted against King Diarmait; King Diarmait in turn fasted against them. They played a trick on him, pretending to eat, so that he broke his fast thinking that they had broken theirs. He was now in their power. He had a night-vision in which he saw a mighty tree, its top among the rafters of heaven and its roots in the earth. A hundred and fifty men approached the tree, each carrying an axe, and they began to hack at it until the tree fell. Diarmait awoke, to hear, not the sound of the falling tree, but that of the saints' bells, and their chanted curse.

Diarmait protested that he had been engaged in good work, maintaining law and order and bringing malefactors to justice, and he told the saints that the vengeance of the Lord would be upon them for bringing law into contempt and protecting criminals. But the saints told him that his sovereignty would fail, none of his seed would inherit Tara, his place would be a desert and swine would root it up with their snouts. Diarmait admitted that they had taken away his sovereignty – 'I know you have greater favour with the Lord than I' – and he told them to take away his prisoner, but pay his ransom. For ransom, Ruadán produced thirty blue horses, which had risen from the sea; they raced the horses of Tara and defeated them. Diarmait distributed the horses among the nobles of his household but in a little while the horses returned to the sea.

This appeared in the series 'Wars and Rumours' in the *Irish Times*, 15 May 1979.

This monastic legend is one of a number which account for the desertion of the ancient royal sites. It is, in effect, an allegory of the triumph of Christianity over paganism.

Diarmait mac Cerbhaill is an historical figure, if a shadowy one, whose reign at Tara is placed by the annalists about the middle of the sixth century. In later times he was regarded as the ancestor and founder of the dyasties known as the 'southern Uí Néill', who controlled the area represented roughly by the modern Meath, south Louth, Westmeath and Longford. They shared the kingship of Tara with the 'northern Uí Néill', based on the Donegal-Derry area. All these dynasts claimed descent from Niall of the Nine Hostages, but Diarmait's relationship to him, on which the southern Uí Néill based their claim, is possibly fictitious.

He is a major figure of saga and legend. The monks of Clonmacnoise regarded him as a patron. It is said that, while an outlaw, he helped St Ciarán build the first oratory of the monastery there and that St Ciarán's blessing secured him the kingship of Tara. Otherwise Diarmait figures in most ecclesiastical traditions as a hostile figure. He celebrated the *feis* of Tara, a pagan inauguration ceremony highly repugnant to the Church; he employed druids and druidic magic. He was the warrior king leading the army opposed to St Columba at the battle of Cúl Dreimhne, according to the late legend which said that this 'battle of the books' was fought, successfully, to assert Columba's right to a copy he had made of a manuscript, after judgment had been given against him. According to this tale, it was in penance for the bloodshed that Columba went into permanent exile and founded his great monastery of Iona, off the coast of Scotland.

In the episode of the cursing of Tara, as in some other incidents and tales, Diarmait figures essentially as the representative of the old paganism. The story is an expression of Christian triumphalism. We find a number of such expressions:

> Sing the kings defeated!
> Sing the Donals down!
> Clonmacnoise triumphant,
> Cronan with the crown.
>   All the hills of evil,
> Level now they lie;
> All the quiet valleys
> Tossed up to the sky.
>   (Frank O'Connor's translation.)

In the ancient pagan tradition, the king was the intermediary between his people and the Otherworld. He was hedged in with tabus. He mated with the goddess of sovereignty, and had himself to be without physical blemish. He was usually killed by his successor. In the saga-like legends which portray the victory of Christianity over paganism in Ireland, the pagan king, with his ally the druid, is portrayed as the chief opponent of the new faith.

We find a number of such symbolic confrontations located at Tara. St Patrick, according to a seventh-century story, there faced the pagan Loegaire, and defeated his druids in a contest of magic.

We may go on to ask, however, what kind of victory it was that Christianity won over Irish paganism. In the medieval legends which celebrate the Christian triumph, the saints are, for all practical purposes, transformed into druids themselves. They are ferocious thaumaturges, shamanistic heroes of sagas. There is no similarity whatever between the Patrick we know from his own writings of the fifth century, the *Confession* and the *Letter against the Soldiers of Coroticus*, and the Patrick who is the hero of the seventh-century story about the lighting of the Paschal fire on Slane, the miraculous safe passage, in spite of ambush, to Tara, the defeat of Loegaire's druids on that 'hill of evil', and the fiery immolation of the chief druid.

The legends wholly distort the reality of the fifth, sixth and seventh centuries; but they tell us something of what happened later. The early missionaries from the Roman provinces who worked in Ireland were straightforward, and doctrinally orthodox, fifth-century Christians, who must have found the barbarian world of pagan Ireland strange and in many ways repugnant.

> And so – as Patrick wrote – I dwell in the midst of barbarous heathens, a stranger and exile for the love of God. He is witness that this is so. Not that I desired to utter from my mouth anything so harshly and so roughly; but I am compelled, roused as I am by zeal for God and for the truth of Christ; by love for my nearest friends and sons, for whom I have not regarded my fatherland and parents, yea, and my life unto death. I have vowed to God to teach the heathen if I am worthy, though I am despised by some.

At the end of the sixth century, St Columbanus was writing, in letters which are still preserved, a good lively Latin, putting forward arguments based on a wide reading and on a firm confidence in the learning and orthodoxy of the Irish schools. The Venerable Bede, writing at the beginning of the eighth century, testifies to the impression the Irish monks had made, by their character, in Britain a century earlier.

But in the writings of Irish seventh-century authors, like Cogitosus, Muirchú, Tírechán and Adhamhnán, we can discern the beginnings of that tendency that was to lead, in the proliferation of hagiographical writing in the tenth, eleventh and twelfth centuries, to the presentation of Christianity as jejune miracle-mongering and of the monastic institution as a shallow competition for prestige and rents. Yet, on other topics, the monasteries remained capable of producing works of some – indeed considerable – intellectual respectability.

What has happened, of course, is that Christianity has been absorbed by native Irish society and has accommodated to it, but unevenly. The first small Christian communities in the pagan Irish world remained largely aloof and distinct. This is very much what had happened some hundreds of years earlier with the earliest Christian communities in the Roman Empire – although those had the added complication of being (in the beginnings) connected with Jewish communities which were themselves somewhat distinct. Some of our earliest Christian texts from Ireland are sets of rules for the Christians. They display a preoccupation with the problems of remaining free from involvement, inadvertently or otherwise, with what was intrinsically pagan in Irish society. This led to some confusion: an insistence on maintaining certain customs which, in fact, were Roman rather than essentially Christian – styles of dress and haircut, for example, which distinguished the Christians.

Irish society did not react as violently to the alien cells in its midst as Roman society had. There was no systematic persecution of Christians – possibly because of the prestige enjoyed by all things Roman among the barbarians beyond the imperial frontiers. On the other hand, the Roman world itself was in rapid decline and change, from the very moment when Christianity was firmly implanted in Ireland.

By the seventh century, orthographic rules had been devised for writing down the Irish language in Latin letters; kings and other representatives of the old order had accepted Christianity and had made some modification in their habits and customs; a place had been found within the legal system for the new institutions of Christianity. This accommodation involved compromises. The social and political impact of the Church must have been considerable. In Ireland, as elsewhere, the Church found it difficult to live with the institution of slavery. In Ireland as elsewhere, the acquisition of property by the Church impinged in a disruptive way on traditional property-holding systems. In Ireland as elsewhere, the Church loosened a stratified social system by providing new careers and immunities for people of low degree.

It appears that the diocesan organisation, based on the civil administrative structures of the Roman Empire, was unable to survive satisfactorily in the highly decentralized and recently tribal polity of early historic Ireland. The Church itself, in its organisation, became partly tribalized. Dioceses faded away, bishops retired into pious withdrawal from the overseeing of Church affairs, and the distinctive system of monastic federations was gradually developed.

These in turn became closely connected with dynastic politics. Many had abbots drawn, generation after generation, from a particular ruling family. The monasteries – the organized Church – had become 'secularized'. It is important, however, to understand that this secularization was incomplete. Large monasteries by the tenth and eleventh centuries had a dual character. They were towns, trading in pilgrimages, in miraculous shrines, in the provision of safekeeping and immunities, in the services, moral or administrative, they could offer local kings. But they also had attached to them genuinely religious communities, the survival of their original purpose. It is necessary to distinguish between the literature produced by the secular shell and that produced by the religious core.

The kings survived. Certain pagan customs (such as polygamy, among the ruling class) continued to be tolerated. But Christianity's triumph was real. The ancient pagan sacred places *were* deserted. The druidic order gave way to the priestly order, although poets retained much of their ancient powers. The kings were deprived of their pagan aura; although in Ireland as elsewhere, the Church found it necessary to commandeer this and create a new sacral and semi-priestly kingship under its own auspices. The bustling monastic cities represented the new order and the new accommodation and had replaced the ancient sacred hilltop sites on which pagan kings had embraced the goddess:

> Navan town is shattered,
> Ruins everywhere;
> Glendalough remains,
> Half a world is there.

12

Raths

It used to be said that there were about thirty thousand raths, or ring forts, in Ireland. The estimate was based on the density as revealed in the six-inch Ordnance Survey sheets. It now seems, from what shows up on air photographs, that the number in fact is, or was, considerably larger. The rath in other words is the country's commonest type of field antiquity, so numerous that it must be regarded as a most significant kind of monument.

For centuries raths in Ireland were protected by superstition. Not only were they themselves often associated with the Otherworld, but quite commonly a 'fairy thorn' growing within the ramparts gave additional protection. This is no longer so, and agricultural improvement and development schemes in the past twenty years or so have, with the aid of the bulldozers, removed a great many from the landscape. Very often this has been done more or less wantonly, or in the interest of tidiness for its own sake, since a rath is not necessarily a dead loss to a farmer. On most of them cattle can graze, and often a growth of trees or shrubs on the ramparts provides some shelter. In a country where so much land is under-utilized, it is only occasionally that a real advantage is gained by the removal of this kind of earthwork.

Probably the commonest word now used throughout the country for a rath is 'fort', often qualified as 'the old fort', and the archaeological term 'ring-fort' is based on this. It is a somewhat misleading term, since it does not seem that the great majority of monuments so described had any military purpose. The word 'rath' itself is, of course, Irish (*ráith*), and is an old word which is found in a very large number of placenames, including those of several Dublin suburbs. The Irish word *lios* sometimes replaces it, but this has a more limited (mainly southerly) distribution as a placename. This word originally appears to have referred to the space enclosed within the rampart, whereas the word 'rath' originally referred to the structure itself. Both terms are frequently found in early texts, and it is plain from the literature that the people who lived in pre-Norman Ireland were familiar with these sites not as antiquities, but as structures in everyday use.

The distinguishing features of a ring-fort are a fosse, dug more or less in a ring, the upcast from which forms a mainly earthen bank or rampart, and

This appeared in the 'Roots' column in the *Irish Times*, 24 May 1972.

an enclosed space within, which may be raised above the level of the surrounding ground. Access is usually provided by a gap in the ring forming a causeway across the fosse. The earthen rath is usually distinguished in archaeological descriptions from the stone forts (built without mortar) which are especially common in the west and which usually lack the outer fosse that characterizes the embanked monuments.

The orthodox teaching on raths is that they were the enclosed farmsteads of people who lived in Ireland over a long period of time which would include the first millennium of the Christian Era. The literature can be called on to show that they were commonly referred to as dwelling places – within the *lios* stood the *tech* or house, and outside the rath was the *faithche*, an open space through which the dwelling was approached.

The story, however, is not quite as simple as it seems at first glance. Although dozens have been archaeologically excavated by now, and although a good deal of survey work has been done in various parts of the country, it is not at all clear that our understanding of these antiquities has greatly advanced in, say, the past thirty years. One of the most important processes in the methodical study of material evidence is classification, and the classification of 'ring-forts' still leaves a great deal to be desired. Enclosed houses are common to different periods and different cultures. We know that there were at least some dwellings enclosed by some kind of wall or rampart in Neolithic and later in Bronze Age times. Indeed this is to be expected for the protection of stock and goods from wild animals and other hazards in early times, and even down to the present day the farmhouse has usually been provided with an enclosed yard and out-buildings. The circular is the most economical plan for enclosing an area, and an easy one to lay out.

Two things remain unclear. Were unenclosed house-sites common when most of the raths were built? In the nature of things these are much more difficult to find, just as the remains of houses within raths can generally be found only by excavation.

Do the raths or ring-forts of Ireland represent a single cultural phase, and did they all serve the same purpose? It would seem that the answer to the last part of the question is that they did not all serve the same purpose. The Irish word *dún* does appear to apply to structures of military or defensive purpose, and would seem to be applicable to some raths. Some, in other words, appear to have had a military meaning. More surprisingly perhaps, a great many of the excavated raths have not revealed satisfactory evidence of occupation as dwelling places. Some have shown little evidence of any occupation at all; others appear to have been used by metalworkers or other craftsmen but to have had no permanent houses.

One very obvious way of classifying the forts is by the number of rings which formed them, for, while the single-fosse-and-vallum is by far the commonest type, there are many in which there are two, three, or rarely more, enclosing ditches, each with its inner bank. The early laws would suggest that this multiplication of defences reflected the higher status of the owner or occupier, but several of the multivallate forts which have been excavated were among those showing no convincing evidence of habitation. We are left with a number of questions about them, and indeed may in part be dealing with monuments of prestige rather than utilitarian value. Something may be learned from detailed study of the distribution of raths. They tend to avoid bogs, mountains and low-lying sites, although there are numerous exceptions. They cluster very densely in some parts of the country, but this unevenness is itself, as it were, fairly evenly spread all over the island. Yet, interestingly, the ring-forts stop at the Irish coast. There are none, for example, in Argyll, although we know that in the middle of the first millennium AD, and for long after, Irish culture for many practical purposes extended across the North Channel to that part of Scotland. There are sites a little more like raths in south-west Wales, another area colonized from Ireland at that period. But by and large the raths are an *Irish* manifestation, and this fits in with the slowly accumulating evidence of date, from excavated sites, which suggests that the greater part of them probably represent the period from after about the sixth or seventh century, and that some may be post-Norman in date.

'The homes of the well-to-do farmers of early Ireland'. This standard explanation probably still conveys most of the truth about the raths, at least so far as we understand it now. But it also seems that this is not all of the truth, and that the raths represent a good deal more. We may well be giving a single label, as so often happens in this kind of study, to several different things which, in our present state of knowledge, we cannot adequately distinguish. The subject at any rate is one for which the evidence, in spite of an increased rate of destruction, is still abundant. It is to be found in every parish in the country and we can all add by our observation to the store of knowledge from which, as it grows, there may develop a better insight into the meaning of these old structures which our ancestors regarded with awe.

13

The Conversion of Britain

The civilization of Europe has been shaped for nearly two thousand years by the powerful force of the Christian religion in its various forms and manifestations. In Britain too this great social, cultural, intellectual – and spiritual – force has permeated the country's life for centuries. But Britain was not converted to Christianity in one simple missionary endeavour. No less than three distinct major enterprises were involved. This gave rise to a complex culture that was ultimately to achieve considerable unity of belief and a measure of harmony and civilization long before political unity came to the island.

The first introduction of Christianity had taken place in the centuries of Roman rule. The Gospel message was brought from the Near East by the merchants, slaves, soldiers and administrators who passed ceaselessly on the roads and seaways of the Empire. The Christian message of salvation was competing successfully not only with belief in the old Celtic gods of the Britons, but also with other exotic salvation-religions brought from Egypt, Persia and other parts through the Roman communications network. By the end of the fourth century, the Christian Church had been establlished in Roman Britain in some form for at least two hundred years. Beyond Hadrian's Wall, to the north, were the Picts, still pagan at the end of the fourth century, and outside the Empire. To the west, across the sea, were the Irish, also mostly pagan, and of Celtic speech. They still lived in tribally organized societies, unconquered by Rome. To the east, beyond the North Sea, were warlike German tribes, again pagan, living outside the Imperial borders. All of these had begun to raid Roman Britain for valuables and slaves. In the fifth century, a society which was still incompletely Christianized was beset on three sides by pagan enemies. The raiders began to settle in increasing numbers both in the west and in the east, taking land for themselves. Irish settlement was on a fairly small scale on the Welsh coast, but more extensive in Western Scotland.

But in southern and eastern Britain the pagan Anglo-Saxons established their own society and economy, which contrasted sharply with that of the Christianized

This is a modified version of 'The Christian Connection', a television lecture broadcast in the LTV series 'The Making of Britain' and published in Smith, ed., *The Making of Britain*, London (1984).

Britons, who still occupied the western and central regions. The organized Christian Church survived among the Britons; it disappeared in the Anglo-Saxon areas. It seems that among the British provinces struggling for their survival against these pressures, Christianity not only survived but continued to expand. In the west, the British dialects of the ordinary people completely replaced the Latin of the ruling classes for general purposes, and these dialects survive as modern Welsh. However, Latin continued as the language of the Church. It is probable that in Britain, as elsewhere at this date, many of the Church leaders may have been drawn from the administrative class, trained in Roman schools. They by no means confined their leadership to Church matters, but regularly concerned themselves with such affairs as the distribution of food supplies or the mustering of defences against barbarian attack.

Even while Christianity was being wiped out in eastern Britain, Christians seem to have regrouped in the west and to have organized the Church among the barbarians beyond the frontiers. This occurred especially in the buffer states between the Empire and the barbarians, such as Strathclyde and the lands of the southern Picts. There were also Christian communities in southern and eastern Ireland, in coastal areas that had been visited for centuries by traders from Roman Gaul and Britain.

Two new developments affected the British Church in this time of turmoil. One was a movement of total withdrawal from the world. People retired into desert or remote places to live celibate lives of prayer and fasting, following a rule of discipline laid down by some holy person. The custom was already established in Gaul, and there is some evidence of its introduction to Britain at about this time, although the settlement at Tintagel in Cornwall is no longer thought to have been a monastery.

The other development was the emergence in Britain of a heresy, or unorthodox teaching, known as Pelagianism after its founder Pelagius. Earlier, while there had been fierce controversies in the Christian Church concerning what it was that Christians should believe, Britain had been reported to be quite orthodox. But the new heresy led to several interventions from the churches of Gaul acting in consultation with the church in Rome, where the popes took over the direction of the effort to restore orthodoxy.

An imporant result was the organization of missions in Ireland. This began when Pope Celestine consecrated the deacon Palladius and sent him in 431 to be the first bishop of the Irish Christian communities. It is likely that this was intended to foresetall the spread of Pelagianism outside Roman Britain. It suggests that, for the church in Gaul, Ireland was to be reckoned an extension of its fraternal British responsibilities. Many other Gaulish bishops were to work in Ireland in the fifth century, bringing the Church into the interior.

The Britons themselves sponsored the extension of their Church organization beyond the Imperial frontiers. It was perhaps from Carlisle that bishops – St Nynia, St Patrick and St Maughold – were sent to south-west Scotland, north-east Ireland and the Isle of Man. Most of this expansive activity took place after the Romans had left the Britons to their own devices. There seems to have been a brief period of some fifty years of comparative stability – perhaps even some prosperity – in the decades after 500 during which the British Church had time and opportunity to strengthen its position.

However, the animosity between the two peoples, Celtic Britons and the invading Germanic Anglo-Saxons, went so deep that no British attempt to convert their pagan adversaries is known. In spite of the warfare and of the breakdown of order, not only in Britain but also in Gaul, the Roman and Gaulish Church continued to maintain contact with western Britain. Shortly after the middle of the century, for example, it seems that the British accepted from the Bishop of Rome a revised method of calculating the dates of the moveable festival of Easter.

From about 550 onwards, the renewed expansion of the Anglo-Saxon settlement provoked a major collapse of British political culture and some demoralization in the Church. At the same time the monastic movement came to dominate Church organization, and there were necessary realignments in both the British and the Irish churches. With the British defeats and retreats towards the highland refuges of the west, the Irish pupils, not their British teachers, began to take the initiative in Church matters.

Here began the second distinct mission to convert Great Britain to Christianity, this time led by Celtic monks. Monasteries of the Eastern type now became the chief Christian centres of the West. The best preserved is off the south-west coast of Ireland, the Skellig Rock, about twelve kilometres from the County Kerry mainland. It is not quite typical, since in this timberless situation, its buildings are of stone, not wood, and since its community plainly wanted more than most to be remote and alone. There are six huts here, with a couple of tiny oratories or chapels. Each hut, whose interior measured about four square metres, would have housed two or three monks. Establishments such as these were probably modelled on those of western Britain; they rapidly became numerous in Ireland.

The monks followed rules of extreme austerity, attempting to discipline body, mind and spirit. In Irish society of the time, ties of kinship were of overwhelming legal, social, and therefore psychological importance. Separation from kin was a severe penance. Total separation, from kin and homeland, was the greatest deprivation. After the middle of the sixth century, Irish monks, seeking this ultimate renunciation, began to leave Ireland in some numbers. One of these migrations was to have important consequences in Britain.

In 563, the priest Columba, born Cremthann, a member of the inner kin-group of the most powerful royal dynasty of the northern half of Ireland, sailed to western Scotland with some companions. He founded a monastery on Iona, a little island off the larger island of Mull. This brought him just beyond the northern limit of the colonial kingdom established in Scotland by the east Ulster kingdom of Dál Riada, rivals of Columba's own dynasty. To certify his right to the island, Columba travelled up the Great Glen to meet Brude, the king of the Picts, whom he converted to Christianity. In the following years many further monasteries were to be founded in Scotland and Ireland; from Iona many hermits went, as Columba's biographer puts it, 'to seek a solitude in the pathless sea'.

From the start, Iona also played its part in the political realignment of Scotland, establishing a scriptorium for the copying of manuscripts and the keeping of records, influencing the counsels of kings, and becoming a safe repository of charters and chronicles. In 574 Columba himself solemnly anointed and inaugurated Aidán as king of Dál Riada – an act of great political significance. Within a couple of generations, Iona was the head and centre of a federation of monasteries in Britain and Ireland, all of which followed the rule of Columba and were responsible and subordinate to his successor on the island.

For a number of generations, the rulers of the federation, Columba's successors, were members of the same royal kin-group (whose centre was in Donegal) and so commanded great influence in the politics of the north. The island monastery was closely in touch with the wider world, and developments – for example, in the Eastern Church, in the distant Byzantine Empire – were perhaps more quickly reflected there than anywhere else in the West.

Meanwhile, throughout the second half of the sixth century, the Anglo-Saxon expansion continued spreading over all of lowland Britain, overwhelming not only the culture of the Britons but also the Christianity which that culture had accepted. This was the position when a carefully prepared plan for the recovery of England (as we may now begin to call that country) was put into effect by Pope Gregory the Great. Gregory belonged by blood, training and instinct to the old Roman ruling class. His Rome, however, was a shadow of its former Imperial self. No Emperor had ruled there for more than a hundred years. He had been Prefect of Rome as a young man, then became a monk following the rule of St Benedict, and gained administrative and diplomatic experience in the papal service before becoming Pope himself. He envisaged a restoration of the Western Roman Empire; but in his vision the new legions would be priests and monks. The Franks who had overrun Gaul were (at least nominally) Christian by now; the Anglo-Saxons who occupied what had been Roman Britain were pagan. Gergory proposed their conversion. This was the third great mission to convert the peoples of Britain.

Gregory's officials consulted the old Imperial records, and the plan of conversion was based, not on the existing division of Britain into warring Anglo-Saxon and other petty kingdoms, but on a restoration of the old Roman administrative divisions. Bishops were to be appointed to these, with metropolitans in London and York, and twelve other bishops in each of these provinces. In practice, this plan had to be modified to fit in with the political realities of Britain at the time.

A monk called Augustine, provost of the Benedictine monastery in Rome where Gregory had been trained, was chosen to carry out the enterprise. He was supplied with numerous letters to clerics and rulers along the way, and was sent with a band of monks to England in 596. Augustine and his monks appear to have been fainthearted about their hazardous and difficult mission, but they were not permitted to flinch, and in due course they arrived, like the first Roman legions more than five centuries earlier, on the coast of Kent.

The King of Kent, Ethelbert, was married to a Frankish princess who was a Christian. She had a Frankish bishop as her chaplain, and had restored to use an old Christian church at Canterbury. Ethelbert himself, however, was a pagan and was surrounded by priests and retainers who had a vested interest in the old pagan beliefs.

Ethelbert and Augustine met in the open air, the monks carrying a silver cross and an image of Christ painted on wood. Generally speaking, in such confrontations, whether with the old Celtic or old Germanic religions, Christianity has considerable advantages. First, it carried with it the great prestige of Roman civilization, backed since the time of Constantine by the power of the state. And even those barbarians who had contributed to the decline of Rome in the West held the Empire in awe and admiration. But by now the Christian faith also offered a coherent and systematic body of doctrine, moulded by Hellenistic philosophy, which had much more appeal to the educated or intelligent mind than had the amorphous pantheons of gods and goddesses who were personifications of natural forces or spirits of places, trees, rocks or pools. For uneducated peasants or workers, it had another appeal, that summed up in Marx's phrase, 'the opiate of the people'; it offered consolation for the hardships of their lives. It promised personal salvation and the joys of paradise in an afterlife.

Bede sums this up well. In his account of the conversion of another Anglo-Saxon ruler, one of the King's advisers says:

> When we compare the present life of man on earth with that time of which we have no knowledge, it seems to me like the swift flight of a single sparrow through the banqueting hall ... This sparrow flies swiftly in through one door of the hall, and out through another. While he is inside, he is safe from the winter storms, but after a few moments of comfort, he vanishes from sight into the wintry world from which he came ...

Christianity offered a comforting certainty to replace this austere, if touching, image of human life. But there was of course some resistance to it, and the quickest way to change these comparatively simple societies was through the ruler – who commanded not only military power but also to some extent unseen forces of the Otherworld – being a sacral person descended from a god.

In Kent, King Ethelbert's conversion was not immediate; he was baptized probably in 601. And Pope Gregory's grand design proceeded slowly. Augustine never established himself in London as was originally intended; he remained at Canterbury, which was to become the metropolitan see of the south. Within a few years he sent to Rome for more helpers. Some of these became bishops of neighbouring centres, including London. One of Gregory's instructions on prudent missionary procedures is interesting:

> The idols are to be destroyed, but the temples are to be aspersed, altars set up in them, and relics deposited there.

It is probable that in this way several Christian stone churches of the Roman period, converted after the Saxon invasion to pagan use, were now converted back to Christian worship. When Augustine died, sometime in the first decade of the seventh century, he left an established and slowly expanding Church in the south-eastern corner of England.

There was one major problem which Augustine could not overcome: the British bishops refused to acknowledge his authority. His mission represented a direct reassertion of Roman authority in Britain. But the Christian churches which had weathered the storms of the previous two centuries were not prepared to give way readily to this new order. Besides, Augustine's church was firmly associated with the Anglo-Saxons, and between them on the one hand and the Britons on the other, there was still continuing warfare.

After the death of Ethelbert the mission passed through a very difficult period. But an opportunity to expand northwards came when Ethelbert's daughter, a Christian, married Edwin, King of the Anglian territory of Northumbria. One of Augustine's companions, Paulinus, was consecrated bishop and travelled with Ethelbert's daughter to the north. In 626 Edwin accepted baptism, and as he was at that time the most powerful English ruler, his example was followed by many. Edwin was succeeded in the kingship of Northumbria by Oswald, who had been educated in Irish monastic schools, both in Ireland and in Iona. As soon as he had established himself as the ruler of Northumbria, he sent to distant Iona for monks to come and help to establish Christianity in his kingdom. Bede tells us that on the site of Heavenfield – where Oswald defeated his chief enemy, Cadwallon – he set up a wooden cross before the battle. This idea he may well have acquired from the Irish monks of Iona, where the ancient stone crosses are derived from wooden prototypes.

From Iona came the monk Aidan, with a number of companions, bringing the monastic culture of the Atlantic to the shores of the North Sea. They settled on the island of Lindisfarne and were followed by reinforcements from Iona, who founded other churches and monasteries. These carried on with enthusiasm the work of preaching the Gospel to the Anglians.

By this date, the middle of the seventh century, the traditions of Roman learning and culture which had been brought to the British and the Irish and had been preserved by them since the twilight of the Roman Empire in the West, had blended with older traditions rooted in a remote Celtic past. The result now was the flowering of a distinctive literature, matched by brilliant productions in metalworking, stone sculpture and manuscript painting. In the north these interacted with the equally brilliant decorative and craft traditions of the Anglo-Saxons. The Anglo-Saxons in turn began to acquire literacy through Christianity and to produce their own literature.

However, the Roman and the Celtic concepts of ecclesiastical order were not wholly compatible, and there were difficulties. It was in the field of organization, and in connection with questions of authority, that discrepancies came to a crisis. The question of the authority of Canterbury remained unresolved. The churches of the west and north, claiming antiquity and tradition, were not willing to yield their claim to the new mission. The Irish missionary Columbanus, working in Gaul, had expressed this view at the beginning of the century in letters to popes of the time; he enjoined one of them to follow:

> the hundred and fifty authorities of the Council of Constantinople, who decreed that churches of God planted in pagan nations, should live by their own laws, as they had been instructed by their fathers.

He wrote to Pope Boniface that 'the inhabitants of the world's edge are disciples of Saints Peter and Paul', and that 'the Catholic faith, as it was delivered by you first, who are successors of the holy apostles, is maintained unbroken'.

This conflict between the new mission in Kent and the older established churches in Britain was not centred around doctrine. But, quite apart from the refusal of the British churches to accept Rome's authority, there was also great lack of uniformity in custom and practice. In particular, differences in the methods of calculating the dates of Easter from year to year led to anomalies, this major Christian festival being celebrated on one Sunday in some parts of Britain and on a different Sunday in others. In Northumbria Oswiu celebrated Easter according to the Iona calendar; his Kentish Queen with her clergy celebrated it according to the Roman, or Canterbury, calendar.

It was in Northumbria that the major confrontation between the two systems took place, in 663. The King, Oswiu, presided at a meeting in Whitby in 664, at which differences in practice as between the church of Canterbury and the Irish and British churches were argued out, with the result that Canterbury prevailed. Our chief account of this meeting is partisan; it comes from Bede, writing about half a century later. He perhaps exaggerates the importance of some of the technicalities discussed – he had strong feelings on the matter in-favour of the Canterbury view – but the decision did have a considerable effect on Northumbria. Most of the Irish withdrew from Lindisfarne to Ireland, or back to Scotland, leaving the field to their opponents.

The meeting at Whitby was to set the pattern for the Church in Britain, which had been divided between two Christian traditions. Full unity was to take time, but by bringing the dominant English kingdom of the time over to Canterbury the Whitby meeting was to prove crucial. The victory was won probably because it was seen by the secular rulers to bring the Church in Britain into line with Continental practice. Although the merits of the Celtic churches were acknowledged, their customs were seen to be extravagant and eccentric. The sober practicality of the Benedictine form of monasticism and the methodical organization now supervised from Rome had greater appeal, especially to kings and rulers.

The process of union was spread over a series of conferences and agreements between the two traditions, but it was given new impetus by an appointment which had the effect almost of a new mission from Rome. Theodore of Tarsus, an elderly, widely experienced, highly cultivated Greek, was appointed Archbishop of Canterbury, where he arrived in 669. He was a man of great learning and administrative ability, and he was to survive as Archbishop for more than twenty years. In that period, he reorganized and revitalized the Church. He had protégés such as Benedict Biscop, a Northumbrian who founded and endowed many monasteries and schools. He brought artists and builders and other craftsmen from Italy, imported manuscripts and generally encouraged the reintroduction of Roman civilization. In the north and west in particular, this blended with the cultural revival already occurring, to produce what has been called the golden age of the English Church, in the eighth century. It was a Christian golden age too for Scotland and Ireland.

The blend of Roman, Celtic and Anglo-Saxon is exemplified in that remarkable work of sculpture, the cross of Ruthwell, erected in about AD 700, which is inscribed in runes with a version of the poem known as the *Dream of the Rood*. The Cross speaks:

> Unclothed himself God Almighty when he would mount his Cross, courageous in the sight of all men ... I durst not bend. Men mocked us together. I was bedewed with blood ...

It is exemplified too in the pages of great Gospel books, such as that of Lindisfarne, whose majestic, mysteriously ornamented pages drew on the cultural history of the different peoples who, through conversion to a common belief and through the restraints which it attempted to impose on their enmities, began to create a shared culture.

In England, one of its most remarkable ornaments was Bede. He was a product of the twin monasteries of Wearmouth and Jarrow – founded by Benedict Biscop – which possessed the best library, it was said, outside Italy. Bede wrote many learned works, in particular the history of the English Church, a history centred on the Gregorian mission and celebrating the imposition of Roman order and uniformity. He gives credit, however, to the Celtic tradition. Writing, about the year 730, he says:

> At the present time there are in Britain, in harmony with the five books of the divine law, five languages and four nations – English, British, Irish and Picts. Each has its own language; but all are united in the study of God's truth by the fifth – Latin – which has become a common medium through the study of the Scriptures.

The enthusiasm, gentleness and austerity of the Celtic founders had made a deep impression on the north, which remained long after the new order had replaced their tradition. In Scotland, Columba in particular was revered, and his relics were honoured. In Northumbria, special affection continued for Cuthbert, a saint of the Celtic tradition, whose figured coffin and pectoral cross have survived the centuries because of the care bestowed on them.

By the eighth century, Britain was, by and large, a Christian land. The Church entered more and more fully into the life of society as a whole. It took over the pagan and warlike institution of kingship and gave it a special Christian – and undoubtedly more civilized – meaning, by adapting the traditions surrounding the sacred person of the god-descended King to the models of Biblical kingship and priesthood. Columba, as was mentioned earlier, anointed Aidán King of Dál Riada – the first such occasion we know of in the West – and the ceremonials of anointing, crowning and enthroning, which Christianized pagan rituals, were intended to give authority and dignity and to assist the process of political centralization and State creation. Church and State went hand in hand in this process, whose rituals have survived in Britain to the present day.

14

St Brigid's Birthplace

There are certain places that have an atmosphere of magic and seem to be the focus of spiritual, or natural, or historic forces. It is usually possible to work out why. It is not because of any actual magic, of ley lines, or earth magnetism, or the power of a supernatural *genius loci*; but the result, generally, of topography. They are places, often on eminences, often on boundaries between one kind of country and another, where things are constrained to happen in human affairs: armies to be ambushed; people to realise that there are different kinds of world and to have visions; the configuration of valley and summit, rock and flowing water to offer revelation through suggestions of potentiality. Faughart, in County Louth, is such a location.

It is a steep place, in the extreme north of the county, on the Irish Border. To the east are the Cooley Mountains of the Carlingford peninsula, where the Brown Bull lived, in pursuit of whom Queen Medb mounted the *Táin*. To the west is the cone of Slieve Gullion rising from its rim of foothills among mountainy small farms and close-set clachans where the Irish language, its poetry, music and storytelling, stubbornly hung on when all around had changed. To the south, the rolling drumlins of *Magh Mhuirtheimhne* extend to a dim horizon, while to the south-east is the shining expanse of Dundalk Bay. To the north, a rough passage to a notch in the hills is plain: the 'Gap of the North', the Moyry Pass, the entry to Ulster. The pass so impressed both the imagination and the eye for country of the early Irish that they located several mythological battles here. When Cúchulainn defended the North against Medb's armies, she was troubled at the number of men he was killing and decided to trick him. She arranged to meet him at Faughart for a parlay: he was to be unarmed; she was to have with her only her attendant women. But his charioteer advised otherwise. In the words of Thomas Kinsella's translation of the *Táin*:

This is previously unpublished but incorporates the substance of an article that appeared in the 'Roots' column of the *Irish Times* on 2 February 1972.

'Medb is a forceful woman', the charioteer said. 'I'd watch out for her hand at my back'.

'How should I go?' Cúchulainn said.

'With your sword at your side', the charioteer said, 'not to be caught off guard. A warrior without his weapons is not under warriors' law; he is treated under the rule for cowards.'

'I'll do as you say,' Cúchulainn said.

'The meeting was fixed for the hill Ard Aighnech, called Focherd today … '

The queen arrived with fourteen warriors, all of whom hurled javelins at Cúchulainn. But he performed what is called elsewhere '*cathcles cu foceardaib*' – a 'battle-feat with subordinate arts', and killed all fourteen with his marvellous weapon, the *gae bulga*. So we have the spurious derivation of the place-name:

> '*Foichaird Muirtheimne, bhaili a nderna Cú Chulainn in foicherd gaiscid ar sluaiged tána bó cúailgne*' – 'Faughart of Muirtheimhne, where Cúchulainn did the heroic spear-feat at the hosting of Táin Bó Cúailgne'.

Another purely legendary battle was fought here by Cormac mac Airt when, with the aid of Fiachu Mullethan of Munster, he defeated Fiachu Airide, the eponymous ancestor of Dál nAiride of Ulster.

Those imagined encounters were located at Faughart because Faughart is a place for battles. There are ruins of a medieval church in the pass, whose graveyard has more than once received the bodies of the slain. At a summit just around a bend of the steep by-road that comes up from the plain to Faughart there is a Norman motte commanding the broad view to the south and guarding the way north. Beyond the narrow road the grassy fields conceal a complex of souterrains. There were real battles here, although they too have soaked up legend, as it were, from the place. In AD 732, Áed Allán with the northern Uí Néill defeated Áed Róin, king of Ulaid, at Faughart. The Ulster king, it is told, was beheaded on the stone called *Cloch an Chomhaoigh* at the door of the church. In 1146 the place was totally destroyed by fire. But the most famous of the battles of Faughart was fought on 14 October 1318. Robert Bruce, brother of the King of Scots, had invaded Ireland three years earlier and had himself been installed as King of Ireland near Dundalk. In those three years, marching with a host through the country, he had done much damage to the English in Ireland and to the country at large. Now he came south from Ulster, through the Moyry Pass not for the first time, and an English force mustered by John de Bermingham met him and defeated him at Faughart. Bruce too was decapitated, and his head was sent to King Edward in England. Several centuries later, in the Nine Years War, the pass was twice held by the Irish against the English. O'Neill and O'Donnell blocked the passage there against 1,000 soldiers sent north by the Lord Justice in 1595. In 1600, Lord Mountjoy, with 3,000 foot and 300 horse, camped at Faughart, but was beaten back by O'Neill in a series of combats over a three-week period of incessant rain and intermittent bloodshed, and failed to force the Moyry Pass. In recent years, visitors to Faughart could watch, across the Border which is only a few hundred metres away, the British helicopters hovering over the soldiers squatting in their dugouts in the dreary countryside around Forkill and Crossmaglen, seeming to the natives of these parts like Martians descended from the outer cosmos, and to themselves like earthlings burrowing under the alien surface of Mars.

There are other associations in Faughart, connected with a different kind of frontier, the border between this world and the Otherworld, between death and life, between Winter and Spring. A thousand years ago the Irish had, on the first of February, one of the principal celebrations of their ecclesiastical year. This is not yet quite forgotten, and there are still some parts of the country where the observance of the old customs marks St Brigid's Day. One of these centres is Faughart.

Like many festivals of great antiquity, this one is not Christian in origin, but comes down to us from prehistoric paganism. It is a celebration of the coming of Spring, marking – according to *Cormac's Glossary* – the moment at which the lactation of the ewes begins. We know the Irish name of the pagan festival to which the feast of Brigid has succeeded. It was *Imbolc*, one of the four major turning points of the pagan year, the others being *Beltine* (the beginning of Summer, the first of May), *Lugnasad* (the beginning of Autumn, the first of August) and *Samain* (the beginning of Winter, the first of November). It is noteworthy that the other three festivals also survive stubbornly, as secular or ecclesiastical celebrations. They too had continued in their old form as long as the Gaelic tradition lasted.

St Brigid's Day was the end of winter:

> *Anois teacht an earraigh beidh an lá 'dul chun síneadh,*
> *'S tar éis na Féil' Bríde ardóidh mé mo sheol …*

The early references to *Imbolc* indicate that it was an occasion which had to do with the calendar of a pastoral people, being connected with the fertility and renewal of flocks and herds. It is the time of renewal. There is much stress on the topic of milk. For all this there are parallels elsewhere. The ancient Roman festival of *Lupercalia*, also in February, appears originally to have been a holiday of shepherds, in honour of the fertility god Lupercus, who was said to keep the wolves from the sheep. The Luperci, the priests of the god, assembled on the festival day and sacrificed dogs and goats. One of the Luperci then smeared the blood of these animals on the foreheads of two young noblemen who were brought to take part in the ceremony; others immediately wiped off the blood with milk. The skin of the sacrificed goats was cut into strips, some of which the Luperci bound round their waists, and then, otherwise naked, they ran through the streets carrying thongs of goatskin, with which they touched or struck people, especially young married women, who were made fruitful as a result.

A somewhat more remote parallel may be seen in the Hindu Spring festival of *Holi*. The god who is the equivalent of Lupercus (or Pan) in this is the Indian god of desire, Kama. Caste restrictions are suspended for Holi, and all kinds of people run about the streets throwing red powder or water (a harmless survival of an original blood sacrifice) over their neighbours, or striking them with bladders or other phallic substitutes.

Brigid herself, the patroness of the festival of the first of February, was, with Patrick and Columba, one of the three principal saints of the Irish. She differs from the other two, however, in an important respect. Both Patrick and Columba are figures of history. Under an accumulation of legend and folklore we can discern, for each of them, some historical reality, with a location in place and time. Some of Patrick's own writings survive, and for Columba we have the *Life* written by his successor in the abbacy of Iona, Adhamhnán, about a century after the saint's death. While this work is full of conventional hagiographical wonder-working, and while it undoubtedly contains much legendary material, there can be little doubt that Columba himself did live and work and have his place in the affairs of sixth-century Ireland and Scotland.

The oldest surviving *Life* of an Irish saint is probably the work on St Brigid written by Cogitosus of Kildare and it too, like the work of Adhamnán on Columba, was written about a century, or a little more, after the date given for the death of its subject. But in other ways the two *Lives* are quite different. Cogitosus gives us not much more than a list of miracles concerned with buttermaking and the like, together with some interesting information on the monastic city of Kildare in his own time – which was probably just past the middle of the seventh century. There are several other *Lives* of Brigid, quite early in date but offering us no more real information about a real historical person. They include a very early work in the Irish language (the other hagiography being in Latin).

This is not altogether surprising, for Brigid not only inherits the attributes but bears the name of one of the chief deities of the pagan Irish, the triple goddess who was also, it would seem, honoured by the Continental Celts of late prehistoric Europe. It is *Cormac's Glossary* again which gives us some basic information:

> Brigit, that is a learned woman, daughter of the Dagda. That is, Brigit woman of learning, that is a goddess whom poets worshipped. For her protecting care was very great and very wonderful. So they call her goddess of poets. Her sisters were Brigit woman of healing and Brigit woman of smith-work, daughters of the Dagda, from whose names among all the Irish a goddess was called Brigit.

This Brigit or Brigid appears to have belonged to the class of mother–goddesses, whose equivalent is known from altars and inscriptions in Roman Gaul (the '*Matrones*'). According to T.F. O'Rahilly, her name derives from a form like *Briganti*, meaning something like 'the high goddess', which has derivatives also outside Ireland, as in the tribal names, *Brigantes*, *Brigantii*. *Brigantion*, a tribal capital of the *Brigantii*, survives still in the name of the western Austrian town of Bregenz, at the eastern end of Lake Constance. In Ireland, the goddess watched over childbirth, brought prosperity, and patronized poets and healers. A fowl was buried alive at the confluence of three streams in sacrifice to her, clearly marking her triple character.

Brigid the Christian saint, if she lacks historicity, inherited a great deal of the qualities of the goddess. Milk and butter, flocks and herds, figure largely in her *Lives*. According to the Old Irish *Life* she was reared on the milk of a white red-eared cow, which saved her life when she was failing to survive on food given to her by a druid. One of her miracles was to change water into milk (she could also, on occasion, turn it into ale). Another, occurring in several versions and variations, concerns the increase of flocks, or the marvellous re-placement of beasts lost or stolen from a herd.

The scene of the life and miracles is mainly set in the south midlands; the time, the fifth or sixth century. Croghan Hill (*Brí Éle*) in Offaly plays a central part in the legends, as does Ardagh, Co. Longford, and its bishop, St Mel. But, of course, the place especially associated with St Brigid was her 'city', later known as *Cell Dara*, or Kildare. Gerald the Welshman, the chronicler of the Norman invasion, visited Kildare in the late twelfth century, and described the fire which was kept perpetually burning there:

> Although in the time of Brigid there were twenty servants of the Lord here, Brigid herself being the twentieth, only nineteen have ever been here since her death until now, and the number has never increased. They all, however, take their turns, one each night, in guarding the fire. When the twentieth night comes, the nineteenth nun puts the log beside the fire and says: 'Brigid, guard your fire. This is your night'. And in this way the fire is left here, and in the morning the wood, as usual, has been burnt, and the fire is still burning.
>
> The fire is surrounded by a hedge which is circular and made of withies, and which no male may cross ... Moreover, because of a curse of the saint, goats never have young here.

He goes on to describe what is probably the Curragh:

> There are very fine plains hereabouts which are called 'Brigid's pastures', but no one has dared to put a plough into them. It is regarded as miraculous that these pastures, even though all the animals of the whole province have eaten the grass down to the ground, nevertheless when morning comes have just as much grass as ever.

Kildare may well have been, as Macalister and others have suggested, a pagan sanctuary before it became Christian. It was a dual monastic establishment, of monks and nuns in separate communities. In the seventh century, according to Cogitosus, the tomb-shrines of Brigid and her collaborator in the foundation, Bishop Conlaedh, stood by the altar of the divided church. However, it was the abbess who ruled.

According to the Old Irish *Life*, St Mel said of Brigid, 'This virgin alone in Ireland shall have the episcopal ordination.' And the same work tells us that Brigid, and after her her successors or abbesses, always had a priest as charioteer to drive her about. Cogitosus claimed primacy over the churches of 'almost the whole island' for Kildare, but not long after he wrote it seems that the community of Armagh came to an agreement with Kildare by which priority, on terms, was allowed to the northern church.

Wherever the truth about the origins of the monastery of Kildare and its mysterious founder may lie, St Brigid is surely a suitable patron for the Irish women's liberation movement. If things had gone a little differently in the seventh century, the church in Ireland might (it is a fanciful thought) have come under the rule of a woman. But the whole subject is clouded in a mist. None of the *Lives* give any solid information about Brigid herself. The anecdotes of her wonder-working, which fill them, clearly derive in large part from the folklore of the pagan divinity who was her predecessor.

In Cogitosus's account, her father was named Dubhthach and her mother Broicsech; they were 'noble Christian parents', descendants of Eochaidh. Some later accounts of her origin say she was born at Faughart, in the country of the Uí Eachach. An Eochaidh Finn Fuath Airt, however, was the ancestor of the ruling family of the Fotharta, a Leinster people of the south midlands, the area with which Dubhthach is associated in most accounts; so there were Uí Eachach there too. It is probable that the similarity of the names *Fochart* and *Fotharta* gave rise to this duality. Be that as it may, it became firmly established that her birth-place was Faughart. And the place wholly suits her, who was born on the border of reality and unreality, 'neither by night nor by day; neither within nor without the house', neither in Winter nor in Spring, the saint and goddess of the threshold, of the turning of the year, of the borderland.

Her curing well is in the graveyard of Faughart, where, like Kali, she can wear a necklace of skulls. Her shrine is there, her festival is celebrated. There her three faces still regard us: the soothsayer, the healer, the armourer.

15

The Leek and the Shamrock

Last Saturday was St David's Day, the Welsh equivalent of St Patrick's Day in Ireland. The significance of St David of Wales, however, is quite different from that of St Patrick for Ireland. He was not the missionary chiefly associated with the conversion of the nation to Christianity. Far from it; Christianity had long been established in Britain when David was active (in the sixth century), and indeed it is just possible (although unlikely) that Patrick's Christian home, from which he was carried off by Irish raiders as a boy, was in some part of Wales.

That was in Roman times, when most of Britain could still be reckoned part of the Empire, even if it was after the last of the legions had abandoned the country. Just what proportion of the British people was then Christian it is difficult to say with any confidence, but there certainly were many Christians, and, after the withdrawal of the legions (when the Britons had to face, on their own, attacks from pagan enemies) their Christian faith and their Roman heritage must have become ever more closely associated.

Although not a great deal is known about St David, the traditions agree in giving special emphasis to the Irish connections, both of the man himself and of the movement with which he is especially associated. By the middle of the sixth century, Roman Britain had shrunk considerably in extent – because of the inroads of the Anglo-Saxons from beyond the North Sea – and the Romans themselves were hardly more than a memory. The Britons, or Welsh as they might begin to be called at this point, retained some of the traditions and institutions of the Roman province, but they had lost control of its more prosperous regions and larger towns. They had the Pictish and Irish intrusions to contend with as well as the Anglo-Saxon settlements.

For a long time, British-Irish relations had been close, if not always friendly, as Irish colonies and settlements had been established at points along the west coasts of Britain. The most enduring of these was the colony planted by the Antrim kingdom of Dál Riada in western Scotland – which brought the Irish or Gaelic language to that country – but there were others in Wales and Cornwall. The Dési of Munster had settlements in Pembrokeshire and

This was published in the 'Roots' column in the *Irish Times* on 4 March 1975.

elsewhere, settlements which are marked not only by forts and earthworks but by the spread of ogham stones from their dense areas of concentration in Waterford and Kerry across to Wales. There, many of the inscriptions are bilingual, in Irish and Latin.

This situation was already developing when the Christian missionaries from Gaul and Britain (including Patrick) were at work in Ireland.

The Church in western Britain and Ireland came to have a number of peculiar features in common which gave rise to much controversy in the seventh century. This sharing of peculiarities is an indication of the intimate cross-Channel relations which had been established in the period of missionary activity and early ecclesiastical development in Ireland, that is to say in the fifth and sixth centuries. Legends of the early saints reflect this intimacy, recording the names of British missionaries, such as Mochta of Louth, Mel of Ardagh, Lommán of Trim, who established churches in Ireland, or of Irish churchmen who are said to have studied in Britain, such as Búite of Monasterboice, Finnian of Clonard and Brendan of Clonfert. The early Christian monasteries of Ireland and Wales again display many features in common, and indicate that the two sides of the Irish Sea shared customs of discipline in Christian, but especially in monastic, life.

Monasticism, of the kind derived ultimately from the Egyptian desert, was the chief peculiarity of the western churches of those centuries, and the basis for their further peculiarities. This system came in time completely to eclipse in Ireland the episcopal organization of the Church introduced by the earliest missionaries. It is a development associated with the Britons, and the names of those who introduced the monastic movement to Britain constantly recur in the Irish legends as teachers of the Irsh monastic founders – Iltud of Llan-Iltud, Cadoc of Llan-Carvan, David of Menevia, Teilo of Llandaff, Samson of Dol (in Brittany) and others.

The chronology of all this is obscure, because the records are confused and defective, but it seems unlikely that David was one of the earlier of the Welsh founders. It is more likely that he was asscociated with a particularly strict form of monasticism, and that this was the form that had most influence in Ireland. In this he represented, perhaps, direct influences from Egypt rather than the Romanized and moderated monasticism derived from Gaul. His monks, according to one account, had to labour (food being denied to those who did not work) in the fields and workshops, doing such tasks as pulling the plough themselves rather than using draft animals, while their diet and regimen in general were severely ascetic and penitential. This was resisted by some ecclesiastics as extravagant and intemperate, but it seems to have had a particular appeal to Irish churchmen of the day.

Such stories of David as survive (and they are unreliable because they were gathered into narratives too many centuries after his time) serve to illustrate the point that the Irish-British relationship was two-way. In one story, David is said to have been baptized by Ailbhe of Emly. In the document known as the *Catalogue of the Saints of Ireland* (a kind of stylized summary history of early Christianity in Ireland, composed in early medieval times) the Irish early monastic founders are said to have received a Mass 'from Bishop David and Gildas and Docus, the Britons'. Another legend tells that Finnian, the Irish monastic founder who was reputed to have been the teacher of some of the most famous abbots, adjudicated in favour of David in a dispute over the 'headship and abbacy of the island of Britain'. This too is a story inspired by events much later than the time it deals with, but it reflects again the close ecclesiastical relationships between the two islands.

The Biblical form David was given by the church writers to the name Dewi, and it was near the south-western tip of Wales, in the territory called '*Moniu* of the Dési' that St Dewi founded his church, of which he was bishop. '*Moniu*' in turn was later Latinized as '*Menevia*', but the place is nowadays known, as it has been for centuries, as 'St Davids'. It became, as a result of ecclesiastical developments long after the time of its founder, the chief see of Wales, the Welsh Armagh, and its fine old cathedral testifies to this pre-eminence.

St David's Head looks straight across the Channel to the south-eastern coast of Ireland, and ever since St David's time there has been constant traffic on these narrow waters, as there still is to the modern port of Fishguard. St Davids itself was the old port, and in the founder's time there were Irish-speaking people, descended from the Dési settlers, living in the hills around. On the shore near the cathedral are the ruins, reduced to little more than foundations, of a chapel of St Patrick – probably a dedication which reflects the reflex of the Norman invasion of Ireland, manned so largely by people from this very district.

The two patrons, Patrick of Ireland and David of Wales, have much in common, then, in spite of the different rôles they played in the countries which honour them. In particular, they both represent ancient links across the Irish Sea.

16

Early Irish Writing

Professor James Carney of the Dublin Institute for Advanced Studies last week delivered a lecture to a large and keenly interested audience at the Royal Irish Academy, in which he demonstrated among other things that the origin of the *Ogham* cipher may be a good deal earlier than had previously been believed, and that its place of origin was probably in Continental Europe; most likely Roman Gaul.

Professor Carney's paper raises some interesting questions about the whole matter of writing in Ireland. It has long been conventional to associate the beginning of literacy with the beginning of Christianity here, and to date both to about the fifth century. But there certainly were Christians in Ireland before then, and it seems very likely that there were people in Ireland acquainted with writing much earlier than the fifth century. The early Irish literary tradition, like that of the Continental Celts, was oral, and the absence of early writings may be a reflection not merely of ignorance but also of an opposition to the writing down of lore which people were expected to memorize.

Christianity however required the existence of books, and once the new religion was spread in Ireland we find that the making and the decorating of books became outstanding features of Irish culture. The book, along with the bell and the crosier, is one of the conventional symbols used to identify ecclesiastics in early Irish art, and the interest of the Irish in books was one of the characteristics for which they were noted abroad. We have no evidence at all that any form of painting was practised in pre-Christian Ireland (although we should accept the possibility), but once psalters and Gospel-books had to be provided, we find that the scribes and craftsmen soon developed a style and technique for ornamenting their manuscripts with rich and elaborate paintings, using pigments some of which must have been imported.

This development happened at a time when significant changes were taking place in written materials. The ancient Graeco-Roman world had depended largely on supplies of papyrus from Egypt for the making of written records. This was a comparatively fragile and perishable material, but it was also comparatively cheap. It was usually manufactured and produced in long rolls,

This appeared in the 'Roots' column of the *Irish Times* on 3 July 1973.

which could be kept in tubular containers, and this was the common form of early books. Changes in economic and trading patterns in the post-Roman period, including the major changes brought about by the Muslim conquest of North Africa, caused a diminution in the supplies of papyrus reaching northern Europe and the West. Our earliest surviving manuscripts from Ireland are all on a quite different material, vellum, that is, specially prepared calfskin; and they are in codex form; in other words, they are bound with gatherings of leaves in the general fashion to which we are accustomed in present-day books. Vellum, properly prepared and reasonably well looked after, will last almost indefinitely.

In the library of the Academy there is one fragmentary manuscript of the Psalms which may be as old as the sixth century, and may indeed be the handiwork of St Columba himself. This is the book which is known as the *Cathach*, because for centuries, treasured as a relic of St Columba, it was carried into battle by the O'Donnells as a charm to bring them victory. Another fragmentary very early manuscript, dating probably from the early seventh century, is housed in the library of Trinity College, Dublin, where it is known as *Codex Usserianus Primus*. This is part of a Gospel-book. There are a few other similarly early fragments of manuscripts which give us a glimpse – no more – of what would appear to be the first stage of Irish book production. In them, simple ornaments to the text are used, which do not go much beyond the flourishes and decorations that flow naturally, as it were, from the scribe's task of producing an elegant and pleasing script. There are small touches of colour, followed by a few letters diminishing to the normal text size, at the beginnings of important passages, and emphasis produced by outlining initials or other ornaments with dots made with the quill, or little freehand decorative motifs.

The language of the early books is Latin, but we know that the Latin alphabet had already been adapted to serve the purposes of Irish by this time. The *Ogham* inscriptions, which are in Irish, are in a kind of cipher based on a Latin alphabet. They are of course brief, and of a funerary or memorial character. A system of notches and strokes, such as *Ogham*, is suitable for brief inscriptions on sticks or wooden posts, or on the edge of a rough stone pillar, but is far too cumbersome for use in books. The writing in the books, therefore, is in no sense a development from or an 'improvement' on *Ogham* writing, but something with quite a different purpose. Instead, the *Ogham* inscriptions may tell us about the early borrowings of the Latin alphabet which have not survived in the form of straightforward writing. In part at least, this alphabet was associated in Ireland with the Christian mission. In seventh-century versions of St Patrick's legend, for example, we find stories telling how he wrote alphabets for his converts, or left alphabets with them when he moved on. And in Kilmalkedar, on the Dingle Peninsula in County Kerry, there is an early cross-inscribed pillar which has an alphabet incised, rather clumsily, down one face.

The big change in the character of the books came when the scribes, or perhaps specialists working in collaboration with the scribes, began using them as a medium for elaborate paintings, which may illustrate or adorn the text but seem sometimes to be quite independent of it. One of the earliest examples, again a fragmentary Gospel-book (just a few pages) is kept in the cathedral library of Durham, where it is known as MS *A II 10*. This has part of the text tabulated and divided into panels by a framework of broad-ribbon interlacing.

The motif was soon to become one of the commonest in the Hiberno-Saxon art of the seventh and eighth centuries; here in the Durham manuscript we can see it making its entry into the repertoire – a borrowing from the decorative art of the Mediterranean.

For the people who were inventing the new style of book-painting could not find ornamental ideas to suit them in the mere script itself – beautiful though they made that. They looked around at other media, and they copied especially the patterns and ornaments of the enamellers and bronze-smiths, who practised a long-established craft. They copied the designs of fine metalwork not only of Irish origin, but also of Saxon or Pictish or Continental derivation – since the missionary monasteries provided opportunity to see the products of other cultures. Soon the book-painters had blended and mixed these designs to produce the extraordinary, elaborate and obsessive style which we fisrt see taking shape in the seventh century in the 'carpet pages' of Gospel-books like the Book of Durrow, and which somewhat later produced the mysterious complex ingenuity of the Book of Kells.

17

'Gaelic' Lettering

It would be very interesting to know what the earliest writing used in Ireland looked like. Presumably, once Roman rule was established across the Irish Sea in Britain, people who were literate would have visited our shores fairly frequently, and there may even have been a few in Ireland itself who had some knowledge of letters.

While the pre-Christian traditions in law and lore were plainly oral rather than written, the appearance of the *Ogham* script, based on some alphabet like the Roman, indicates an acquaintance with writing. And a sealbox of Roman origin, found in the excavation of the 'Rath of the Synods' at Tara in the 1950s, suggests that quite some time before the coming of Christianity there may have been correspondence between literate Roman Britain and pre-literate Ireland.

At any rate it is certain that by the fifth century, when Christianity was being established here, with it there was also established the use of writing. Apart from the fact that Christianity came to Ireland under the aegis of Roman civilization, it created an immediate need for copies of Scriptural and other texts. But, since the western provinces of the Roman Empire were overrun by invaders just at the period when the first missionaries were active here, there was a break in contact which left the infant Church in Ireland to develop in semi-isolation. Our very earliest specimens of writing date from about the year 600, and show us that in the period of a century or so since the coming of Christianity, the Irish had developed a distinctive script.

The *Cathach* of St Columba, an incomplete manuscript of the Psalms, dating from about the end of the sixth century, is probably the oldest piece of writing from Ireland (as distinct from *Ogham*) which still survives. It shows the distinctive Irish version of Roman script, already fully developed. The Irish scribes had devised an elegant round hand which is, in its grace and clarity, one of the earliest major achievements of Christian art in the country. It draws, somewhat eclectically, upon the book-hands of the Late Roman world, to produce in fact two scripts – majuscule and minuscule, or upper case and lower case – of which it is the miniscule that has the character which was to distin-

This appeared in the 'Roots' column in the *Irish Times* on 22 March 1972.

guish in particular the writings of the Irish. Since this script was brought across the sea and became the standard hand of the decorated manuscripts of seventh- and eighth-century England too, it is often described in the text-books as 'Hiberno-Saxon'.

The script of the luxury manuscripts of early Ireland – of the Book of Durrow, the St Gall Gospels, and the Book of Kells – still seems eminently clear and legible after the lapse of twelve or thirteen centuries. This is partly because of its inherent qualities of legibility. It is partly too because the Irish script was one of the main ingredients in the book-hand which was developed in the Carolingian renaissance of the ninth century for use in major Continental manuscripts of that period. The Carolingian book-hands in turn contributed greatly to the design of early type-faces when the Italians, at the time of the Renaissance, began to produce printed books – to which they devoted the same skill and taste in design as they did to coins, medals, clothes, buildings, or anything else that could appeal to the eye.

The Italian style of lettering was to prevail, ultimately (and very recently, so far as some parts of Western Europe are concerned) over 'Gothic,' 'black-letter' and other manuscript-derived styles of lettering. These styles are inherently much less legible, but were once widely used. Anyone who lives within reach of a medieval church, abbey or friary which still has tombstones of the fifteenth and sixteenth centuries can readily verify this and ascertain that they were current in Ireland, or at least among Irish masons, at that period. But the type-face in which this book is printed today is in quite a different tradition, which owes something to developments in Irish scriptoria of twelve to fifteen hundred years ago.

The script, evolved in the churches and monasteries of early Ireland, did, of course, change, like everything else, over the centuries. A more angular and crabbed style of writing became usual, and when, at the end of the Middle Ages, the invention of printing began to be applied in Ireland, the type-faces for books printed in Irish were based on the manuscript hands customarily used in writing that language at the time. Printing has its own special demands and requirements, and naturally, therefore, while early type-faces were based on manuscript hands, type soon tended to impose its own discipline on the characters.

While the earliest type-faces for the printing of Irish were based on the 'pointed' or angular hands that had gradually displaced the earlier half-uncials, they had certain defects from the printer's point of view, and later founts tended to be based more and more on the early Irish book-hands. In this they came closer to their chief competitors in Ireland, the so-called 'Roman' type-faces, belonging to the family derived from the Italian Renaissance. Nowadays, most books in Irish are printed in 'Roman', since such standardization simplifies life for printers and publishers – and in the long run for readers too. The change, however, came about only after a prolonged controversy, since there were many who felt that in some way the 'Gaelic' type-faces were bound up with the very nature of the language itself, and there were many more who felt (with much more justice, it would seem to me) that such type-faces as those of the Irish Archaeological Society in the mid-nineteenth century, or the Colm Cille type designed by Colm Ó Lochlainn, had a beauty which in itself justified their use.

In 1924, Edward Lynam, a scholar who was actively interested in Irish topics and who became superindentent of the Map Room in the British Museum, published a paper on 'The Irish Character in Print, 1521–1923', in *The Library* (Transactions of the Bibliographical Society). The paper was offprinted as a pamphlet the same year and was re-issued a few years ago, with an introduction by Alf MacLochlainn, in the series of reprints published by Irish University Press. The paper traces the history of the type-faces used for printing Irish, including Scottish Gaelic, since the first fount for the purpose was made in London by Queen Elizabeth's order in 1571. This face was in fact very mixed in its basic design, since many of the letters were Roman. It was in Louvain that the first fount which was wholly derived from Irish manuscript sources, by Irishmen, was produced for the Franciscans about the year 1611. This rather angular face had a character which was to prevail. Anyone who learned at school or elsewhere to use 'Gaelic lettering' will immediately feel at home with the early Louvain type and will have no difficulty whatever in reading it.

Lynam's book is a standard text, and all who are at all interested in the subject should have it. It is unlikely to go seriously out of date, although it was written as long ago as 1924, since standardization has taken over from the effort to maintain a separate and distinctive type for printing Irish. The Irish University Press reprint includes as an appendix specimens of founts designed since the original publication, and the reprint therefore is a fairly comprehensive handbook on a subject which is of considerable interest for our cultural history.

18

St Brendan the Navigator

After Patrick, Brigid and Colum Cille (Columba), the chief figure of the early Irish Church, in the estimation of the early medieval hagiographers and story-tellers, was St Brendan of Clonfert. There was a real person, who founded Clonfert; we know comparatively little about him. There is a Brendan of story, dealing in the legendary affairs of sixth-century Ireland. And there is the Brendan of the mythical voyage – an allegory of Christian quest – whose exploits on the ocean were a tale told all over medieval Europe. We have, in his record, a striking example of the blending of myth, legend and history.

Anecdotes and tales concerning him are numerous in the saints' *Lives* and other texts, and there exist several versions, in Latin and Irish, of a *Life* of St Brendan, as well as variations on the famous romance, *The Voyage of St Brendan the Abbot*. Most renderings of the *Life* have incorporated in them, to a greater or less extent, matter from the *Voyage*.

Like his namesake (or double), Brendan of Birr, with whom he is closely associated, he is said to have been of West Munster origin. His father was Finnlug moccu Allta, his mother Broinngheal. In the *Life* of St Mac Creiche, it is told that Brendan's mother, Broinngheal, Mac Creiche's mother Brig, and St Cainneach's mother Mainesc, were three daughters of a king 'who had many a harbour'. The Alltraige Caille, his reputed people of origin, were a sub-group of Ciarraige Luachra (whose territory was in north Kerry), and his homeland would appear to have been the Killarney area, although much of his activity is associated with the western part of the Dingle Peninsula, where there was a strong tradition of seafaring.

The *Life* describes a birth announced and accompanied by wonders. His mother's breast shone like gold before he was born (*Broinngheal*: 'bright breast'). Bishop Erc, who was present, interpreted this as a sign of coming greatness. The prophet Bec mac Dé, visiting a wealthy neighbour of Finnlug's, Ardi son of Fidach, told Ardi that his king would be born between him and the ocean, and Ardi, when thirty of his cows calved that night, hastened to give both cows and calves to the newborn infant. Meantime Bishop Erc saw all of Alltraige

---

This is adapted from an entry in *A Dictionary of Saints of Ireland* (Four Courts Press, forthcoming).

Caille ablaze with light all night. These are more or less standard omens of the spiritual hero's birth, the stock-in-trade of the hagiographical storytellers.

We are told that he spent his first year with his parents, then five years with St Ita, tended by angels; then he went to Bishop Erc 'to learn his Psalms' (to learn to read and write: the Psalms were the schoolchildren's reading primer in early Christian Ireland). While he was with Erc he gave evidence of virtue. He rejected a young princess who jumped playfully on his chariot, and drove her off with blows. For that beating, Erc imposed on him as a penance that he spend the night in a cave. All night the sound of his psalm-singing in the cave filled the countryside, and after he came out, no one could look directly on the glory of his face – except Finán Cam. This is attributed in the story to Finán's great virtue; but surely the original meaning was that since Finán was *cam* – squint-eyed – when he was looking directly at Brendan, he was really looking elsewhere – a rare hagiographical joke.

Having performed a few standard miracles and having learnt the Scriptures, he decided it was time to learn 'the rule of the saints of Ireland'. He consulted St Ita, who advised him, to avoid scandal, not to learn the rule from women saints (there is the intriguing implication here that the primary authorities on monastic rule were women). He went to Connacht, to Iarlath son of Lug son of Tren, to learn the rule. Iarlath offered to enter his service, but Brendan said to him, 'You are too old', and told him his place of resurrection was not where they were. He bade him have a chariot built and then travel in it to the place where its two hind shafts would break. Iarlath did so; the chariot broke at Tuam, and there he made his church and stayed until he died. Brendan wrote a rule dictated by an angel, returned to Erc, and was ordained by him. In a number of texts he is listed among those who attended St Finnian of Clonard's school of saints.

Now he felt the desire for penitential pilgrimage, to leave his home and people, and endure exile. At this point he met Barrinn and heard the story of the Land of Promise of the Saints, which inspired him in his great quest, the Atlantic voyage. The narrative of his quest for the Land of Promise over the ocean was the most widely told story of an early Irish saint. Manuscripts of it exist all over Europe.

The narrative begins at Clonfert. Here, according to the story, Barrinn *ua Néill* came to Brendan and told his tale. Barrinn's monk Mernóg (Ernán) had gone to seek solitude, and had established a community of coenobites on an island near Slieve League (in County Donegal). Barrinn decided to visit Mernóg and was well received. The coenobites, who lived on apples, nuts, roots and herbs, came out of their separate cells to greet him 'like a swarm of bees'. (The narrator here appears to be borrowing, perhaps at second hand, from descriptions of the early monks of the Egyptian desert.) Mernóg took him to sea and they sailed for an hour through a thick mist until they saw the Promised Land of the Saints, shining in a great light, full of fruiting trees and shrubs, where all the stones were jewels. After fifteen days on the island they came to a stream and were told by a man of great beauty who approached them, that this was as far as they could go; it was not permitted to cross the stream to the other half of the island, and they must now return. He told them that this island of unending light was where people would live if they avoided sin. So, after two weeks' absence, they returned to Mernóg's monastery, with the scent of Paradise on their clothes, and were joyfully received by the monks.

When the story had been told, Brendan went into retreat with St Malo and thirteen others of his brethren, and told them he wished to go in search of the Land of Promise. He then set out with his fourteen companions, going first to spend three days consulting St Enda on Aran. Then he went to Mount Brandon (in the Dingle Peninsula), and from the foot of the mountain they set sail in a ship covered with oxhide, the joints smeared with pitch and grease, the sails made of sewn animal skins, and materials for two other ships within it. A mountebank and three brethren from the monastery arrived at the last minute and, with misgivings, were taken along. Again they visited Enda, and Pupeus and Ronad, in Aran, and then set sail westward.

In time they came to an island on whose shore they saw numerous ugly mice as large as cats. The mountebank died at this point, having received the Viaticum, and they threw his body on the shore, where the mice ate it, all but the bones. Then, having buried the bones, they sailed for forty days with a favourable summer wind, without rowing. They reached an island where there was a guesthouse containing many ornamented vessels and golden bridles. For three days they were fed and refreshed, and as they prepared to leave, Brendan warned them to take nothing from the island. They protested that none would do so, but he showed them that one of the three brothers who had arrived late for the start of the voyage was concealing a golden bridle in his armpit; then he expelled the little black demon who had been living in the man's bosom for seven years. The man repented, received the Sacrament, and died. As they boarded their boat, a steward came to the shore with a vessel of bread and a vessel of water, and told them that they had a long journey ahead but would not lack provisions until Easter.

They came to the Island of Sheep, with fish-filled streams and so many flocks of sheep that they could hardly see the ground. They intended to keep Easter there, and Brendan told them to take from the flocks what they would need for the feast. But a holy man, a steward, came to them with bread and other food, and told them that in eight days he would supply them with provisions to last until Pentecost. Brendan asked him where they would be then, and the man indicated a nearby island where he said they would keep the vigil of Easter; then they would sail to another island called 'the Paradise of Birds'. When they came to the nearby island they found it bare of vegetation and without sandy beaches, so that landing was difficult. Brendan stayed on board and the priests chanted their Masses. The brothers brought ashore meat and fish for salting – the supplies given them by the steward – and set a fire, at which the island began to move, and they abandoned their supplies and fled in terror towards the ship. Brendan helped to pull them on board and told them that God had revealed the island's nature to him. It was a great fish, named Jasconius.

They rowed to the west to the Paradise of Birds, lush with trees, flowers and fruit, and pulled the boat up a stream by the lines, and came to a well. There was a great tree there so densely covered by white birds that leaves and branches were invisible. One flew down to the poop of the ship and explained that the birds had been part of Lucifer's host but had not consented to his rebellion. Nonetheless, they had been expelled from Heaven with the fallen angels, and were wandering spirits, except at the times of the great festivals, when they could come in this form to the island, where they might praise and see God. The angelic bird further told Brendan that he had now been one year at sea and would be at sea for six more, but finally would achieve his heart's desire. After the octave of Easter, the young steward arrived as he had promised, with provisions until Pentecost. They stayed for that period; then he returned with all necessaries for the feast of Pentecost, and told them it was time to resume their great journey.

For three months they saw only sea and sky, but were provisioned every two or three days. They came within sight of an island, but contrary winds held them off for forty days, until they were exhausted. Eventually they found a landing place and were greeted, in total silence, by a very old monk. He led them to his monastery, and they were entertained by the community of twenty-four, who had lived there, they were informed, under the strictest discipline of silence and obedience for eighty years, nourished by Christ and in good health, 'since the time of St Patrick, and of St Ailbhe, our father'. When Brendan asked if they might stay there, the abbot told them that was not God's will; he must return with his fourteen brethren to his own place. Of the two survivors of the latecomers to his company, one would make his pilgrimage to the island of Antoninus (actually no island, but a desert monastery), the other would go to hell.

Having celebrated Christmas, they went their way. They reached an island whose well gave soporific water. They sailed through a three-day storm after which the wind dropped and the sea curdled. Brendan told them to ship oars and trust in God. After twenty days the wind rose again, from the west, and they completed the circuit they were to repeat for a total of twenty years. Each year they visited the Island of Sheep, and kept Easter on the back of Jasconoius, Pentecost on the Island of Birds and Christmas on the Island of Ailbhe's community.

In the intervals of the seasonal rounds they saw many wonders. Once a huge monster of the deep blew a great spout of spume from his nostrils and came at speed to devour them, but another sea-monster intercepted him and chopped him to pieces with his jaws. Later, on the shore of an island the voyagers found the hind parts of the first monster, and Brendan told them they might now subsist for a time on the flesh of him who had meant to eat them. They came to a broad flat island without trees or shrubs but covered with great white and purple gourds. On this island there were three singing choirs, of boys, of youths, and of seniors, who sang psalms and hymns day and night, sometimes in unison, sometimes in parts, and whose repertoire included the Eucharistic hymn attributed to St Secundinus, '*Hoc sacrum corpus Domini*'. When they were leaving this island two of the boys gave them a basket of gourds, and, pressing the juice from just one of these, Brendan was able to provide the ship's company with sustenance for twelve days. Then they fasted for three days, and a large bird, of an unknown kind, alighted on the ship with a grape-bearing branch in its beak, which it presented to Brendan. This sustained them for another twelve days; then, after a three-day fast again, they came to the Island of Grapes, where they pitched camp for forty days. As they sailed in a bay they saw above them a griffin, as big as an ox, with terible claws, but before it could attack them it was killed by the bird that brought them the grapes. They were threatened by whirlpools, and more than once by the devil. They found the body of a fair young woman, a hundred feet tall, who had been killed by a spear-thrust. Brendan restored her to life, learned she was of the people of the sea, baptized her, gave her the Viaticum, and buried her when she died again. They came to a beautiful island on which they were unable to land, although they circled it for a week and could hear voices raised in song, praising the Lord. Eventually a waxed tablet was lowered down the cliff telling them they might not come ashore there but that in the end they would reach the Land of Promise. In one part of their passage, the sea was so clear and transparent that they could see the innumerable creatures on its sandy bottom, like the flocks and herds of the upper world, and the monks were so afraid of the monsters they saw below that Brendan made fun of them.

One day, when they had said Mass on board, they saw a column, so large that although it was three days' journey away, it seemed quite close. This vast column was as if made from glass and crystal. When they reached it, they found it marvellously transparent, and full of huge doors through which their vessel could pass in and out. On a bench near its base they found a Mass chalice. Another day they passed a dark mountainous island, full of fire and smoke, where hellish smiths were at work with hammers and tongs. The smiths flung fiery charges at them, which passed over them and fell into the sea, causing it to seethe up. They passed another great hellish mountain vomiting smoke. Here, one of the late-coming monks was carried off by demons, and when they looked back they saw the island belching fire into the air. When they left that place, they saw a man marooned on a small rock in the ocean, being buffeted by the waves and by a flapping cloak which hung before him and repeatedly struck him in the face. He told them that he was Judas Iscariot, and that this was not his punishment but his reprieve, for he was relieved of his real torment on Sundays and major festivals. At the hour of vespers a great cloud of demons came to carry him off to burn in the fiery mountain; but Brendan constrained them to allow him another night's reprieve. They came on another solitary on a small steep island where here were two caves and two fountains. This was an aged naked man, who told them he was Paul, formerly a monk of St Patrick, who had been ninety years on this island, sustained for thirty years by fish and for sixty by the fountains, having been for fifty years before that in Ireland. The hermit bade Brendan take some of the island's water with him on his way.

Eventually they came to the Land of Promise, where they were greeted by an ancient man, naked, but covered with a white down, who showed them the delights of Paradise. Brendan asked him if God willed that he and his company should stay, but the elder told him to depart and instruct the people of Ireland.

In some versions of the story it is told that Brendan made not one but two voyages before finally reaching the Land of Promise. He returned from the first after five years, having failed to find what he sought. He consulted St Ita, who reproached him for failing to come to her before his first voyage. She pointed out to him that his ship had been made with the skins of dead animals, and that such could not reach the Land of Promise, where no blood was shed. He went to the coast of Connacht and had a large timber vessel built, and it was in this that he finally achieved his desire.

After his adventurous years at sea, Brendan and his company arrived back to Inishmore in Aran, where they were greeted with joy by the monks. Saints Enda and Pupeus tried to persuade them to stay, but Brendan insisted that his place of resurrection was elsewhere. He sailed on to Inis Dá Droma (now Coney Island in the estuary of the Fergus in County Clare), where his company lived a life so ascetic that four of them died from the severe fasting. The fishermen of the Fergus refused them any of their catch, and Brendan cursed the river so that it would bear no more fish (he also cursed, we are told, fifty rivers in Ireland). He laid waste fifty forts in Bruis (near Tipperary). However, he blessed a stream in Clíu. While they were on Coney Island he was guilty of a grave fault which caused him to move on again. He had left his psalm-singer to guard a boat on the shore, and this man was sitting in the boat when a sudden storm carried it out on the estuary, where it was lost. The psalm-singer's brother blamed Brendan, who turned on him in fury because the man showed more concern for his brother than he himself had shown, and sent him out after the psalm-singer. He drowned, but the psalm-singer came alive from the bottom of the sea. Again, at Dubh Daire in Thomond, a man called Dobharchú ('Otter') killed Brendan's oxen which had strayed into his meadow. Brendan turned him into an otter. Dobharchú sadly warned his son and his wife against eating otter-flesh; then he wandered away and died.

Troubled in conscience, Brendan went to Ita to know what penance he should do. She bade him cross the sea, and with thirteen companions he travelled to Britain and visited Gildas. 'And he baptized all the men of Alba', says a poem by Macua mac Dolcáin about this journey. Gildas, having tested him, declined to be his judge. He built a church on Islay. When he was praying on a clifftop there one day he saw two sea-monsters fighting in the air. One, which was about to be overcome, called on the name of St Brigid and was saved. Straightaway Brendan set out and visited St Brigid, asking her how it was that the monster was saved by calling on her name, when she was absent, rather than on his, when he was present. She bade him confess, and he declared that he never crossed seven furrows without turning his thoughts to God. He bade her confess, and she said: 'Since I first set my mind on God, I have never turned it away and never will.' Apparently satisfied by this that she outranked him in sanctity, he returned to Britain and, on Tiree, built a monastery named Bleit.

He went to Connacht, to Inchiquin in Lough Corrib, and he baptized the people of Iarconnacht. Then he told the brethren that he had seen that the place of his resurrection must be in Uí Mhaine. In Uí Mhaine he built his monastery at Clonfert.

He came to the aid of Ruadhán, along with Brendan of Birr and other saints, in the quarrel with King Diarmaid mac Cearbhaill over that king's infringement of Ruadhán's sanctuary. It was he who suggested the tricks that defeated the king. He supplied the ransom of horses – actually seals from the ocean, which took the form of horses but then reverted to their true nature when the king had been paid with them, and returned to the sea. When the saints were fasting against the king outside the ramparts of Tara, and the king, inside, was counter-fasting, it was Brendan who suggested that the saints pretend to eat, so deceiving the king into breaking his fast and losing the contest.

He visited his sister Brig, accoring to the *Life*, at the fort of Áed, son of Eochaidh Tirmcharna, at Annaghdown on the shore of Lough Corrib, where her monastery was established. There he became mortally ill. He directed that his body should be brought back to his monastery at Clonfert for burial – but unostentatiously so that the tribes would not contest for it. The dates given for his death are all within a few years of 580. His festival is 16 May.

What are we to make of all this mishmash of myth, legend and fiction? Brendan would appear probably to have been an energetic organizer of the Church, expanding the monastic movement out of south-west Ireland into Connacht. He is credited with missionary endeavour in west Connacht, in Pictland, by some accounts in Brittany and Normandy, and in north Munster. It would seem that he built up, like Columba, a largely sea-linked federation of monasteries. Adhamhnán tells us that, in company with Comhghall, Cainneach and Cormac ua Liatháin, he visited Columba on Iona. There are church dedications to him in Scotland and Brittany, and St Macutus (St Malo) is mentioned as his disciple. He was possibly one of the churchmen active in the important work of building centralized and orderly Christian kingdoms in place of the tribalism of the past, and is said, for example, to have been involved in negotiations to bypass the local West Munster kings and transfer the allegiance of the coastal peoples directly to the high-king of Cashel. He is also said to have helped the Corca mRuadh of northern County Clare to secure remission of tribute claimed by the Connacht king Áed son of Eochaidh Tirmcharna. The story of his dealings with Bishop Iarlath may be a parable of the supersession of the episcopally organized Church of St Patrick's day by the monastically organized Church of later times. At any rate, under the great accretion of legend there must be a real person, probably one of the founders of the Church in Ireland.

The narrative of the *Voyage* has the very smell and feel of the North Atlantic, and for all the fancifulness of the story, it has many details showing knowledge of those waters. Some of the details are found in other Irish voyage tales. They are drawn from the lore of people who had seen whales, icebergs, volcanoes, island white with birds and, perhaps, floating branches bearing strange fruit. It is not surprising that the suggestion has been made that St Brendan may have reached America, and Tim Severin has shown that it was physically possible. However, the narrative is the story of a religious quest, not a geographical exploration. It should be read as an allegory, coloured by the knowledge of people who were familiar with the ocean. That St Brendan rather than another is the central figure is probably no more than chance – although he was, like so many of the monks of his time, a seafarer. He is, in the *Voyage*, the Christian soul seeking Paradise. Paradise, in turn, as imagined here, is partly modelled on the old idea of the location of an Otherworld, a land of ageless youth and eternal promise, beyond the western sea, the end of the terrestrial world.

The question is rather, since such knowledge of the Atlantic is revealed in the *Voyage*, did Irish people reach America at so early a date? There is no good evidence that any Irish preceded the Vikings in either Greenland or Newfoundland; but the first Viking settlers on the Faroes and in Iceland found Irish monks and hermits there before them, and there were many small islands of the ocean inhabited by holy men from Ireland. The skin-covered boats of the early Irish were capable of making the passage; but the object of the hermits was not to find new lands but, as Adhamhnán put it, 'to seek a solitude in the pathless sea'.

There are architectural remains at a number of the places associated with St Brendan, although they are all of much later date than his time. Ardfert Cathedral in north Kerry has remains of the early Romanesque period. Clonfert Cathedral has one of the most striking Romanesque doorways in Ireland. At Annaghdown, on the shore of Lough Corrib, where he is said to have obtained the site for a monastery for his sister Brig from the King of Connacht, there are also Romanesque fragments among the later medieval ruins. His name is attached to a number of features of the Dingle Peninsula, notably Mount Brandon. St Bredan's Creek, from which he was believed to have set out on his great voyage, looks out from the foot of the mountain to the open ocean. Interestingly, there is another Brendan landscape, with another Mount Brandon, by the Barrow near St Mullins (County Carlow), where his legend intersects with that of the local patron, St Moling. But he will always be chiefly known as the subject of a major medieval bestseller.

19

The Art of Enamelling

The Continental Celts were known to the ancients as being, among other things, skilled in enamelling and it is probably from them that knowledge of this craft spread to Britain and Ireland. At any rate, enamelling is one of the elements of our early art for which a more or less continuous history can be traced from pre-historic times down to the period of the Anglo-Norman invasion in Ireland – and there are not many such elements.

Enamel is a vitreous glaze or a combination of vitreous glazes fused on to a metallic surface, the glaze usually being composed of easily fusible salts such as silicates and borates of sodium, potassium and lead, to which various metallic oxides are added while the vitreous base, or flux, which is itself colourless, is in a state of fusion; and they stain it throughout. It is by these means that for centuries in Ireland colour was added to ornamental metalwork – and among a non-urban people like the early Irish, who lacked monumental arts, the metal-worker's craft was an important one, producing the showy personal ornaments, horse-trappings, decoration of weapons, bucklers and chariots, which formed an essential part of aristocratic display.

Glass was made by Egyptian craftsmen from very early times, but glass-making and enamelling, although so closely akin, do not necessarily go together. The ancient Syrians were skilled glass-makers, while, on the outskirts of the classical world, in south Russia, there were barbarian enamellers who were not glass-makers. The peoples of Central Europe, however, in Late Hallstatt and La Tène times, practised both arts. Coral from India, cut into little plaques or balls, was widely used as an adornment for metalwork, and the earliest enamels may have been simply a replacement for this when supplies were interrupted.

The first Early Iron Age enamels were in one colour only – red – and the technique itself appears to have spread westward from the Caucasus, although this is by no means clear. Various simple settings were used, the small size of the earliest mountings being determined largely by the small dimensions of the utilizable stem of the coral tree. Very often the little coral or enamel set-tings formed the eyes in figures of birds, animals or humans, and they depend for their effect simply on their colour. Then rather more elaborate setting

This appeared in the 'Roots' column of the *Irish Times* on 31 May 1972.

began to be used. In Britain the *champlevé* technique was developed, in which a sunken panel of the required shape is made in the surface of the metal and then filled with the enamel, which is finished flush. The *cloisonné* technique, in which a kind of little box is formed on the surface with thin strips of metal, which is then filled with enamel, was also practised in Britain and was common on the Continent. In Ireland it was the *champlevé* technique which prevailed. Here, the beginnings of enamelling are considerably later than on the Continent.

Some of the earliest specimens of the technique in this country come from the great nineteenth-century find of Iron Age swords and other objects, at Lisnacrogher in County Antrim. The objects were dispersed among several collections and can be seen in the Ulster Museum, the National Museum and the British Museum. A scabbard top with red *champlevé* enamel and a ring-headed pin with a stud of red enamel were included in the Lisnacrogher finds. Red remains the only colour used in Irish enamels right into the early Christian period.

In Britain, spots of blue or yellow began to be introduced shortly before the Roman conquest of the first century AD, but these were not themselves true enamels, but pieces of coloured glass set in the red enamel, which was used as a cement. Obviously there was a technical difficulty – perhaps a matter of furnace temperature – to be overcome for colours other than red, but polychrome work was already being done by this date in the western Roman provinces, somewhere along the lower Rhine. Soon after the conquest, yellow enamel appears in Britain in imitation of provincial Roman fibulae, or safety-pin brooches. The best early British examples are on horse-bronzes.

In Ireland too, enamel, but in red only, was being used about this date on horse-trappings, but these were of quite a different character from the British examples. There is a bronze 'pendant' (a piece of horse-furniture of a peculiarly Irish form and of uncertain function) in the National Museum, which has a sub-ovate head filled with a large stud of red enamel; and a horse-bit from Lough Beg on the Bann has red enamel fused in deep cavities.

Quite suddenly, it would seem, the technique of enamelling in yellow, green and blue, as well as red, became widespread in Ireland soon after the advent of Christianity. It would also seem that this was part of the flood of Roman influence associated with that event. Not only do these techniques closely resemble those which had long been practised in Roman Western Europe, but the patterns do too, especially the L-, T- or rectangular-shaped panels found on some early reliquaries, brooches and buckles (dating from the seventh and eighth centuries). There is, however, a problem. The enamellers' workshops of the Gaulish frontier seem to have gone into a steep decline after the disastrous Germanic raids of the mid-third century which plunged much of Gaul into anarchy for nearly a generation and which permanently altered the ethnic character of the frontier areas. There appears to be something of a gap beween this decline and the appearance of the western Roman techniques in Ireland. The real gap, however, is probably in our knowledge.

At any rate there are indications of the Roman connections of some of the early enamelled objects – a bronze hooked toilet implement, for example, imitated from Roman types, or a number of finger-rings with enamel settings, which again have Roman analogies.

Of special importance in this respect is the series of early penannular brooches of a type antecedent to, and greatly simpler than, the Tara Brooch. There are many of these. They have broad terminals, which are commonly enamelled, the *champlevé* panels taking increasingly elaborate forms. Often little tablets of millefiori glass are added to the enamel – another Roman provincial technique. Seán P. Ó Ríordáin, excavating the trivallate rath at Garranes in County Cork, found evidence for the manufacture of millefiori glass actually on the site at a date round about AD 500.

By the seventh century at any rate, the craftsmen, with the experience of centuries in their tradition, had developed two skills to a superb degree – that of working bronze, by casting, chasing, beating, shaping, and that of *champlevé* enamelling. When they were suddenly introduced to the techniques and the motifs of other metalworkers, such as those of the Anglo-Saxons, mainly as a result of the expansion of Irish Christianity in the late sixth century, their skills formed the basis for the achievements of a golden age of masterly and versatile craftsmanship.

Melting their bronze and mixing their glazes in little crucibles about the size and shape of egg-cups, held with tongs in charcoal fires, the enamellers produced works which have never since ceased to astonish the eye and the imagination.

20

Iona

One of the principal and most revered sites associated with early Irish Christianity is not in Ireland but in Scotland, a land which has for thousands of years had the closest connections with Ireland. The island of Iona, off the Ross of Mull in the Hebrides, is a place which, more than any other, is central to the early traditions of the two nations.

In the year 563, to take the most acceptable date on the evidence we have, St Columba, or Colum Cille, founded there the monastery which was to become one of the chief centres of Christianity of the far west of Europe, important not only ecclesiastically but also artistically and culturally. It is commonly referred to as an early example of Irish missionary activity; the word 'missionary' may however be somewhat misleading in this context. Asceticism was the driving force in the early days of monasticism here, and would seem to be the intention which impelled groups of monks to sever their connections with home and kindred and venture into the outer world on their 'pilgrimages for Christ'. The later legend of Columba tells how exile from Ireland was imposed on him as a penance. According to this story, which seems to be unknown to his earliest biographer whose work is extant, Adhamhnán (his successor in the abbacy of Iona), the penance was imposed as a result of the battle of Cúl Drebene, for which Columba is said to have been responsible. His confessor, Laisrén, according to the legend, imposed on him the penance that he should endure perpetual exile from Ireland. Accordingly he sailed away to the north, looking for a place from which he could no longer even see any part of Ireand on the distant horizon. The island of Iona was the place from which, even when he climbed its highest hill, he could see no trace of Ireland to the south.

This legend is contradicted by the story Adhamhnán has to tell, for he gives an account of visits to Ireland by Columba after he had founded Iona; but it came to be widely accepted in the Middle Ages and is preserved in some of the placenames of Iona itself. *Carn Cúil ri Éirinn* is the eminence on the island which commemorates, in its name, the final turning of the back on Ireland, which is otherwise celebrated in verse:

This appeared in the 'Roots' column in the *Irish Times*, on 26 June 1973. Since it was written, Iona has been developed for tourism, and there are much more frequent ferry services in the summer. A cast of St John's cross now (1996) stands on the site of the original.

Fuil súil nglais
fhéachas Éirinn tar a hais;
nochan fhaicfe iarmho-thá
fiora Éreann nách a mná.

(There is a grey eye
Looking back towards Ireland;
to see no more
Ireland's men or women.)

The island was commonly known as Icolmkill, '*Í Choluimchille*', its old Gaelic name, when it was visited by Dr Johnson in the course of his Hebridean journey, on 19 October 1773. Boswell was with him, and both have left us accounts of the island which show it to us as it was not long after the old Gaelic polity, introduced to western Scotland by the Irish some thirteen hundred years earlier, had broken down, and while the Scottish form of Irish was still spoken on Iona. Johnson remarked on the other-worldly atmosphere of the island, which has been noticed by many visitors since his time.

> Whatever withdraws us from the power of our sense; whatever makes the past, the distant, or the future predominate over the present, advances us in the dignity of thinking beings. Far from me and my friends be such frigid philosophy as may conduct us indifferent and unmoved over any ground which has been dignified by wisdom, bravery or virtue. That man is little to be envied, whose patriotism would not gain force upon the plain of *Marathon*, or whose piety would not grow warmer among the ruins of *Iona*.

The island is a small one, five kilometres by two-and-a-half, lying less than two kilometres west of the large island of Mull, in Argyll. From its western shore no land is visible, but the main focus of Columba's monastery was on its eastern side, looking across the narrow straits to Mull and towards the Scottish mainland beyond. When it was founded it lay a little beyond the boundary of the territory then controlled by the Irish kingdom of Dál Riada and within, it would seem, the territory of that mysterious ancient people, the Picts. It was with the Pictish king that Columba negotiated when he made the settlement, and his monks in time played a part in evangelizing such parts of Pictland as were not yet Christian. It was from Iona too that part of the evangelizing of northern England was undertaken in the seventh century, when St Aidan went with a group of monks from the island to be bishop in the Anglian kingdom of Northumbria. The first Viking raids found the monastery in the late eighth century, when it was the head of a great monastic federation in Ireland and Scotland, and within twenty years, after several other raids from the sea, the main body of monks had moved to central Ireland, where they founded the monastery of Kells, to which they transferred the relics of Columba and other valuables, including probably the famous Book of Kells.

It is still a place to visit. The port of Iona is Oban, a few hours from Glasgow. From there there is a daily steamer in summer, which circumnavigates Mull and allows passengers a couple of hours on the small island, or, rather better, a ferry-boat to Mull, connecting with a bus which crosses that island to Fionnphort, from which a small ferry-boat departs at regular intervals for Iona across the narrow sound.

Not much remains of the old Irish monastery. This was replaced in the Middle Ages by a Benedictine community, with the more grand and formal architectural ideas of that Order. They built an abbey which attained cathedral status, and a nunnery. Ruins of both survived, in the Romanesque style of the end of the twelfth century, and the cathedral has now been restored by the Iona Community, a Presbyterian group (of rather un-Presbyterian monastic tendency) who have endeavoured to fulfil the second part of the reputed 'prophecy' of Colum Cille:

> In Iona of my heart, Iona of my love,
> Instead of monks' voices shall be the lowing of cattle,
> But ere the World shall come to an end
> Iona shall be as it was.

Traces of the old monastic vallum may still be seen, and there are, as at so many early ecclesiastical sites, remains of high crosses. It is said that there were once more than three hundred crosses on Iona, and it is thought that the early destructiveness of the Reformation may account for their disappearance. It is unlikely, however, that these were high crosses; the reference may well be to cross-inscribed gravestones.

At any rate there is now only one intact early cross – the cross of St Martin. This has carvings of bosses and scenes from the Scriptures and a ringed head. Its date and its precise place in the high-cross series as a whole are disputed, but it seems likely that it was erected in the eighth century and that it is one of a number of crosses in western Scotland which exerted a great influence on the development of this type of monument in Ireland. St John's cross is stylistically perhaps more interesting, and probably earlier. Unfortunately it has suffered badly from the Atlantic storms. Having been shattered and then re-erected (by R.A.S. Macalister, who was for long Professor of Celtic Archaeology in University College, Dublin), it was again blown down about twenty years ago, and the fragments lay for a number of years where they had fallen, a melancholy sight. They have since been gathered into the shelter of one of the buildings.

The beaches are still white and clean, the sea breaking on them clear and fresh. Seals still sport and bask along the shore, as they did in Columba's time. But the 'prophecy' that 'Iona shall be as it was' is unlikely to be fulfilled.

21

St Aidan of Lindisfarne

Aidan, the first Bishop of Lindisfarne, according to one tradition was originally of Inis Cathaigh (Scattery Island, County Clare). He was a monk of Iona in the time of the abbacy of Ségéne, when the English king Oswald, who had just fought his way to control of Northumbria, requested Iona to send a bishop to preach the Gospel among his people. Oswald was a member of the royal family of Bernicia, the more northerly part of Northumbria. His father Aethelfrith had created the unified Northumbrian power but had been defeated and killed in 616 by Edwin, of Deira, the southerly part. Aethelfrith's sons fled to refuge in the far north, among the Picts and the Irish. They were baptized, probably on Iona, and learned the ways of the Irish church. They returned to Northumbria when Edwin was killed in 632, and the kingdom was invaded by Penda, the pagan King of Mercia, and by the Christian Briton Cadwallon, King of Gwynned. Oswald's brothers, who apostasized, were both killed in the warfare that ensued, but Oswald finally triumphed when he defeated and killed Cadwallon at Heavenfield in 633. Before the battle he set up a cross on the field – a custom he may well have learnt from his Irish mentors. After his victory, he immediately turned to Iona for help in establishing Christian rule.

Ségéne sent one of his monks, but the man was unsuccessful; the English refused to listen to him. He returned to Iona to report failure, saying that the English were obstinate and barbarous. A council was held to decide what was to be done. Aidan, who was present, told the man that he had been too hard on his ignorant hearers in Northumbria; he should have followed the example of the Apostles, first offering the pap of simple teaching, then gradually introducing the word of God. The Iona community saw evidence in this of Aidan's discretion. They consecrated him bishop and sent him south to Oswald.

At Aidan's request, Oswald gave him the island of Lindisfarne in the North Sea as his base. The island could be reached twice a day on foot at low tide. It was close to the King's fort at Bamburgh, and Aidan probably chose it for convenience of communications, since he would have been used to easy travel by water. His knowledge of English was imperfect (Bede tells us that when he preached to Oswald's ealdormen and thanes the King himself, who had

---

This appears as an entry in *A Dictionary of Irish Saints* (Four Courts Press, forthcoming).

learnt Irish in his sojourn in the north, interpreted for him), but he set about spreading the Gospel. He began by teaching the faith to a chosen group of twelve English boys. As time went by, more and more Irish came to assist him, dispersing under his direction throughout Oswald's realm. Those who were priests baptized the people, and some built churches. Most were monks, persuading the English, where they could, to follow the monastic way of life, while the King gave land and endowments for the foundation of monasteries.

Bede (who was born about twenty years after Aidan's death and must have met some who knew him) writes that Aidan gave an example of self-discipline and continence:

> 'The highest commendation of his teaching to all was that he and his followers lived as they taught'.

He fasted until None throughout the year on Wednesdays and Fridays, except for the fifty days after Easter. He was not afraid to mix with the wealthy and the powerful, nor was he afraid to speak out when they did wrong. He offered them food and entertainment but not money. What gifts they gave him he distributed to the poor, or used to ransom captives. One Easter he was dining with Oswald, and the food was served on a fine silver dish (possibly part of a splendidly ornamented Late Roman dinner service, of a kind of which examples occasionally turn up in Britain and, even, by way of loot, in Ireland). It was reported that poor people were outside asking for alms, and Oswald straightaway handed the silver vessel to his servant to be broken up for distribution to them. Aidan took hold of the hand that had passed the dish to the servant and praised the King, saying: 'May this hand never wither!' Bede goes on to tell that afterwards, when Oswald died in the battle of Maserfelth (in 641), the victor, Penda, severed his head and arm from his body; they were later enshrined in St Peter's church in Bamburgh, where they remained incorrupt.

Oswald's brother Oswy succeeded him, sharing the Nothumbrian kingship with Oswin of Deira until he killed Oswin in 651 and became sole ruler. When a priest, Utta, was sent to Kent to bring back Eanfleth, daughter of Edwin, as a bride for Oswy, Aidan, according to Bede, blessed some oil and gave it to Utta, telling him to pour it on the sea when a storm – which he prophesied – would rise. The storm occurred but the oil stilled the waves. Bede also tells us that Aidan had a retreat, for solitary meditation, on one of the smaller Farne islands, and that from there one day he saw Bamburgh, three kilometres across the water, being burnt by King Penda. He prayed, and the wind changed, driving the flames back.

Another anecdote concerns Oswin, who had given Aidan a finely caparisoned horse. Aidan preferred walking to riding – because it was easier to meet people that way – and when a beggar came asking for alms he gave him the horse with its rich trappings. Later, when he went to dine with the King, Oswin asked him why he had given away so valuable a gift. 'Is the offspring of a mare worth more to you than a child of God?', answered Aidan. The King, who had just been hunting, warmed himself at the fire before dinner, thinking about what the Bishop had said. Suddenly he unbuckled his sword, handed it to a servant, and knelt to Aidan, asking his forgiveness. Aidan assured the King of his high regard, raised him to his feet, and asked him to sit to his meal without regret. Oswin did so, but as he grew merry, Aidan grew sad. Aidan's chaplain asked him in Irish (which neither Oswin nor the servants knew) why he wept, and Aidan answered that it was because the King would not live long: 'I have never before seen a humble king ... he is too good for this nation'.

Oswin was murdered by Oswy shortly afterwards, and eleven days later, on 31 August 651, Aidan died. At the time, he was staying in one of the royal demesnes, where he had a church. When he became ill a lean-to bothy was built for him against the church exterior, and he was within this, leaning against one of the posts of the church, when he died. The body was taken to Lindisfarne and buried in the monks' graveyard. When the larger church of St Peter was built, his bones were removed there and given the place of honour to the right of the high altar. Bede reports that the post against which he was leaning when he died was twice unscathed when the church to which it belonged was destroyed by fire. After the second rebuilding it was set up within the church, and scrapings from it, immersed in water, worked cures.

Bede paints a vivid picture of Aidan: a man of subtle mind and simple ways, devoted to his duty, gentle, but unafraid of the powerful, uninterested in possessions or outward show, diligent and wholly free from sluggishness, prudent and not fanatically ascetic, but prepared to deal as unostentatiously with high as with low. His disciples included Chad, Eata, Cedd and Wilfrid, and he presided over the foundation of nunneries and gave direction, among others, to Heiu of Hartlepool and Hilda of Whitby. His achievement was great, and Bede, our source for such details as we have of his life, while deploring his persistence in the old Irish observances in relation to Easter and the form of the tonsure, nevertheless says that he cultivated peace, love, purity and humility, raised himself above anger, greed, pride and conceit, kept the laws of God as well as he taught them, studied and prayed, checked the powerful, and comforted the sick and the poor.

22

Monuments of the Dead

The pre-Norman centuries have left us with so rich a heritage of works of art that some whole groups which, if they existed in isolation, would be recognised as having great value and importance, receive in fact little notice. The elaborate monuments, whether manuscripts like the Book of Kells, pieces of metalworking like the Ardagh Chalice, or stonecarvings like the Cross of Muiredach at Monasterboice, are well known and are often reproduced in photographs. They leave an impression that the Irish art of the time depended on a dizzying intricacy and complexity of pattern. The impression registers part of the truth: the taste for a pedantic intricacy of pattern, following a kind of mad logic through bewildering convolutions without making a mistake was, and perhaps still is, a feature of the Irish temperament. But some of the achievements of our early civilization obey quite other laws.

Among these is the Irish, or Hiberno-Saxon, script, which pleases by simplicity and elegant proportions, and was so satisfying that, through its contribution to the Carolingian book-hand, it forms part of the basis of the type-faces most widely used to the present day, including that which the reader is now perusing. This script was a manuscript hand, and may be seen in its stately elegance on the written pages of the Book of Kells, the Book of Durrow, the Lindisfarne Gospels, and other manuscripts, pages from which perhaps too many eyes quickly turn aside to marvel at the neurotically perfect minuteness of the painted decoration.

The same lettering is to be found on a group of monuments which receives less notice than it deserves, the inscribed gravestones to be seen at many early ecclesiastical sites. These are usually thin slabs, most often of sandstone, which were laid on the graves either as simple markers of position or, in developed examples, as a covering for the full length of the grave. The inscriptions themselves are usually short and simple, following one of a few formulae of which the most common simply asks for 'a prayer (oróit) for N ... ' The word oróit is almost invariably contracted in the inscriptions to OR̄, so that the text appears on the

---

This appeared in the 'Roots' column in the *Irish Times* on 15 January 1974. Since it was written, the theft and destruction of grave-slabs has continued, and now (in 1996) there is no longer, for example, an open-air gallery of them at Clonmacnoise; they have had to be taken into more secure keeping.

slab in the form, to quote one of the many Clonmacnoise examples, '$\overline{OR}$ DO THUATHAL', with the mark of contraction shown as a horizontal stroke over the abbreviated word. Sometimes the personal name alone appears, especially on very early examples; sometimes a personal name with a word of description, as in another Clonmacnoise example reading 'COLMAN BOCHT', which is unique because the word *bocht* ('the poor') is written in *Ogham* script. Sometimes there is a simple variation on the basic formula, as in the Iona example which reads: '$\overline{OR}$ AR ANMAIND FLAIND' ('A prayer for the soul of Flann'), and, rarely, an expansion which tells us something about the dead person other than his profession or calling, as on the Clonmacnoise slab asking for a prayer for Feidlimid, which goes on to tell us, in Latin, *qui occisus est sine causa* – 'who was killed without cause'.

The slabs have been the subject of a number of studies. Petrie, early in the last century, provided what is now a most valuable collection of engravings of as many of them as he could find, in his two-volume work, *Christian Inscriptions in the Irish Language*, which also dealt with inscriptions on high crosses and on objects of metalwork. In the present century, R.A.S. Macalister dealt with them several times, first in monographs on Clonmacnoise, Inis Cealtra and other sites, when he tried to deal with questions of style and chronology, and finally in his comprehensive two-volume work (which also attempted a full listing of *Ogham* inscriptions), published by the Manuscripts Commission under the title *Corpus Inscriptionum Insularum Celticarum*. Subsequently, in 1961, Pádraig Lionard published a long paper on 'Early Irish Grave-slabs' in the *Proceedings of the Royal Irish Academy*. Scholarship, therefore, has by no means neglected the slabs, although there is still a good deal that could be done towards their study.

What does emerge is that, of many thousands of such grave-slabs must once have existed, perhaps as many as a thousand are still available for study, some however being represented only by small fragments. These span a period of five or six hundred years and can, for purposes of study, be divided into groups representing not only different periods but also different localities. They are a product of monastic culture, European and Latin in their early background, but gradually, as the centuries went by, showing more and more the influence of the indigenous artistic tradition. Wherever numbers of inscribed slabs are found there are also other slabs, similar in design and marked with similar Christian symbols, which do not bear inscriptions. It seems probable that some uninscribed grave-markers with Christian symbols are among the very earliest memorials of Christianity in the country.

At the time when the first missionaries were working in Ireland, the memory of the martyrs was still powerful in the early Christian Church, and cemeteries were cult centres of primary importance. Many of the great churches of medieval Europe began as cemetery-chapels which sheltered and honoured the bones of Christian dead.

One of the commonest manifestations of Christianity, in a material form, was the symbol of the cross, often enclosed in a wreath or circle, or the Monogram of Christ symbol formed by combining the Greek initial letters of the name of Christ, *chi* (x) and *rho* (p). By the exercise of but a little ingenuity, the *chi* could be turned through 45 degrees to become +, and combined with the *rho* to give a symbol which is at once the Cross and the initial of Christ. All over the early Christian world such symbols are common, especially in the cemeteries, on tombs and gravestones. With the missionaries they were brought to Ireland, where in due course, as time went by, the masons who carved them began to elaborate them. We find different kinds of Monogram, different kinds of cross (including very frequently the Irish ringed cross) and different kinds of combination of the two.

Collections of slabs can be seen at a number of the major monastic sites, including Glendalough, Inishmurray off Sligo, Iona, Durrow, Inis Cealtra, and Clonmacnoise – which has the greatest and most impressive range. At Gallen, in Offaly not far from Clonmacnoise, a large number of interesting slabs and fragments was turned up in an excavation before the Second World War. They were housed for many years in a sad state of neglect in a bicycle shed, but are now displayed in somewhat better circumstances in an open-air gallery like that erected (also by the Commissioners of Public Works) at Clonmacnoise.

There are many other sites throughout the country which have one or two slabs each. There is nothing elsewhere – that is, outside the area of influence of the early Irish Church (which does include parts of western Britain) – quite like this series of memorials to the dead. The slabs form, collectively, a major monument, and a major testimony to the beliefs and outlook of our ancestors. Yet they have been little regarded. Many even of those recorded by Macalister can no longer be found. And they are still, today, being casually stolen, casually defaced.

23

The Book of Durrow

Ireland in the earliest centuries of her recorded history became renowned as an island not only of saints but of scholars; a place where books were written and books were valued. Indeed, in representations of ecclesiastics in the early art of Christian times, the book, together with the bell and the crozier, appears as it were as the badge of office of the monk. The craftsmen and artificers of early Ireland wrought costly and elaborate shrines for famous books. The Venerable Bede, the historian of early England, writing in the first half of the eighth century, says:

> At this period there were many English nobles and lesser folk in Ireland who had left their own land during the episcopates of Bishops Finán and Colmán, either to pursue religious studies or to lead a life of stricter discipline. The Irish welcomed them all kindly and, without asking for any payment, provided them with books and instructors.

It is fitting then that among the principal monuments of our country's early culture which still remain for study, books are among the most important. These, of course, are hand-written books – manuscripts – for the invention of printing came not long before the final downfall of Gaelic society in Ireland. The importance of manuscripts is of different kinds. Some, especially of the earlier books, are of interest chiefly as outstanding examples of early Irish art. Others are valuable because of their content, which may be of interest to historians, to linguists, or to students of our native literature.

With the coming of St Patrick and his fellow missionaries to Ireland in the fifth century of our era there was established immediately a widespread need for books for use in the churches. There probably had already been some

---

This was the first lecture in a series of Thomas Davis Lectures which I edited in 1963 and which were broadcast from Radio Telefis Éireann in 1964 under the general title 'Great Irish Books'. The series was published under the title *Great Books of Ireland* in 1967. The lecture is printed here as it was published; but since 1963, not only has there been much new scholarship investigating the period of the Durrow Gospels and the historical problems of that time, but there have been important new discoveries of material. Therefore, a short appendix is added, embodying some revisionist thoughts.

knowledge of the use of writing in the country; this now became common, but it is likely that for the first hundred years or so almost all the books in Ireland would have been in Latin, the language of the Church, and most of these would have been copies of the texts chiefly used in Christian worship, especially the Four Gospels and the Psalms. Those few centuries were the very period in which Western Europe, formerly governed by the Romans, was being over-run by barbarian peoples. As a result, the Church in Ireland was left to develop in comparative isolation. One of the effects of this was that the copying of manuscripts went on independently of the influence of examples imported from overseas. A very distinctive style of script was developed in this period by the Irish scribes. This script in itself, rounded, elegant and clear, is one of the first major achievements of the Irish monastic schools. It is based on a combination of elements from several ancient scripts, which presumably the fifth-century missionaries brought with them, and in itself it is really two scripts: a majuscule and a minuscule ('upper case' and 'lower case' in other words).

Our earliest manuscripts are all on vellum, that is, specially prepared calf-skin, and are in codex form – in other words they are bound with leaves in the form with which we are familiar in present-day books, but which was still comparatively new in the fifth and sixth centuries, more ancient books being in the form of long rolls. One little fragmentary book, the *Cathach*, may be as old as the sixth century; and may just possibly be from the hand of St Columba himself. This is a manuscript of the Psalms now preserved in the library of the Royal Irish Academy in Dublin. For the best part of a thousand years it had been encased in an ornamental silver reliquary which was in the possession of the O'Donnells of Tír Chonaill. The metal shrine is now in the National Museum. The book in its shrine, treasured as a relic of St Columba, was carried into battle by the O'Donnells – hence the name *Cathach*, from the Irish word *cath* – 'battle'. As it now remains the manuscript consists of 58 leaves containing 64 psalms. The scribe has ruled most pages with evenly spaced lines lightly scratched on the surface of the vellum, to enable himself to write neat orderly pages. The text is written in Latin, in a dark brown ink. Each psalm opens with an enlarged initial letter; this is followed by a few letters which diminish down to the normal size of the text – a feature characteristic of Irish manuscripts. A light red and a few touches of yellow have been sparingly used, chiefly on the initial letters. Many of these are outlined with vermilion dots and some are decorated with simple ornaments, spirals, animal heads, a Maltese cross, and scrolls. These are in the style found on early Christian monuments in Western Europe; very similar motifs occur for example on early cross-inscribed stone slabs in Ireland. The *Cathach* is distinctively Irish not because the illuminator has borrowed any themes from the art traditions of pagan Celtic Ireland – he has not – but because its decorated initials represent an original Irish contribution to the Western scribal tradition.

Another early manuscript, again very fragmentary, dating probably from the first half of the seventh century, is housed in the library of Trinity College,

Dublin, where it is known as *Codex Usserianus Primus* (Ussher Codex No. One). This is a fragment of a Gospel-book. The script is Irish but the book has generally a Continental Late Antique character. It may be the work of an Irish monk at St Columbanus's monastery of Bobbio, in Italy. Its only ornament is in black and red on the colophons to the Gospels. The *Cathach* and the Ussher Codex, together with a few other fragments and incomplete books not now in Ireland, represent the achievement of Ireland's period of comparative isolation. The distinctive insular script was being developed, and an elegance worthy of the sacred text was attempted in the manuscripts, but no great elaboration of ornament had yet appeared. This elaboration when it came was in part the result of contacts which Ireland made with other cultures through the Irish missions overseas, especially through the establishment of monasteries in the north of England. The first evidence of the enriched art style, due to the contacts in England and elsewhere, appears in the manuscripts; and the earliest of the great series of richly decorated manuscripts (that we still possess) is the Gospel-book known as the Book of Durrow.

This manuscript is so called because of its association with the important Columban monastery of Durrow, in Offaly, where it was kept for centuries. Towards the end of the eleventh century there was entered into the back of the book the record of the handing over of a parcel of land by the monastery of *Glenn Uissen* (Killeshin, in Laois) to the monastery of Durrow in settlement of an old claim, with the signatures of witnesses to the transaction. This is good evidence for the presence of the book at Durrow in the eleventh century. Nothing more is known of its history until the seventeenth century. In the 1620s it was still at Durrow and in 1627 Conall Mac Eochagáin, the translator of the Annals of Clonmacnoise, recorded that the book was in the custody of an ignorant man and was used as a cure for sick cattle, the manuscript being dipped into water which was then given to the cattle to drink. Round about this time also the book was consulted by the scholarly James Ussher, then the Protestant Bishop of Meath, later Archbishop of Armagh. Ussher was assisted in his work on manuscripts by Henry Jones, who gave the Book of Durrow to the library of Trinity College. How he obtained it is not known. When it came into the library the book was enshrined in a jewelled silver reliquary, which subsequently disappeared – probably during the military occupation of the College in 1689. Before this happened, however, in 1677, the antiquary Roderick O'Flaherty made some notes on the book and its case, and he recorded an inscription in Irish on the shrine, which in translation reads:

'The prayer and blessing of Colum Cille for Flann son of Maolsechnaill, King of Ireland, who had this shrine made.'

King Flann, who died in the year 916, was also responsible as patron for two other works that we know of: the Cross of the Scriptures and the Cathedral at Clonmacnoise – not so very far away from Durrow.

The ordinary visitor to the Long Room of Trinity College Library is in danger of paying little attention to the Book of Durrow, open in its glass case not far from the larger and resplendent Book of Kells. Durrow is a much smaller manuscript and in every way more simple and restrained. Yet it would be a great pity, even for the visitor with limited time, to ignore this first master-piece of Irish Christian art. It is a work of great beauty, and in some ways more interesting than the Book of Kells. To begin with, the Book of Durrow, unlike the earlier manuscripts referred to, is almost complete, in spite of the ill usage to which it was subjected in the past. The page size is quite small: about 245 x 145 mm; and there are 248 leaves. These contain the Latin text of the four Gospels, together with some introductory matter, and the book has been designed to present the sacred scriptures in a worthy format. The script is a handsome clear firm Irish majuscule written in a black-brown ink. On the ordinary text pages only one other colour appears – red – which is used largely in the form of dots outlining initials or groups of letters. Yellow, green and brown are the other colours used in the book; these are concentrated on the ornamented pages which illuminate and vary the text. Among these orna-mented pages are the opening pages of the Gospels and of the introductory texts. Other pages are used like frontispieces and are devoted to the symbols of the evangelists. But the most original feature of the decoration is the oc-currence of full pages devoted wholly to ornament. These are sometimes known as carpet pages and they were to be a recurring feature of the Irish manuscripts; when you think of it, a somewhat strange feature in works which were pro-duced with infinitely painstaking and minute workmanship, for the carpet page is neither an embellishment of the text nor an illustration or symbol, but a pure luxury, a gratuitous addition to the book.

The arrangement of the Book of Durrow is straightforward and orderly. Like many other old manscripts it had suffered in re-binding and the original order of the pages had been disarranged; this, however, has been carefully restored in recent years. The book opens with three ornamental pages, the first and third being carpet pages, the one in the middle having the symbols of the four evangelists arranged in a centre panel around a cross. Then there follows the preliminary text known as the *Novum Opus*, which opens with an enlarged and decorated initial, followed by a group of letters diminishing into the text, which occupies several pages. The *Novum Opus* was a letter written by St Jerome in the year 383 to Pope Damasus. The Pope had asked St Jerome to produce a new Latin translation of the Gospels to replace the Latin version which was already available. In the letter St Jerome defends his translation (which is known as the Vulgate and which is the Latin version still used). The presence of the *Novum Opus* in the introductory matter of the Book of Durrow is an indication that the book contains the Vulgate text of the Gospels. There follows a glossary of Hebrew names, for St Matthew's Gospel. Then come the Eusebian canon tables. These, set out in tabulated form, and by numbered sections, show a harmony or comparison of the four Gospels, to display at a glance where the same topic or episode may be found in more than one Gospel. The tables occupy a number of pages, each of which has an ornamented frame. Then come chapter-headings and summaries for the Gospels; each of these is followed by an obscure passage about the relevant Gospel which is known as an *argumentum*. There are illuminated initials on a modest scale in this section.

After these preliminaries we come to the main part of the book: the Gospels themselves. Each is preceded first by a page devoted to the symbol of the evangelist and then by a carpet page (except that there is no carpet page before the beginning of Matthew), and there is also a carpet page at the end. Each Gospel opens with an elaborate initial letter followed by a line of ornamented letters diminishing to the normal script size. There is a tendency for these initials to increase in size and elaboration in succeeding Gospels; the initial at the beginning of Luke spans the full height of the page. There is one other point in the text, apart from the openings of the Gospels, which has been singled out for illumination. This is on the third page of St Matthew's Gospel, where the words occur: *Christi autem generatio sic erat* ('And this was the manner of Christ's birth'). The name of Christ here is illuminated. It is written in abbreviated form – *CHRI* – and with the Greek letters *Chi Rho*, equivalent to the Roman Ch R. These letters *Chi Rho*, which look like the Roman capital letters XP, form the Monogram of Christ which was one of the most widely used symbols of the new faith in Early Christian art. In later and more elaborately ornamented manuscripts than Durrow, this *Chi Rho* initial in Matthew was to be given even more prominence – in the Book of Kells it occupies a full page.

The general arrangement of the book seems clear and orderly, but there are a few discrepancies – all connected with some confusion between the Old Latin and the Vulgate versions of the Scriptures. It would seem that, in the usage of the Irish Church, St Jerome's Vulgate was just about replacing the Old Latin version at the time that the Book of Durrow was written. Its main text is basically that of the Vulgate, with some survivals of the older text, and the Gospels are arranged in the Vulgate order, Matthew, Mark, Luke and John; but the symbols of the evangelists, preceding the Gospels, occur in the old order, Matthew, John, Luke, Mark, and some of the preliminary matter, especially in the *argumenta*, is taken over from the Old Latin version.

These matters, with other aspects of the text and of the ornaments, have a bearing on the time and place of the origin of the Book of Durrow, both of which have been the subject of much controversy. This is in spite of the fact that Durrow, like some other lavish manuscripts, has a colophon – in other words a note by the scribe added at the end of the book. Unfortunately the note in Durrow been shown to consist of two parts, only the first of which is the colophon proper. It reads simply: *Ora pro me frater mi Deus tecum sit* ('Pray for me, my brother; the Lord be with you'). The second part of the inscription contains the names Patrick and Columba, and Columba is named as the scribe. But the most recent and most detailed study of the text, by Dr Luce of Trinity College, has shown that alterations had been made in it, including the insertion of the name Columba – in other words, a forgery had been carried out. From the colophon, then, we learn nothing of great value about the source of the book. As to the date when it was written, this has been established approximately in various ways – by the study of the text, by the study of the script, by the study of the ornament – and of these the ornament is the most accurate determinant. There is now general agreement among scholars that the Book of Durrow was copied in the seventh century, and most, but not all, would narrow this down further to somewhere around AD 660–75.

But was the Book of Durrow always at Durrow? In other words, was it written there, and if not there, where was it written? This is a question on which agreement has by no means been reached; indeed around this question there centre most of the controversies concerning early Irish Christian art. Some students of this art and of the early manuscripts believe that the book was indeed a product of the monastic scriptorium at Durrow; that it represents therefore in its ornament, in its script and in its text, the culture and scholarship of Ireland in the mid-seventh century. Others hold, however, that the book represents not the culture of Ireland at that date but that of the northern English kingdom of Northumbria, where Irish missionaries had been working among the Anglo-Saxons since St Aidan came south from Iona to found the monastery of Lindisfarne in the year 636. From Lindisfarne, for about thirty years, Irishmen worked in the evangelization of the north of England, while simultaneously, in the south, the mission begun by St Augustine, who had been sent from Rome at the end of the sixth century, laboured for the conversion of Kent and southern England. It soon became clear that there were differences in the practices and customs being established by the two Christian missions working so close to each other; especially in the calculations used for arriving at the date of Easter and the other moveable feasts. These differences led ultimately to a confrontation of the two systems at a meeting held under the presidency of the Northumbrian King at Whitby in 664. The King decided in favour of the Kentish customs and the Irish monks withdrew from Lindisfarne to Ireland, preferring to continue the observances which they derived from their own tradition. Now, all this happened round about the probable period of writing of the Book of Durrow, and it can be plausibly argued that a manuscript copied in Lindisfarne at about this time could well have found its way to Ireland (especially to a Columban monastery, such as Durrow was) as a result of the Irish withdrawal, or partial withdrawal, from northern England.

The Gospel text of the Book of Durrow is a fairly pure Vulgate text, unlike the mixtures of the older Latin versions of the Gospels with St Jerome's which are found in Irish Gospel-books of later date than Durrow. This has been put forward as an argument for a Northumbrian origin of the book; not a wholly convincing argument, since the version of the Vulgate found in Durrow does not agree with that found in manuscripts of known Northumbrian origin. However, arguments about the origin of the book which are based on the text will remain inconclusive, unless a more detailed study of the text than has yet been carried out may shed fresh light on the subject. Studies of the script seem to be equally inconclusive so far as this question is concerned. But the chief interest of the Book of Durrow lies in its art, and here a partial answer at least can be found to the question.

When we examine the ornament of the carpet pages, the enlarged initials, and the borders to the other illuminated pages, we soon see that an effect of variety and of richness of pattern is in fact produced with the aid of comparatively few decorative elements. Those which play a main part in the decorative scheme may be summed up under four headings: first, repeating patterns of frets, chequers and other simple rectangular forms; second, elaborate compositions of triple spirals, their coils expanding into clusters of trumpet-shaped terminals; third, patterns of interlacing, made up of broad bands with double-contoured edges, which are plaited in and out in great sweeping loops; last, a strip, or sometimes allover ornament, consisting of ribbon-like animal forms, biting and intertwined with each other. Then, the traditional symbols of the evangelists, the man of St Matthew, the lion of St Mark, the calf of St Luke, and the eagle of St John, are drawn in so stylized a way that they can be added to the list of motifs. Now the artist who set out and painted these designs was not inventing purely with his own unaided imagination: like every other artist of any time or place he was working within a convention; his imagination was drawing on ideas with which he was familiar from the work of others. The spiral patterns, for example, can be found in almost identical form in engraved or brightly enamelled patterns of sixth- and seventh-century metalwork in Ireland and Scotland – the very best examples being found on a type of large bronze bowl, fitted with hooks and chains for hanging up, which is commonly found in pagan Anglo-Saxon graves of that period but was of Irish or British, not Anglo-Saxon, manufacture. Tracing the motif back further in time, we can see that these spiral patterns are simply a development of an old metalworking ornamental style of the Celtic west. The inspiration of the patterns and techniques used by bronze – and goldsmiths can be seen elsewhere in the book: the man who is the symbol of St Matthew, for example, has a multicoloured patterning on his coat which seems to be derived from the polychrome glass inlays known as millefiori which were used by Irish jewellers at this time, while some of the angular patterns used in the carpet-pages derive – although this is possibly an indirect derivation – from patterns of inlays in Anglo-Saxon jewellery. Interlacing is a type of ornament which would be thought of by many people as typical of so-called 'Celtic' ornament; in the seventh century it was a foreign element which was just being absorbed in the West, and which points to contacts with the art of Mediterranean countries. The animal ornament of Durrow has some distinctive features which indicate that it is based on patterns found in Anglo-Saxon art of the early seventh century. Finally, some of the stylized symbols of the evangelists more than hint at Pictish influence from Scotland. In other words, in the art of the Book of Durrow, we can see the coming together of several cultures – and just such a coming together as would fit conditions in one of the great Columban monasteries of the mid-seventh century, when Lindisfarne in England, Iona in Scotland, Durrow in Ireland, were linked under a common monastic jurisdiction as well as by the comings and goings of monks, craftsmen, students and guests of different races.

In this coming together of cultures lies much of the permanent fascination of this earliest major monument of Irish illumination. Here we can see the first synthesis of the diverse elements which went to produce the art of Ireland's golden age.

Now, the synthesis was Irish and could have come only from the cultural background of the Irish Church as it was being modified by contacts with other cultures in the seventh century. This is what is important, rather than where, within the widely extended province of Columban monasticism, the Book of Durrow was written. In my own opinion, it is slightly unlikely that the models for some of the motifs in the art of the book would have been available to an illuminator working in central Ireland in the seventh century; in other words, I think it slightly more probable that the Book of Durrow was written at Lindisfarne, or possibly Iona, rather than Durrow. Since there was much coming and going of monks, much carrying to and fro of manuscripts, between the two islands, it is very difficult to arrive at a final conclusion about this, and eminent scholars would disagree with my view. The question is not really one of great moment: whether by the shores of the bleak North Sea or among the great bogs of central Ireland, the Book of Durrow was written where the rule of St Columba was followed, where Irish was spoken, and where Irishmen were learning from the peoples they taught. Wherever it was written, the Book of Durrow is the oldest of the great books of Ireland.

Date and provenance of the Book of Durrow remain controversial but, in light of research and discoveries in the more than thirty years that have gone by since the above lecture was written, I would wish to modify the concluding opinion expressed in it. Detailed argument is for another place; but it has now become clear that important works for which a Northumbrian origin was then suggested plausibly enough, are in fact of Irish provenance – including the Tara Brooch and the Sutton Hoo hanging bowl.

It is the innovations that mark the Book of Durrow as the first major work of the new composite style. Of these, the chief is the profuse use of broad-ribbon double-contoured interlacing. This is usually said to derive from Mediterranean art, but it is difficult to adduce any plausible prototypes of suitable date, except in Germanic (Lombard) metalwork in Italy. Uta Roth has argued compellingly that the background was the 'loop-ornament' (*Schlaufenornamentik*) widely found on ornamented Germanic objects in the late sixth and early seventh centuries, including the great gold buckle from Sutton Hoo. The date of the deposit of the ship-burial at Sutton Hoo has now been firmly revised to about AD 625, on coin evidence. The buckle (closely matched by one from St Denis) illustrates convincingly a background for the Durrow double-contour ribbons with dotting, and also (on its loop) for the narrow strands of the border of the interlace carpet page.

Another major innovation of the Book of Durrow is certainly derived from Germanic metalworking. One of the carpet pages is devoted largely to panels of ribbon-animals, long-snouted, biting one another or themselves. These are derived from an early phase of Style II of the Germanic animal styles classified by Salin (now shown to be more complex than in his exposition), a style of the early seventh century. In its borrowed form in Durrow there is some modification of the Germanic prototypes, notably in the fluid irregularity of the interlace, but also in some details. The symbols of the Evangelists appear to be derived from Pictish animal representations, but lack the liveliness of those originals and are handled stiffly and awkwardly by the artist. Throughout the book the painter is inspired by Irish enamels employing predominantly red-and-yellow designs. And the great hanging-bowl from Sutton Hoo, with its triple spirals, has now been shown conclusively (on chemical and metallurgical analysis) to have been made in Ireland – so greatly diminishing the arguments for Northumbrian origin.

The case is for argument elsewhere; but the Book of Durrow was probably written in the 630s. It displays the three elements that went to the making of developed Irish art: ribbon interlacing, Germanic animal ornament and the Ultimate La Tène tradition. It stands somewhat apart from the main stream, simply because the borrowed elements hadn't yet been fully assimilated. The text is a rendering of St Jerome's Vulgate. Irish manuscripts of later date used the Old Latin version of the Gospels, mixed with St Jerome's text. This relatively pure text may well derive from a version of the Gospels brought back from Rome in 632, after a deputation from the churches of the south of Ireland had gone there to verify the Roman practice in the calculation of Easte dates. The scholar Cummian, who organized this, seems to have been abbot of Durrow. A date in the 630s is appropriate for the writing and painting of the book, which may well have been commissioned as part of the Romanization process.

If so, considerable revision is necesary in the dating of the art of the seventh and eighth centuries. But such revision appears to be called for on other grounds too, and it seems likely that the Book of Durrow, apart from its intrinsic merits, may for quite some time to come retain importance as the key to an intriguing and important chapter in the history of art.

24

The Tara Brooch

We are all reasonably familiar in this country with at least the most important of the treasures which have now gone on display in New York. If the number of Irish people who have seen the actual Book of Kells, Ardagh Chalice or Cross of Cong is limited, there can be very few who have not seen photographs or reproductions of them, and fewer still who have not encountered ornaments or patterns derived from them. Since they were discovered or rediscovered in the last century, these objects have been admired, imitated (often with unfortunate results) and exploited commercially, nationalistically, sentimentally.

They will now be seen by very large numbers of people to whom they are not familiar in this way. They may be seen by fresher eyes. What will an intelligent, reasonably well-read person, interested in works of art or the history of art but not conversant with that major by-way in art history that passed through early Christian Ireland; what will such a person make of this highly distinctive style? There are many objects in the New York exhibition, and they span a lengthy period of time. One of them which will certainly draw special attention, even among the remarkable works already mentioned, is the Tara Brooch.

This, for several generations of Irish people, was almost a symbol of the civilization of Ireland in the remote past before the Viking and Norman invasions. Its general shape and outline have been copied in ten thousand trinkets. It has helped to sell chocolates, insurance and holidays in Ballybunion. But, aside from its modern symbolic function, what does it signify for the time in which it was made?

Unlike some of our treasures, the Tara Brooch was not handed down through a chain of hereditary custodians from the days of antiquity. It was found in the middle of the last century, in circumstances which are not altogether clear, on or near the beach near Bettystown, County Meath. It came into the hands of a Drogheda jeweller, and then to a Dublin jeweller. It has no connection whatever with Tara, but was given the name by which it is still known because this sounded romantic and appropriate. When first it became known to the modern

This appeared in the 'Roots' column in the *Irish Times* on 13 October 1977, when the exhibition 'Treasures of Ireland' had been organised to be shown in New York, Boston, San Francisco, Philadelphia and Pittsburgh.

world, therefore, it already had attached to it what were considered suitable associations to link it with the 'Golden Age', which was dimly known to the public from Tom Moore's lyrics and similar works.

The Brooch is quite a small object, its ring (it is not penannular) being just eight centimetres in diameter. It is made of silver but is richly gilt on the pin and the ring head. What makes the brooch quite remarkable is the profusion of ornament, executed in various techniques on a minute scale, which covers its surfaces. There are interlacings, intertwined fantastic and distorted animal forms, animal-head reliefs, elaborate compositions of interlocking spirals, and geometric settings of coloured glass and amber. Every surface is ornamented, and the back of the brooch is slightly more elaborate in its decoration (which is also better preserved) than the front. The pin, which has an elaborate keystone-shaped head, with a loop by which it is loosely attached to the ring, is also minutely ornamented and gilt. A hinged attachment fits a cable of woven metal (in what is called 'trichinopoly work') to the brooch-ring. This cable is now broken and incomplete. Possibly it had at its other end another Tara Brooch, one being worn on each shoulder.

The techniques employed include a very fine filigree, which is used in the main triangular panels on the front of the brooch. The equivalent panels on the back, ornamented with complex spirals, employ a remarkable technique. The patterns were first produced as a fine line relief on copper plates. Molten silver was then washed over the copper and burnished down to leave the fine copper lines of the design set off against the silver ground. Other patterns are cast and finished in the angular faceted relief (derived from a woodcarving style) which is technically known as '*Kerbschnitt*'.

The whole piece is a luxury article produced by a master craftsman of superb skill. It must have cost a great deal. It is the kind of brooch which only a king or a nobleman of equivalent means could commission – the fanciful romantic name 'Tara Brooch' may therefore not be too wide of the mark.

Although antiquarianism and antiquarian nationalism have made the patterns of the Brooch and of contemporary objects familiar, indeed hackneyed, ornaments in this part of the world in the past century and a half, the style of the work is far removed from modern taste in general. Even at the height of 'Celtic' revivalism, no one quite reproduced the minuteness and the assurance of ornament in the eclectic style of the eighth century. Even the best attempts at reproduction in modern times have produced little better than a pastiche. One age can never do the work of another.

Perhaps for this reason, we have never really got to grips with some of the real art-historical problems posed by objects like the Tara Brooch. Why the emphasis on smallness? This is probably chiefly a demonstration of skill and craftsmanship, with something in it of the kind of virtuosity displayed in the ability to write the Book of Genesis on the back of a postage stamp, but with something more as well. Complete command of the craft is revealed. Photographic enlargement of details of the Tara brooch does not – as with photographic enlargement of, say, a coin or print from a book – reveal flaws and imperfections: it reveals perfection. There may be something barbaric about the glitter of the object, and the inability to leave a space unornamented, but the finish, which extends to the last detail, reveals the imperatives of a civilization.

We know a lot about some superficial features of that civilization. But, when we look long and thoughtfully at something like the Tara Brooch, we realise that there are many important aspects of that distant world about which we know nothing. Certainly, it is very far removed from present-day Ireland, where virtually nothing is done or made that is not in one way or another slipshod. The great and important non-event of early Irish history is the failure of the Romans to invade and conquer our island. Their order and regularity did not reach our shores. But some other compelling and successful discipline is manifest in the Tara Brooch and the other major objects of the New York exhibition. It is a discipline whose roots we cannot trace; it informs a civilization which is ours only by a convention of continuity but which in reality is as remote as Nineveh and Tyre.

25

The Derrynaflan Altar Set

Every now and then an unexpected archaeological discovery reminds us that our knowledge is still very fragmentary – even of well-explored periods for which the material evidence seems reasonably abundant. In general, this kind of knowledge accumulates gradually and steadily; the cry 'Eureka!' is one rarely heard and little favoured among the patiently methodical archaeologists. Field-work, excavation, settlement and burial studies, build their evidence (largely contextual) slowly. But the case of what we might term 'archaeological art history' is different. Here we are concerned not merely with the sociological, the average or the repetitious, with objects simply as evidence. We may depart at times from the archaeological canons and take an interest in the unusual or outstanding, the personal and the psychological, appreciating that a master-work is not merely representative; it is to be enjoyed and studied for its own sake.

For the study of an art such as fine metalworking a major new discovery has a special importance. A run-of-the-mill pin or buckle-mounting has little to add to our knowledge of the past unless its provenance and context are precisely known. Hence the emphasis archaeologists lay on the slow work of controlled excavation. They are not looking for 'finds' as such; they are seeking information. A master-work of art, however, can teach us a great deal in and of itself – although of course our understanding is deepened if we have good evidence of context.

Irish Christian art of the pre-Norman centuries had two periods of high achievement. The first reached a peak about the beginning of the eighth century, the second about the beginning of the twelfth. As it happens, the major works of the first period come to us with little background information. Even the painted manuscripts – such as the Book of Durrow – are comparatively uninformative about themselves. Whole groups of carvings, like those on the slopes of Slievenamon, are at sites about which we have scant historical information or none. Some of the chief works in metal come as accidental or

In March, 1979, I gave a short discourse to the Royal Irish Academy on Byzantine prototypes for the Ardagh Chalice, and was preparing a longer paper when, within a year, a new find at Derrynaflan in County Tipperary provided material to open up the whole subject. The following appeared in *Art About Ireland* for June-July, 1980, under the title 'The Derrynavlan Hoard'.

stray finds. The Ardagh Chalice was part of a hoard accidentally found by a boy digging potatoes in a rath in County Limerick in the last century. The 'Tara Brooch' (the name is the conceit of a Victorian jeweller) was found at the foot of an eroded cliff on the shore of Bettystown, County Meath, also in the last century. The Moylough belt-shrine was found by turf-cutters in County Sligo in the present century. We are better informed on the background of major works from the second flowering of Irish Christian art. Some of the objects, like St Manchan's shrine (now displayed in its own shrine, commissioned by the then Bishop of Ardagh and Clonmacnoise, Dr Cahal Daly, and made by the sculptor Ray Carroll, in the church of Boher, County Offaly) remained in the hands of hereditary keepers until modern times. Others, like the Cross of Cong, the shrine of the Bell of St Patrick's Will and the shrine of St Lachtin's Arm, bear inscriptions recording the names of royal and ecclesiastical patrons and sometimes of the artificers. It helps our understanding of the objects to know that it was one of the functions of royal greatness in the twelfth century to commission such splendid and luxurious pieces for the altars, and to know that the artists had status, a dignity and a name.

The hoard recently found at Derrynaflan, County Tipperary, stems from the more anonymous earlier period. It immediately sheds an oblique but revealing light on much-studied older finds, such as the Ardagh Chalice.

Derrynaflan itself is a place of some interest; indeed the site has long been a National Monument in State care. A green drumlin-island in a great expanse of dark bog, it was the site of an early monastic foundation and has ruins of medieval ecclesiastical buildings in stone as well as some medieval grave-slabs which are associated in folklore with that energetic and travelled character the *Gobbán Saor*. The new discovery therefore, compared with other finds of early Christian master-works, has an unusual measure of background, although it was unscientifically removed from the earth. But the background may be somewhat misleading.

Derrynaflan was originally *Daire-ednech* – the 'ivied oak-wood'. It is said to have been founded by St Ruadán of Lorrha, and there is a description of the place in the medieval Latin *Life* of St Ruadán. He is a figure of considerable significance in the early hagiographical tradition. He appears as the champion of the new Christian Church against the old pagan monarchy in the story of the 'cursing of Tara', in which his antagonist is the sixth-century king Diarmait mac Cerbheoil. His monastery at Lorrha (in north Tipperary) was an important one and itself has specimens of ninth-century art in the form of fragments of sculptured high crosses which may still be seen on the site. Lorrha was also a centre of the eighth-century reforming and ascetic monastic movement of the Céli Dé ('God's Men' – a term which originally probably simply meant 'monks'), one of whose principal leaders was Máel Ruadáin ('devotee of Ruadán') of Tallaght. The attribution of the foundation of Derrynaflan to Ruadán may well mean no more than that the place was an offshoot of Lorrha. It was probably what might be described as an eremitical out-station, bearing to Lorrha a relationship like that which Inis Locha Cré (now Mona Incha) bore to St Crónán's monastery at Roscrea.

The oldest antiquity now visible on the site itself is an ornamented small Romanesque window, in sandstone, of the later twelfth century, re-used as the piscina of a late medieval church. It was compared by Thomas O'Connor (in the *Ordnance Survey Letters* in 1840) to work at Cormac's Chapel at Cashel, but more closely resembles work at other Romanesque sites in Tipperary, such as St Peakaun's. The island stood within the territory of the Eoghanacht of Cashel, the lands of the Cashel branch of the great royal dynasty of pre-Viking Munster. It is in the extensive bog known as Móin Éile, near its southern edge, and was really in frontier territory between Eoghanacht and Éile.

The hoard found on the island in February [1980] comprised a chalice, a paten, a ring which is taken to be the base or stand of the paten, a strainer and a large plain bowl of thin bronze which was inverted over the other objects, presumably to protect them. The find reached the National Museum very soon after its discovery, and the Museum's Keeper of Irish Antiquities, Michael Ryan, together with some of his colleagues, further investigated the find-spot and recovered small fragments and mountings. The discovery was announced to the press on 6 March, and on 14 April the Director of the National Museum, Mr Breandán Ó Ríordáin, and Mr Ryan gave a general account of the objects to a special meeting of the Royal Irish Academy. A significant point made by Mr Ryan was that the hole in which the hoard had been deposited was shallow, and his opinion was that the deposit had been made at some date after the Norman invasion.

A hoard of valuables hidden in a shallow pit is an indication of some kind of emergency, personal or public. This hoard could have been hidden either by someone properly in possession of the objects, who wished to safeguard them in time of trouble, or by a thief, seeking to avoid detection and presumably intending to return to recover his booty. In either case, it need have no direct connection with the monastery or church of Derrynaflan. The site, being remote and protected by a wide marsh, would have made a good hiding place. On the other hand, the objects are likely to have come from not too far away, and the depositor, whoever he was, probably had some connection with, or local knowledge of, the island. On the whole, it seems more likely that he was in some sense a guardian of the objects, who hid them in an emergency under the protection and friendly shadow of the church walls of Derrynaflan. This might well have happened after the Reformation, and there is a high probability that ecclesiastical vessels of such value and splendour had belonged to some more metropolitan church than the little bogland island retreat – somewhere, say, like the cathedral of Cashel.

The hoard forms a liturgical set, all the objects except the protecting bowl (and just possibly it too) being connected with the celebration of the Eucharist. The strainer is of the type resembling a long-handled spoon or ladle, the bowl being divided longitudinally by a vertical membrane pierced with small holes arranged in a decorative pattern. Wine would be poured into the spoon at one side of this membrane, would flow through the piercings and, thus strained and purified of sediments, would be poured out from the other side of the spoon into the chalice. The chalice itself is large and two-handled, the type usually interpreted as a communicant's rather than a celebrant's chalice. The paten is very large, and slightly dished, with a flat ornamental border which has inlays in small panels around the circumference. It had a separate stand, a strip of metal formed into a ring, which also had small decorative panels. From the detail of the elaborate ornament on these objects it is possible to date the paten and its stand with considerable confidence to the period round AD 700. The strainer, more simply (but elegantly) ornamented and more difficult to date with precision, would fit very happily into the same period. The chalice, however, may well be considerably later, and its different quality and character raise interesting questions about the meaning of the set as a whole. It is clear however that all these objects were intended to be splendid, and that a wealth of skill, sensibility and time was lavished devotedly upon them in their manufacture. While inscriptions and records relating to crafsmanship are few for this period, we have many reasons to believe that royal patronage was as important then as it was (as attested by numbers of inscriptions and annalistic records) in the renaissance of fine metalworking in the early twelfth century. As early as St Patrick's time royal gifts of jewellery were offered to the churches, as he mentions in his *Confessio*. The eighth century was a time when, in Ireland as in other parts of the West, kingship was being given new meaning and, its pagan origins overlooked, was being given Biblical interpretation and having its rituals and customs accommodated to those of the Church. Towards the end of the century, a King of Tara came to be known as 'Áed the Ordained' – the anointed king, like Charlemagne and his immediate predecessors, or like Alfred the Great in England. Early in the century the great Munster king, Cathal mac Finnguine – who is the first on record as having tried for domination of all Ireland through an attempt on Tara in 721 – appears to have been a monarch of this type, ruling with and within the Church. He promulgated some kind of reform, involving acknowledgment of Armagh, at Terryglass, the monastic neighbour and close connection of Lorrha. It is reasonable to assume that costly ecclesiastical vessels and objects were the gifts of such kings in the eighth century, as we know they were the gifts of kings aspiring to greatness in the twelfth century.

Cashel itself became a Céle Dé centre, especially during the reign of the Céle Dé king-bishop Feidlimid mac Crimthain in the early ninth century, and Derrynaflan then was within an orbit which included Lorrha and Terryglass, Tallaght, and such major centres as Lismore and Cashel. It happens that we have, precisely from this grouping, information on the eighth- or early ninth-century liturgy. The 'Stowe Missal', thought to have been written at Tallaght at the end of the eighth century, was kept at Lorrha for hundreds of years, and it is one of our main sources of information on early Irish liturgical practice.

Remote Byzantine origins for parts of the liturgy of the Céli Dé are apparent –
as in the prayer in the Stowe Missal for 'our most pious emperors and for all
the Roman army'. The chalice was prepared before Mass, as it is today in the
Eastern rites. In the Ambrosian rite of Milan, which was a major influence on
the early Irish liturgy, the bread and wine, prepared beforehand, were brought
in procession to the altar by the clergy after the dismissal of the catechumens
at the end of the preliminary prayers, the choir singing a chant whose name
(*Offerenda*) in the Ambrosian rite gave the Irish word for the Mass (*Aifreann*),
as Fr John Ryan pointed out in a paper on these matters. A tract in Irish at
the end of the Stowe Missal explains the hidden meanings which the wor-
shipper was to bear in mind during the Eucharist. In Fr Ryan's words:

> In it a figurative explanation is given of the altar, the chalice, the host,
> the wine, the lections, the uncovering of the host and of the chalice, the
> elevation of the chalice ... the words of consecration, the fraction (a very
> mystical explanation of the various particles, 65 in all), the intinction.
> Examples are: the host on the paten (*meis*) is Christ's flesh on the tree
> of the Cross. The fraction on the paten is the breaking of Christ's body
> with nails on the Cross ...

Processions with the bread and wine are depicted in the well-known mosaics
in the church of San Vitale in Ravenna, executed by Imperial artists when the
church was consecrated in 548 and including portraits of the great Emperor
and Empress Justinian and Theodora as well as of members of their courts.
The Empress carries a jewelled chalice; the Emperor bears a large shallow vessel which is the paten. These vessels may be – probably are – Imperial gifts
for the altar of the newly finished basilica. For our purpose they have a further
interest; they are representative of the prototypes of the Ardagh and Derrynaflan
vessels. Such gifts may not always have gone into everyday use, but may have
been in themselves offerings which remained as contributions to the splendour of the church. Lord Dunraven, in the paper in which he gave the first
detailed description of the Ardagh Chalice, pointed out that at the end of the
eighth century chalices, or at least jewelled cups (*calices*) were hanging between
the columns of the nave of St Peter's in Rome, and that after the plunder of
St Peter's by the Saracens in 847, Pope Leo IV re-ornamented the basilica and
hung new silver *calices* there.

The artefacts in the Derrynaflan hoard show differences and contrasts, already referred to, which raise some interesting questions about the set. Both the
chalice and the paten (with its stand) are of silver, or of an alloy with a very
high proportion of silver. In this they resemble the Ardagh Chalice and the
Tara Brooch. The strainer is of gilt bronze. It is a very elegantly designed object, with a long handle teminating in a disc, which has a cabouchon crystal
backed with foil and set in an inlaid circular frame. There is a moveable ring
for suspending the strainer. Around the rim of the bowl there is a flat strip

divided by small bosses into long panels which contain trichinopoly work (a knitted mesh of fine silver wire). The ornament is comparatively simple, but it is in keeping with the ornament and design of the paten and its stand.

The paten is a superbly made piece, with craftsmanship of the highest quality achieved in that age of supreme mastery in metalworking. The work attempts, and virtually attains, perfection in miniature, like the work on the Ardagh Chalice and the Tara Brooch, with which it closely compares. It too has a flat band around the rim, which in turn is rimmed, and is decorated with mountings and settings both on its horizontal and on its vertical faces. On the horizontal band small beautifully made studs of glass inlaid with silver grilles (like those on the Ardagh and Tara pieces) provide intervals between which are long panels. There is much use of trichinopoly work (found in the cord attached to the Tara Brooch and in some of the settings of the base of the Ardagh Chalice). The panels on the upper surface of the ring were filled with fine gold filigree of the highest quality. The stand for the paten has work of similar character and quality. After the cleaning, technical research and conservation have been completed on these objects it will be possible to say a great deal more about them and to make much more detailed comparisons with the other master-works of the period, but even at this stage there is no doubt whatever of their quality. They compare with the very best of their time, and they open up remarkably our view of the civilization of the eighth century. They show us that such extraordinary masterpieces as the Tara Brooch and the Ardagh Chalice were not sports, but emerged from an atelier broadly and firmly established. They demonstrate that work of this quality was being produced in Ireland (which has been doubted) and may well give us some clues as to the chief centre or centres of production.

The chalice is a different matter. In its general design and layout it closely resembles the Ardagh Chalice, although it is larger, and slightly taller in its proportions. The band of ornament beneath the rim (matched in general layout on the Ardagh Chalice) does not appear to have engravings or inscriptions on the surface of the bowl beneath – in the position where the names of the Apostles appear on the Ardagh Chalice. The three-bossed handle-escutcheons of a broadly triangular shape provide a very close comparison, in outline, but the additional circular escutcheons of the Ardagh Chalice are not matched on the Derrynaflan vessel. The resemblances in form, in construction, in organisation of the ornament, are such that it is reasonable to say that the two vessels come from the same workshop or at least from the same narrow tradition. But here the resemblances cease. The range of techniques employed on the Derrynaflan chalice is much more limited. It is ornamented chiefly with amber studs and a rather coarse (by comparison) filigree and granulation. The work lacks the microscopic precision of the other objects, and interlacing and animal forms are botched here and there, filigree wires crudely or carelessly finished. It looks like an apprentice craftsman's approximation to a copy of the Ardagh Chalice. Since the Derrynaflan pieces appear to form a functional set, is this a replacement for an original chalice which was of similar quality to the paten and strainer and which had been stolen or lost in some other way? What makes the question quite intriguing is that the Ardagh Chalice would much better fit into the set. And the Ardagh Chalice (found with a small plain celebrant's chalice and with some brooches, the latest of which was of tenth-century date) formed part of what looks like a thief's hoard; while the Derynaflan find, as I have suggested, would seem rather to be a custodian's hoard. It is just remotely possible that the Ardagh Chalice *did* form part of the set, was stolen, and was replaced by this vessel. But this is probably stretching coincidence too far. Nonetheless there is a manifest relationship between the two.

The prototypes for these pieces are Byzantine. Gold and silver chalices appear to have come into use in the East in the fourth century, and soon there was the custom of presenting them as munificent gifts to churches. A sixth-century chalice – the chalice of St Stephen – from Rusafa in Syria, now in the Boston Museum of Fine Arts, illustrates in its general form and organisation of ornament the background of the Ardagh and Derrynaflan vessels. It has two handles, a double band with an inscription under the rim, the *Chi-Rho* Monogram of Christ occupying the position taken by the round escutcheons on the Ardagh Chalice, and a stem and base broadly similar in form. Other early examples are referred to by Lord Dunraven in the paper already mentioned, but there are silver chalices without handles as well as chalices of semi-precious stone from the Byzantine East which show the development of the form from earlier Greek cups. A good example is the cup or chalice of the fifth century found at Durazzo in Albania and now in the Metropolitan Museum of Art in New York.

The Derrynaflan find is of the greatest importance for the study of Irish art of the eighth century. It establishes beyond doubt that there was a school of metalworking of superb skill in Ireland at the time – and somewhere broadly in the south midlands seems indicated by the evidence. This work would seem to require a royal patron, and by far the most likely place to look for such patronage is Cashel. The great figure in early eighth-century Cashel is Cathal mac Finnguine, who seems to have taken a Carolingian view of kingship and to have been one of the first to do so. It would be wholly in keeping with this to provide a magnificent set of liturgical equipment to a major church – Emly, perhaps, or Lorrha, or Lismore. We can, at this stage at any rate, only speculate. But some such background must lie behind the new find which has emerged from the earth to give us pleasure, food for thought, and some feeling, it is to be hoped, of considerable respect for those who preceded us more than a thousand years ago.

26

Irish Monks and Frankish Churches

The whole Rhine valley has Irish associations, because of the coming of missionaries in the sixth, seventh and eighth centuries, and then because of the coming of scholars whose erudition or skill was called upon by the Carolingian renaissance. None of these activities have left traces on the ground. If the Irish monks erected their own kinds of buildings, they were flimsy or at least perishable and have long since disappeared. The Irish monastic system itself, which sponsored the peculiar layout of the monastery marked by numbers of small churches and by separate dwelling-huts, did not last for very long on the Continent, being soon replaced everywhere by the Benedictine system. From the quite long period in which the Irish played a part in the affairs of this area, therefore, the material remains are few. They consist mainly of manuscripts scattered through a number of libraries, at Würzburg, St Gallen, Schaffhausen, and elsewhere, and of a very small number of reliquary fragments.

It seems likely on the contrary that the material evidences of the Irish contact with this area are to be found at the other end – in Ireland itself. The Irish high crosses certainly, and possibly the early Irish mortared stone churches, or some of them, were influenced in their design and ornament by styles developed in Western Europe, mainly probably in the eighth and ninth centuries, but perhaps earlier. Unfortunately, it is difficult now to study the background from which some of these influences emanated. Most of the important centres of the early Middle Ages here on the Continent remained important into the late Middle Ages, and very often beyond, with the result that many rebuildings have taken place to accommodate the needs of changing times and growing populations and congregations. Not a single Merovingian cathedral, for example, survives above ground to give evidence of the kind of church building the early wandering monks, like Columbanus, would have found on their arrival.

In spite of this difficulty, the past hundred years or so have seen a steady accumulation of knowledge about the churches and monasteries which were the centres of cultural survival for much of the heritage of the ancient world during the Dark Ages. Excavations under modern or late medieval cathedrals,

This, written in Frankfurt am Main, was published in the 'Roots' column in the *Irish Times* on 13 November 1973.

churches or secular buildings have been carried out as opportunity offered, especially when demolition was in progress in connection with rebuilding or alteration. The wars of the present century, with their effective technology of indiscriminate destruction, have helped.

As one might expect, it emerges that the background to all this building is Rome – in two senses. When the Franks first settled the middle and lower Rhine areas, which they did from the third century on, first as adversaries and then as a kind of peasant frontier militia of the Roman Empire, they were pagans. When at the beginning of the sixth century Clovis the King of the Franks decided that he and his people should be baptized, he chose the Catholic form of Christianity rather than the Arian faith that was held by most of the Germanic tribal groups. This was a political act by whch in effect the Franks came to a kind of arrangement with the Gallo-Roman population (who were in large part Catholic) of the areas over which Frankish rule was extending. It both gave recognition to the bishopric of Rome and ensured continuity in many matters for Roman culture.

The churches of the Franks, then, were essentially Roman churches. But, since Constantine the Great had ended the persecutions at the beginning of the fourth century and given recognition to the church in the Empire, churches, in architectural terms, were still essentially modifications to new purposes of designs for secular buildings. The hall of audience, of justice, with its antechamber and outer courtyard, was the model – the *basilica*. It is interesting to see how the Franks adopted this, for monastic as well as secular churches. Many of the early monasteries of the West, as in the centres of origin of monasticism in the Near East, were settlements within disused Roman buildings, often forts. This model may have been, somewhat vaguely, in the background of the layout of early Irish monasteries, but if so, the Irish type, probably under the influence of native secular practice, soon diverged from the Continental. Even before the Benedictine rule became dominant, Frankish monasteries, centred on a church which was architecturally a city-centre building, were developing the system of formal courtyards within an enclosure which was to characterize the Continental monastic buildings for centuries. It is interesting to speculate what Columbanus and his fellows, and their many successors, made of these large-scale and formally laid out buildings.

In general the peoples whose backgrounds had lain outside the Roman Empire tended to admire greatly the achievements of that Empire and to wish to emulate them. This does not appear to have been so with the early Irish monks. The famous Easter controversy – about how the date of the movable feast of Easter should be calculated – brought Columbanus into conflict with Continental bishops at the end of the sixth century, and the successors of Columba into conflict in England in the middle of the seventh. The controversy brought out fairly clearly that at this early period the Irish, or the ecclesiastical Irish at any rate, were not disposed to admire the heritage of the Empire, preferring their simple little churches and their own ways. Columbanus says as much, pointing out that the honour he gave to Rome was as the place of martyr-dom of Peter and Paul, not as the Imperial city. In this there are reflections of the rejection by the early monks in the Egyptian desert of what they saw as the corrupt civilization of the Roman world.

But such pristine puritanical principles did not long remain universal in the Irish church; the many translations into Irish sculptured stone of motifs and designs found on Continental ivory book-covers and other objects, or on the stucco-reliefs which adorned Carolingian churches, show that some of the Irish came, at least by the eighth and ninth centuries, to admire the Roman mon-umental tradition.

Of Carolingian, as distinct from earlier Frankish churches, a number remain. The most famous is Charlemagne's octagonal palace chapel at Aachen, of which the kernel, it might be said, still stands. This, built at one of the chief centres of the new Empire which the Frankish king founded at the end of the eighth century, was a very conscious attempt at Roman restoration. Some of the very columns and carved capitals were brought from Italy to demonstrate how authen-tically Roman it was. It was part of a large complex, connected, by a corridor-like system of building, with the palace: church and state expressly linked in a formal and splendid architectural symbolism. But Aachen is a modern town, and the foundations of most of this grand scheme lie under its streets. One must look at drawings and reconstructions to envisage the original layout.

Frankfurt, where I write, was an important Carolingian centre, with a sim-ilar palace-and-chapel arrangement, of which all has been overlain by later buildings and activities – although there is a Carolingian church at the termi-nus of the No. 12 tram at the nearby town, now a suburb, of Hochst. But not very far away, to the south, is the town of Lorsch, where one can more readily envisage, in this case not a palace-and-church layout, but a large monastery which came to have a small royal palace attached to it. Only two of the build-ings still stand, the much-altered large basilican church, and a gate building with a half-round tower attached at one end, which stood at the entrance to a large forecourt. This building, which had a small chapel of St Michael over the gate-arch, is much less altered, and is well known, in illustrations at least, to students of early medieval architecture. It shows well, in the details of its pilasters and its ornament, how very Roman the style was, and this can be seen again in the earlier part of the basilican church. In both, the builders have freely used carved stone from the frieze of a Roman temple which presumably stood nearby. And although most of the original buildings are no longer stand-ing, the site is relatively unencumbered, except by one or two small modern buildings which occupy exactly the foundations of their Carolingian prede-cessors. As a result one can walk about the layout and appreciate the scale, and the imperial outlook which built on this scale in the year 774, in a society at that time little different in its basic economy from contemporary Ireland, but very different in its outlook.

27

The World of the Book of Kells

A laconic entry in the Irish annals records raids from the sea made in AD 795 by 'heathens' on island monasteries within the Gaelic world. Two of the monasteries were Columban, one on Iona, in the Inner Hebrides, the other on Lambay, in the Irish Sea. With the advent of these seafarers – who came from western Norway – there began a period of turmoil, migration and new social formation which historians today commonly label 'the Viking Age'.

It is probable that the Gospel manuscript we know as 'the Book of Kells' was copied and painted not long before the first raids occurred. The book therefore survives from a time which is now very distant from us. It is both a record and a testimony. It bears witness to a world of imagination now vanished.

The eighth century has more than once been referred to as a 'Golden Age' in Ireland, in Northumbria, in Scotland. Out of a ruck of tribes and petty local dynasties that succeeded the Roman Empire there had emerged enduring nations. The process is almost uncanny to watch through the medium of historical and archaeological research; it is like the appearance of an image on film in the photographer's developing tank. Suddenly, out of the darkness, there come England, Scotland, Wales and Ireland, kingdoms and principalities with their own identities, their own languages and their own self-esteem. On the Continent, a new distinctive culture similarly emerges in the Carolingian renaissance.

The Germans and the Celts of late prehistory were not town peoples, although they had tribal centres (called '*oppida*' by modern archaeologists) which, in scale and sometimes in design, were not unlike Greek cities. They had an ancestral history of great migrations, and their decorative arts, in leather-work, horse-trappings, personal jewellery, pottery and woodwork, had elements borrowed as freely from the nomads of the steppe and from remote Siberian hunters as from the civilized Mediterranean. But many of them were conquered and ruled by people of a different bent: the Romans – stern farmers in their fantasy, luxurious town-dwellers in their later reality, square-shapers in their ancestrally puritanical modality. And even those barbarians who lived beyond the frontier were to be in close contact with Roman civilization for several

Previously unpublished.

centuries. When that civilization broke down, as it did in Western Europe in the fifth century, the peoples north of the Alps had already acquired much from it.

The Irish borrowed many elements of Roman culture; most importantly Christianity and literacy (with the Latin alphabet). In the Roman world a common medium of ephemeral writing – such as school exercises – was a wooden tablet coated with wax (which could be softened by heat and re-used), on which letters were scratched with a metal-pointed implement – a stylus. Such tablets, with verses of the Psalms, have been found preserved in Irish bogs – the schoolbooks of pupils who were perhaps learning to write and learning the Scriptures at the same time, in the sixth or seventh century.

For texts that were to last a little longer, the Romans wrote on papyrus. If it was used in Ireland, none survives; although we know that there was a continuing trade in wine and oil from its region of origin, the eastern Mediterranean, where the Roman Empire continued to flourish long after it had disintegrated in the West. Papyrus, made from a tall sedgelike plant that grew in the Nile, was processed into long strips which, when written on, were rolled up and kept in tubelike containers. But for written work that was intended to be permanent in a really lasting sense, there had developed, by the time Christianity was established in Ireland, a technique of preparing animal skin, by means of scraping and a form of tanning, with a surface smooth enough for writing in ink. The rectangular piece of prepared animal skin was folded and sewn together with other pieces, and they were bound and cased in a heavy cover of wood or leather or both, the sheets of skin forming the 'leaves' of a book.

The liturgy of the Christian Church required the regular use of the Bible – and in particular the Psalms and the Gospels. Not only was this written material required for daily use; it was also regarded as having a unique permanent value in itself (it was the eternal Word of God) and as having a peculiarly sacred character, demanding special reverence.

Writing about a hundred years before the Book of Kells was made, Bishop Tírechán tells us that he himself has seen in three different churches liturgical vessels made by Bishop Assicus (otherwise Tasach), who had been bronzeworker to St Patrick and who had made book-casings for him. In the eighth century we have a passing reference to the embellishment of books in the words of the Anglo-Saxon poet Aelwolf, who tells us of the Irish scribe Ultán that:

> He was a blessed priest of the Irish race. He could ornament books with elegant scribings, and by doing so he gave a beautiful character, separately and severally, to each initial. In this art no modern scribe could equal him.

From the first century and a half of organised Christianity in Ireland, no manuscripts survive. Then, about AD 600, we begin to get glimpses of the developments that had taken place, and can see that, for formal writing at any rate, the Irish scribes were well advanced in evolving a script that was both legible and decorative. They were already beginning to embellish their texts – copies of the Scriptures in Latin – with decorated initial letters and with some illustration.

In the Roman world the right angle and the square were the symbols of good order. Celtic order was different. It was expressed by the curving line that changed direction: freedom as against constraint. When the Roman system – through Christianity – came to Ireland and met the Celtic order, it produced an extraordinary dynamic, which is nowhere better expressed than in the Book of Kells.

State formation was well advanced in Ireland by the time the scribes and painters went to work on the Book of Kells. Anointed kings ruled in several large provincial kingdoms, patronizing the Church, keeping records, administering law. In spite of dynastic feuding, lay and cleric worked closely together in the creation of this imperium, as they were doing also at the time both in Britain and on the European Continent. The social order was graded from the king (*rí*) at the top to the slave at the bottom. The socio-political unit, the *tuath* (chiefdom), was quite small, with an average population of the order of about two thousand souls – men, women and children, free and unfree. By the eighth century, however, the *tuatha* were no longer autonomous; superior kings ruled, and sometimes administered, 'fifths', or provinces, made up of numbers of the smaller units.

People whose work involved learning and skill had a specially privileged position. Unlike most others, those who belonged to the *oes dána* – the class of the educated – could travel freely throughout the Gaelic world, under the protection of rulers wherever they found themselves. This class was composed of poets, druids, lawyers, historians, certain skilled craftsmen, including goldsmiths, and – after the acceptance of Christainity – clerics, who were given high legal status. The churchman, the artist and the writer were privileged. A bishop, as well as a poet of the highest grade, had the same honour-price as a *rí* (king, or chieftain). Other craftsmen working for the Church may have been lay people, but the scribes were normally priests and monks, and enjoyed high status.

The material basis of this society was the cultivation of crops and the pasturing of flocks and herds, supplemented by the bounty of nature as provided by the nuts, berries and herbs of the forest. Sheep supplied wool, which was spun and woven to make the outer garment worn by the upper order of society – a cloak, dyed and sometimes ornamented with a decorative fringe or hem. Under the cloak men and women of higher social rank wore a linen tunic, which could be embellished with embroidery. The cloak was fastened with a pin or jewelled brooch. Lower orders wore breeches. These are the garments and ornaments shown in the Book of Kells.

The cattle-baron belonging to the upper rank of this society lived in an enclosed farmstead in which the house and outbuildings stood in a round yard bounded by a rampart (sometimes faced with timber) with an external water-filled fosse. It was an open-air world. Buildings were small and were commonly constructed of timber, earth and thatch. There was often a hearth in the centre of the house. There were no glass windows, and interiors must have been smoky, dark and uncomfortable – refuges for the night and shelters from inclement weather, rather than places for the normal activities of the day. The evidence from archaeological excavations suggests that most crafts, such as bronzeworking, enamelling and inlaying, were carried on within enclosures but in the lee of ramparts and palisades rather than indoors – perhaps with screens or open lean-tos to give protection against wind and rain.

Good light would have been essential to the production both of the minutely intricate metalwork and of such extraordinarily complex miniature painting as we find in the Book of Kells. The artists who did the fine work may have been myopic; but it is highly probable that in any case they used polished crystals to magnify the detail, or, as has been suggested, the lenses of eyes freshly taken from slaughtered cattle. We may imagine the scribe, with his high chair, lectern-like desk, ink-horn, quills, scraper, ruler, compasses and stylus (for scratching and pricking setting-out marks on the vellum) working in an open porch or gallery; perhaps moving himself and his equipment every hour or so to follow the sunshine. About the time the Book of Kells was made, a scribe wrote in Irish in a manuscript now in Switzerland:

> ... A clear-voiced cuckoo sings to me in a green cloak of bush-tops, a lovely utterance. The Lord be good to me on Judgment Day! I write well under the woodland trees.

Monasteries, headed by priests, not bishops, had been founded in large numbers from the 540s onwards, and these in course of time came to dominate the ecclesiastical scene. Some were large, some small, and they served different functions. Among the larger, some governed far-flung federations, of houses following the rule of a single founder and under the general authority of the abbot of the principal house of the group.

The large monastery was more like a town or village than an integrated architectural unit such as was to develop from the Benedictine monasticism of the Continent. The type had come to Ireland almost certainly by way of Italy and Gaul; yet it retained something of the character of the original Christian monasteries that had been founded in disused Roman forts and other such sites in desert places in Egypt, Syria and Palestine. The monks or nuns lived, not in dormitories, but in little houses that would accommodate at most two or three each. The churches remained small, but their number within the monastic enclosure could be multiplied to cater for a large community.

In general, Irish monastic buildings were of wood before the tenth century except where they were built in treeless areas such as the exposed Atlantic coasts and islands. The English monk and ecclesiastical apologist and historian Bede, writing in 731, associates this with other pecularities of the British (Welsh), Irish and Pictish churches of earlier times, including an independent way of calculating the date of Easter, and distinctive clerical tonsure – differences that had caused much controversy but that persisted now only among the Britons. He tells, for example, how, in the previous century, the Irishman Finán, arriving as bishop in Northumbria:

> ... built a church on the Island of Lindisfarne, suitable as a bishop's see, constructing it, however, not of stone but of hewn oak thatched with reeds in the Irish style.

And again, he tells us how, about AD 700, Nechtan, King of the Picts (a nation that had been evangelized by the Irish of Iona) wrote to Coelfrid, abbot of Bede's own monastery of Weamouth-Jarrow, asking for guidance on the matters of Easter and the tonsure, and also for architects 'to build a church in the Roman style for his people'.

We have a description, composed more than half a century before Bede wrote, of a great monastery in the Irish style and its wooden church. It is an account of seventh-century Kildare, from the *Life* of St Brigid by Cogitosus. He mentions a cashel (*castellum*), entered through a gate. Within was the rebuilt and enlarged church,

> ... in which the bodies of that glorious pair, the bishop Conláeth and the holy virgin Brigid, lie right and left of the ornamented altar, placed in shrines decorated with a variegation of gold, silver, gems and precious stones, with gold and silver crowns hanging above them.
>
> In fact, to accommodate the increasing number of the faithful, of both sexes, the church is spacious in its floor area, and it rises to an extreme height. It is adorned with painted boards and has on the inside three wide chapels, all under the roof of the large building and separated by wooden partitions. One partition, whish is decorated with painted images and is covered with linen, stretches transversely in the eastern part of the church from one wall to the other ...

The description is valuable because, apart from a few early stone oratories and huts in the treeless west, at no monastic site in Ireland can we now see buildings that were standing when the Book of Kells was being made. Cogitosus lets us know that some at least of the early churches were big enough to accommodate a congregation, and that they housed paintings, jewelled shrines and other valuables. Such, most likely, was the original setting for the Book of Kells.

Kildare was visited by Gerald of Wales at the end of the twelfth century, and he gives an account of the great treasure of the monastery – a manuscript of the Gospels:

Fine craftsmanship is all about you, but you might not notice it. Look
more keenly at it and you will penetrate to the very shrine of art. You
will make out intricacies, so delicate and subtle, so exact and compact,
so full of knots and links, with colours so fresh and vivid, that you
might say that all this was the work of an angel and not of a man.

Kells, like Kildare, was a great metropolitan monastery. Its foundation was
due to the initial impact of the Vikings on the Irish monastic world. After the
first raid on Iona in 795, several followed in quick succession, and it seems
that the Iona community looked for another, more secure, base in Ireland. Then,
Norsemen in 806 killed sixty-eight members of the community. The abbot,
Cellach, and a number of his monks took refuge in Ireland. Iona was the head
of the greatest of the monastic federations and, a century and a half before,
had been virtually the chief church of the western monastic world and of part
of the Anglo-Saxon world too. Although the Roman system had triumphed at
Whitby in 664, and the Irish churches and their protegés in Scotland and
Northumbria had yielded ground stubbornly but steadily on the question of
Easter and of the form of tonsure to be practised by monks, yet Iona continued
until the disaster to be the hub of a system of seaborne communications, a
place of learning and a repository of political as well as ecclesiastical records, a
centre of sculptural art and no doubt a storehouse of reliquaries, altar vessels –
and books.

   In Ireland, Cellach and his monks occupied a new site. The place was a
hill-fort, a royal centre of some considerable antiquity and prestige, formerly
Dún Chúile Sibhrinne. It stood in the small territory known as *Feara-Cúl*, whose
king, Cathal son of Fiachra, lived some miles away in Raith Airthir on the
river Boyne. More important, it was associated with legendary high kings and
was within the immediate spheres of influence, both of the powerful King of
Tara, Áed son of Niall, and of the primatial see of Armagh. The site was granted
in 804, the same year in which Áed presided at an important assembly about
forty km away at Dún Cuair. The meeting was attended by the abbot of
Armagh. It may well have been at this assembly that the transfer of a substantial part of the Iona community to the Irish midlands was first contem-
plated. Iona was not abandoned; for at least another quarter-century abbots
came to Kells with relics. In 825, the Abbot of Iona, Bláthmhach, was murdered by Vikings and, according to Walafrid Strabo who wrote a poem on the
event when he received word of it in Fulda in Germany, it was because he
refused to reveal the hiding place of relics of Columba.

   The move of the politically skilled and powerful Iona clerics into the Irish
midlands was important and must have involved delicate negotiation. In the
graveyard in Kells is a carved high cross, showing the influence of the sculptural school of Iona and bearing the inscription, '*Patricii et Columbe crux*' –
'the cross of Patrick and Columba'. This ratifies the agreement of Patrick's
church of Armagh and Columba's church of Iona (now being replaced in

Ireland by Kells) and acknowledges the prinacy of Armagh. The patronage of the high king, Áed, is almost certainly involved. We are told that the 'new city' of the Iona monks was made at Kells in 807. The Cross of Patrick and Columba was probably erected fairly soon after that date.

The Columban federation had long since yielded to the general West-European practices concerning Easter, the tonsure and other matters, and the new community at Kells built their church of stone. This has been replaced by a later building. Another building, stone-roofed, on the site, which is known as 'St Colum's House', is probably also a replacement (it is no earlier than the twelfth century). It appears not to be a church, but very likely was a relic-house. If so, it probably replaced one built in the ninth century to receive relics of Columba in a place thought to be safer than Iona.

Was the Book of Kells among the valuables brought from Iona at this time? Is it a product of the great Iona scriptorium; or was it produced in the early years of the new settlement at Kells, which seems to have enjoyed freedom from further Viking attack for a century? Or both? – Dr Françoise Henry suggested that it may have been begun on Iona and finished at Kells (or almost finished, for it is in fact incomplete).

The manuscript is, at any rate, the work not of one scribe or artist but of a number. The efforts of a whole scriptorium, and of a well endowed one, must have been devoted to it over a long period: all but two of the pages are decorated in some fashion, and most have a considerable variety of ornament. The leaves are of vellum – calf-skin – which has not been meanly used; on the hoof, the Book of Kells amounted to more than a hundred and fifty beasts. Even in this sense it was a costly production, without reckoning the other materials involved – not to speak of the time and skill of the artists engaged on the work.

The early vellum Gospel-books, Psalters and missals, copied in Ireland and Britain or by Irish and Anglo-Saxon scribes on the Continent, may be divided by size into 'pocket books' – small books which were meant to be carried about (although the usual medium of transport was probably a leather satchel) – and large books for the service of the altars of established, secure and well-to-do churches in which the volumes could be cared for and could render the honour due to the Word of God. At least since the time of Constantine, it had been felt that objects used in worship should reflect the transcendental significance of the liturgy in the quality and costliness of their workmanship: chalices, patens, Gospel-books. It had become an imperial and royal custom to make gifts of such valuables to important churches. Thousands of books had to be copied by scribes for everyday use, but sumptuous Gospel-books were rare, and were for special occasions.

The Book of Kells is in this category. We know that there was a similar volume in Kildare. The detailed decription of it given by Gerald of Wales could apply to the Book of Kells, and it is highly likely therefore that the lost Book of Kildare was a work of the same period and style. But treasures like this were normally safeguarded and, even allowing for the multitudinous losses of manuscripts suffered by medieval Ireland, we can be reasonably certain that there were never many of the type.

Luxurious Insular Gospel books had been produced at least since the beginning of the seventh century, embodying some features, apart from the script, which are fairly distinctively Irish. One such feature is the use of red dots or stippling to outline decorative features. This echoes the use of stippled punching or pricking on the surface of silver or silvered bronze to set off letters or ornament, as on the body of the Ardagh Chalice. Another feature, found in the small Psalter known as the *Cathach* of St Columba, dating perhaps from around AD 600, is the *diminuendo* that was to be a salient feature of the Irish manuscript style: the process of diminution from an enlarged initial through several further letters into the body of the text.

The oldest of the luxurious Gospel books that still survives is the Book of Durrow, dating from the seventh century and produced in a Columban milieu – probably in fact in Durrow itself, Columba's chief foundation in Ireland. The Book of Durrow, however, although lavishly decorated and written in a bold formal majuscule script, is quite small in page size. The Lindisfarne Gospelbook, of about AD 700, is a large volume, very richly decorated in a splendidly serene and orderly way. Written and painted in Northumbria, a generation after the Irish Columban monks had left, it has decoration and script in the Columban style but portraits of the Evangelists which are copied from Greek originals. Other sumptuous Gospel manuscripts that might be compared with the Book of Kells are those of Lichfield and Echternach, along with the very fragmentary Durham manuscript A II 17.

The series displays a number of common features. The scheme of the painting of these books includes, in general, portraits of the four Evangelists (the Book of Durrow, however, substitutes their symbols, treated as portraits); the symbols of the Evangelists; elaborately treated initials at the openings of the four Gospels; introductory matter embodying, in particular, comparison of equivalent passages in the different Gospels in the form of 'canon tables' as devised in the fourth century by Eusebius of Caesarea; 'carpet pages' – that is, pages devoted wholly to ornament; and the singling out for special treatment of the words *Christi autem generatio* ... ('Now the birth of Christ was as follows ... ') at the beginning of Matthew 1:18, where the Greek letters *Chi* and *Rho* are employed for the initial of Christ. The Chi-Rho initial, which is already prominent in the Book of Durrow, shows a tendency to increase in size with time, from book to book, until in the Book of Kells it fills a whole page – the most minutely and fantastically decorated in that whole elaborate work.

The Book of Kells was kept in Kells until 1654, long after the Columban monastery had ceased to be. It was brought to Dublin, and Bishop Henry Jones gave it to Trinity College in 1661. There is a record of it in 1007, when it was stolen. It had been enshrined in a gold-plated casing, which was never recovered. But the book was. It suffered some damage, then and later, including the clipping of its leaves by a nineteenth-century bookbinder.

In its present state it consists of 340 folios (nowadays bound in four separate volumes). Some of its leaves are missing, including some at the beginning which might have shed light on its origin. It contains copies of the four Gospels, written in a 'mixed' text, such as is characteristic of Irish scriptural manuscripts of this period – that is to say, the Vulgate translation prepared by St Jerome for Pope Damasus in the fourth century, with an admixture of the earlier 'Old Latin' text. There is an amount of introductory matter: prefaces; summaries of the Gospels; and the Eusebian canons. Twelfth-century charters were copied onto blank pages.

The script is a handsome majuscule, decorative rather than clear, and virtually throughout the book there are ornamented initials and interlinear decorations and miniatures. It gives the impression that an obsessive intensity went into its manufacture, in marked contrast to the serene and masterly orderliness of the Lindisfarne Gospels. There are misspellings and mistakes; there is confusion in the arrangement here and there; parts of the work are unfinished and there appear to have been illustrations planned that were never executed (one of the Crucifixion, for example). There is a sense of *horror vacui*, as if the miniaturists obsessively wished to pour everything that was in their minds and hearts into an art that gathers the sacred and the profane together in a kind of sustained fantasy.

The pages were large and now measure 250 x 330 mm. For their work on the book the scribes and painters used a variety of materials, some of which had to be brought from distant places and were expensive. Two inks were used for the script and drawing, one made from iron gall (sulphate of iron, oak apples, gum and water) and the other from soot. The painters used red lead and kermes (a vermilion pigment derived from a Mediterranean insect) for their reds; orpiment (arsenic sulphide), ochre and gall for their yellows (gold leaf is not employed); verdigris for green; a Mediterranean plant for purple; indigo or woad for dark blue and lapis lazuli (from the Himalaya) for other blues; white lead for white, and mixtures of these. Sometimes a wash of one colour was laid over another.

After the lost opening of the book, which included lists of names, there come canon-tables, the first eight of them in an architectural framework of columns supporting arches (distinctly graphic, flat and non-architectural in their feeling) and prefaces and summaries. The order of the main part of the book is traditional, with additions, variations and modifications. The Gospels are in the usual sequence: Matthew, Mark, Luke and John. Each Gospel is preceded by a page given to the symbols of the four Evangelists and two by portraits of Evangelists. Each opens with a page occupied by a huge initial and an exaggerated *diminuendo*. The Chi-Rho page in Matthew is the equivalent, in this scheme, of a Gospel opening. It is preceded by the only carpet page in the book, with a pattern based on a double-armed cross. Other passages in the Gospel texts are also singled out as having special significance, and the pages on which they occur are treated elaborately and ornamentally. They are also sometimes associated with pages carrying pictures.

The scheme of illustration was never completed, and two or three pictures may also have been lost. A page showing the Virgin and Child, with angels, accompanies the note of the Nativity in the Matthew summaries. The Arrest of Christ in the Garden of Gethsemane illustrates St Matthew's account of the Passion. A page depicting the Crucifixion was apparently planned but never executed. In St Luke's Gospel there is a full-page painting showing the Temptation of Christ.

Apart from the many set pieces, there is ornamentation throughout the text, including numerous interlinear drawings, often used for highlighting or for indicating the continuity of a passage. Distinctive devices are used, such as the interlocking of decorated initials down the length of a page, as in the Genealogy of Christ in Luke.

Françoise Henry, who studied the book closely, discerned four main hands in the painting, and suggested that other less accomplished artists also helped. This analysis, which is persuasive, has been fairly generally accepted. One miniaturist she calls 'the goldsmith' – the artist of the carpet page, the Chi-Rho page, and the opening pages of the Gospels (apart from Luke) – who used rich colours, made broad firm patterns and then smothered them in a flow of spirals, interlace and animal ornament. He shunned symmetry, eschewed plant ornament and used human forms purely as decorative motifs. The second she called 'the portraitist' – the painter of the two large figures of Evangelists and of the teaching Christ, of the great '*Quoniam*' opening of Luke, and possibly of the symbols of the Evangelists in square frames – who liked symmetry and avoided the unexpected in his ornamental schemes. The third she called 'the illustrator' – a 'wild erratic painter', responsible for the pictures of the Arrest of Christ, of the Temptation, of the Virgin and Child; for the great initials of '*Tunc crucifixerunt*' (fol. 124r), and probably for the symbols of the Evangelists at the beginning of John – who was given to harsh and strange colour combinations. The fourth, to whom she doesn't give a title, is in some ways the most interesting – and is undoubtedly distinctive. This is the artist of a great deal of the smaller details: the interlinear animals, the cartouches of the text, small capitals, the border of the Genealogy page, the little animal scenes on the Chi-Rho page, and some other passages.

The book, whatever its date (and the range of disagreement is small), stems from an age of intense cultural and artistic activity, in which a certain uniformity within diversity was established among the Christians of Western Europe, a process that involved parallel political developments in Ireland, Britain and Carolingian Austrasia, the establishment of standard religious practices between the Insular churches on the one hand and the Continental churches on the other, and the making of a new European civilization from a mixture of Roman and barbarian elements. This can be read in the Book of Kells. Although the text of the book is simply an indifferent copy of the Four Gospels in Latin – a message widely available elsewhere – its illumination speaks of an extraordinary interaction of cultures at the birth of Europe.

Manolis Chatzidakis and André Grabar have written of the Insular manuscripts in general that:

> These illuminations furnish us ... with a rare and magnificent example of the transference to painting of the ornamental forms and 'programmes' created by a metal-working craft, as well as an example of the prolongation (at the cost of some slight alterations) of a pagan art for the uses and needs of Christian ritual books.

This neatly sums up one important aspect of the ornament of the Insular manuscripts. It is an aspect clearly seen in the Book of Durrow, where the carpet pages maintain a separation between the three principal elements in the decorative scheme – trumpet spirals, ribbon interlace and intertwined animal forms. Each of the three elements has a carpet page devoted to it. The trumpet spirals derive from metalwork of the 'ultimate La Tène' phase of late Celtic art, spanning the transition from paganism to Christianity in Ireland. The animal ornament copies Germanic zoomorphic designs categorized by Salin as 'Style Two' and found on metalwork in Scandinavia and England – although, as Étienne Rynne has pointed out, 'blunderings' of the animal style reveal the Irish adaptor of the art. The ribbon interlace, ultimately of Mediterranean origin, may derive from goldsmith's work in the Germanic world. There are other details in the earlier manuscripts that imitate rectangular, L- or T-shaped inlays in red and yellow enamel – a style found on early ecclesiastical metal objects in Ireland in Scotland and itself originating in Roman industrial art of the Imperial frontiers.

Almost all of this may be found in the Book of Kells, but the elements are no longer held apart, but mixed. Ribbons, threads and strings that may or may not, in their weaving and interlacing, have human or animal attributes; coiled spirals that may faithfully reproduce the old trumpet forms or may develop into serpents; clawed and fanged animals that bite one another, or their own bodies; or architectural members framing the pages: all endlessly wind and unwind, crisscross and intertwine on the pages. There are many details copied from metal objects: for example, the two roundels at the base of the side panels flanking the portrait of Christ (fol. 32v) are copied from impressed glass studs set in protruding escutcheons such as are found on metal reliquaries and similar objects.

The whole book gives the impression of jeweller's or goldsmith's work, an impression reinforced by the enamel-like pigments, laid on in such a way as to give a tactile quality to the miniatures and a third dimension to the surfaces equivalent to that produced by impasto or mosaic.

But there is much more to the book than that, and it reflects the influence of cultures far from the Atlantic islands. Throughout, there is the all-pervasive influence of Mediterranean, and specifically Byzantine, art. Peacocks recur, feeding on vines set in urns, symbols of immortality such as are found in mosaics in Ravenna and in reliefs on altar frontals from Constantinople. The portraits, gazing wide-eyed directly out from the page, in calm hieratic pose, immediately recall the figures that stare at us from the walls of Byzantine churches. The bearded faces, as of Christ in both the portrait and the scene of the arrest, all have a curious downward sickle shape of bare skin low on the chin, looking like a second mouth. It reproduces, as an ambiguous stylization in the drawing, a Byzantine fashion such as can be seen quite clearly, for example, in the much more naturalistic mosaic medallion portrait of St Paul in the late-fifth-century Archbishop's Chapel in Ravenna. The whole composition of the painting of the Virgin and Child is based on something like the panel showing the Virgin and Child receiving the Magi on the sixth-century ivory throne of Bishop Maximian in Ravenna (where the Child, however, faces the other way). The Virgin's headdress, represented as a rather confused veil, reproduces the shape of the diadem worn by the Empress Theodora in the famous San Vitale mosaic, and by other empresses in later works. Indeed, if we could imagine the whole choir and transepts of San Vitale flattened out onto the pages of a book, the overall richly coloured effect would be not unlike that of the Book of Kells. The immediate Byzantine prototypes of many of the details are probably lost to us because of the effects of the iconoclastic movement, which created something of a hiatus in the course of Byzantine art just in the crucial period – the eighth century.

Another very important influence, manifest throughout the book, is that of Pictish art. Françoise Henry didn't go so far in her discussion of the matter, but it is hard not to believe that her fourth, untitled, miniaturist was a Pict. The little interlinear drawings so liberally distributed throughout the book are acutely observed from life and are more naturalistic than any of the other miniatures. But they are naturalistic in a style that had long been established among the Picts, on picture stones and elsewhere. And, as Isabel Henderson has pointed out in detail, the snake-boss motif, found widely in Pictish and Ionan sculpture as well as in some metalwork, is extensively used in the Book of Kells.

As more and more detailed study is done on this remarkable manuscript – which offers almost endless scope for such work – it comes to seem highly probable that the book was made not in Kells but on Iona. That its unfinished state is due to the events beginning in 795 is likely; but considerable problems of relative chronology and mutual influence arise in connection with the relationship of the Book of Kells to certain Continental manuscripts. It clearly fits into the great main series of Hiberno-Saxon books of the seventh, eighth and ninth centuries; but scribes and miniaturists were mobile people, and Irish monks in that period were particularly mobile, throughout the Merovingian and Carolingian realms. The problems have yet to be resolved, so that at present it is possible only to suggest – and somewhat tentatively – that the book was a product of the Iona scriptorium in the last quarter of the eighth century. If so, it came to Kells early in the ninth century, either with Cellach and his companions in AD 807, or, perhaps more likely some years later, when the community was established and a repository had been built for the reception of 'the relics of St Columba'. Its custodians, possibly at the cost of their lives, were worthy of their trust. According to the Annals of Ulster, Connachtach, 'eminent abbot and scribe' of Iona, was killed by raiders in 803. His successor Bláthmhach was killed in 824 when he refused to tell where he had hidden a reliquary of St Columba. And we have further accounts of the comings and goings between Ireland and Iona later in the century by people carrying 'relics of Columba'. At any rate, the manuscript was saved, so that we can still marvel today at the most extraordinary work of its age.

28

The Church of the Irish

When people speak of the early Irish monks who went abroad and founded monasteries in the centuries before the Anglo–Norman invasion, they are usually thinking of the movement associated with the names of Columba, Aidan, Columbanus, Gall and others of their time. This was the earliest and most striking exodus of missionaries, or, as they called themselves, 'pilgrims for Christ', and it took place in the sixth and seventh centuries.

Later movements are less frequently referred to. But the wanderlust, or penitential urge, or both, which stimulated the monks into seeking exile, continued to be effective long after the time of Columbanus and Columba. Throughout the eighth century, we have evidence of journeys, of at least a semi-missionery character, made by Irishmen to the Continent. A little later the mission becomes, in part at least, not so much spiritual as intellectual and cultural.

Irish scholars were among those from many lands who gathered together in the palace schools which were centres of the Carolingian Renaissance; indeed, were sought after because of the reputation of their homeland for learning. But later still there was yet another movement of monastic enterprise into Europe, when in the eleventh and twelfth centuries Irishmen founded the monasteries which are known as *Schottenkloster*. This late movement brought Irish influence farther afield than any of the previous ones, deep into Central Europe, and even beyond, as far as the Ukraine.

The first such foundation in southern Germany was here where I write, in Regensburg (or Ratisbon) on the Danube. It was not a case of finding a desert or a lonely place for a monastic retreat. Regensburg was already an ancient city in the eleventh century. In pre-Roman times there was a Celtic tribal centre here, known as Rathaspona, and after Roman rule had been extended to the Danube, the Empire built a fort to the south of the Celtic centre to house a cohort as frontier garrison. This was in the first century AD. The Emperor Marcus Aurelius, much of whose activity was concerned with frontier defences, completed a massive and impressive *castra*, or fortified camp, here in the year 179. It was known as *Castra Regina*, and considerable parts of its masonry still remain, including the *Porta Praetoria*, the main gate, with its flanking fortification. The praetorian gate of a Roman military town usually opens onto the main road

This, written in Regensburg in Bavaria, was published in the 'Roots' column in the *Irish Times* on 18 December 1973.

from the town, which carried on the line of the principal street within the walls. At Castra Regina, however, the gate looks out onto the dangerous rapids and whirlpools of the swift-flowing Danube.

The gate, in fact, was largely for show, part of the menace of the long masonry walls with their frowning battlements and towers, which confronted the barbarians across the river to the north. These by the second century AD were no longer Celts but Germans.

The Roman Empire in due course went the way of empires, but the lay-out of medieval buildings in Regensburg would indicate that for long the Roman walls stood, even when there were no longer legionaries to man them and maintain them. The medieval town was a good deal smaller than the Roman town, so here was plenty of space to spare within the walls. These served to protect a local ruler of the pagan Bavarians, who were in due course converted by the mission of the Anglo-Saxon St Boniface. He appointed a bishop here, and numbers of churches and monasteries were built before the Irish foundation, although Irish churches were already established to the west in Würzburg and to the east in Salzburg.

It was not, therefore, as a missionary to a pagan land that the monk Muirchertach came here from Ireland in the eleventh century. He was a pilgrim, on his way to the Holy Land, like so many from Ireland and from all other parts of Western Europe in that century of intensive pilgrimage development. He arrived here in 1040, delayed, and never went farther, having chosen to become an anchorite living alone in a small cell.

In 1068 he persuaded one Marianus and two other pilgrims, also from Ireland, to stay like him also in Regensburg instead of continuing their journey. In 1075, from this little pilgrim community was formed the first monastery, to the south of the city. Pilgrims from Ireland continued to join them. The count, or burgrave, of the city, Otto, gave the monks a house outside the walls to the west in the year 1090, and here about a decade later they built the church and monastery whose dedication, appropriately for a pilgrim community, was to St James.

Parts of this building of about 1100 still remain, most notably the two square towers at the east end, as well as part of the eastern apse. The resemblance of these to Cormac's Chapel at Cashel has struck some observers. Cashel had close connections with Regensburg in the early twelfth century, when there was a MacCarthy abbot here, related to the royal Eoghanacht family of Munster. In fact, when money was being raised for the building of the first *Jakobskirche* outside the west gate, two of the community went to Munster, and visited Cashel itself, to obtain Irish help in the collection. For these reasons it has been suggested that Cormac MacCarthy, who became King of Cashel in 1127, and who immediately set about building his famous Chapel on the Rock, may have sent to Regensburg for masons.

However, study of the architectural and sculptural details of Cormac's Chapel, which was completed in 1134, shows that its inspiration was almost certainly in the west of England rather than in Bavaria.

But the connection is an interesting one. Most of the existing fabric of the Jakobskirche at Regensburg is of the later twelfth century, when the abbot Gregory set about a handsome rebuilding of what had apparently been originally a hasty and poor construction. The same Gregory, who died in 1193, built a small church of St Nicholas, to the north of St James's, for the community. He was helped in his work by contributions from Ireland and Rome, while the Grand Duke of Kiev sent him furs, gold and silver to help pay for the building.

The richly carved north facade of the Jakobskirche, with its elaborate doorway and many symbolic figures, is the result of this effort, and has survived in good condition. German art-historians have seen Irish influence in much of the carving, and there is no doubt that it has the kind of surface richness that was very much to the taste of the Irish of the time – as we can see in the more-or-less contemporary doorways of Clonfert, Clonmacnoise (the Nuns' Church), Killeshin and Kilmore. But the mouldings and other details are not Irish in character, and the lavish use of figure-carving in relief is something we find on only one Irish Romanesque church. That one exception, however, raises interesting questions about the possible architecural connections between Ireland and Regensburg, because it is the cathedral of Ardmore in County Waterford, dating from about the last decade of Abbot Gregory's lifetime, and right in the part of Ireland where we would expect such connections to manifest themselves.

Only a few miles from Ardmore is the site of one of the most important southern Irish ecclesiastical centres of the twelfth century, the great monastery of Lismore, where Cormac MacCarthy had built two further churches or chapels. These, however, have not survived the centuries. There is room for further research in all this. At any rate, we have the evidence for a continuing connection of some kind between Munster and Regensburg throughout the twelfth century.

It is not the only Irish connection here. The much older Irish foundation of St Gall in Switzerland had a cell, or small house, here in Regensburg too, part of which still remains. Indeed Regensburg is remarkably rich in medieval buildings, including the old bridge over the Danube, and is worth visiting for a great deal more than merely its historical links with Ireland.

Apart from the numerous ecclesiastical buildings (one feels there must have been more clerics than merchants here in the Middle Ages) it has many secular buildings, including a Gothic Rathaus, and a number of family towers, like those of medieval Florence, in which the quarrelsome upper-class families defended themselves in feuds and vendettas just like those of early Renaissance Italy.

In this season, with snow falling on towers and battlements, with Christmas candles lighting the winter dusk and carvings in wax and wood on sale at the stalls in the open-air Advent market, the medieval atmosphere is enhanced, while the figure of St Patrick looks down from its place over the arcade of the 'Church of the Irish'.

29

The Monastic Ideal: a Poem
attributed to St Manchán

In the anthology which they edited and translated, and published in 1967, *A Golden Treasury of Irish Poetry AD 600 to 1200*, David Greene and Frank O'Connor wrote of one item in their selection:

> This lovely little poem, which Gerard Murphy would place in the tenth century, has the pure singing note of early Irish poetry.

The tenth-century poem is attributed to St Manchán, of Lemanaghan in Offaly. His period was the second half of the sixth century; but such attributions of later works to famous figures of the past are quite common; they gave currency to the work of the later poets, who intended not so much deception as creative fiction, and who sought to associate themselves with the eminent.

In Louvain in 1629, the Franciscan Michael O'Clery (the chief of the 'Four Masters') compiled a calendar of saints, since known as *The Martyrology of Donegal*. He wrote in his entry for 24 January (Manchán's festival day):

> Manchán, of Liath, son of Indagh. Mella was the name of his mother, and his two sisters were Grealla and Greillseach. There is a church called Liath-Mancháin, or Leth-Mancháin, in Dealbh-na-Mhec-Cochláin. His relics are at the same place in a shrine, which is beautifully covered with boards on the inside, and with bronze outside them, and very beautifully carved. It was Manchán of Liath that composed the charming poem [*an dán taithnemhach*], i.e.:
>
> > *Dutraccarsa a meic Dé bhi,*
> > *A ri suthain sein! &c.*
>
> ... A very old vellum book, in which are found the Martyrology of Tamhlacht-Maoilruain and the saints of the same name, and an account of many of the mothers of the saints, &c., states, that Manchán of Liath, in habits and life, was like unto Jerome, who was very learned.

Previously unpublished.

The church of Lemanaghan is in ruins now, but the shrine is still nearby, in the parish church of Boher, where it has been doubly enshrined in a display case commissioned by Dr Cahal Daly when he was Bishop of Ardagh and Clonmacnoise and designed by Ray Carroll. It is a work of the middle of the twelfth century; so it was not in existence when the poem was composed, although no doubt an earlier reliquary then housed the saint's relics. The poem was not necessarily written in Lemanaghan: Manchán had a posthumous reputation for learning and piety that would have tempted many *literati* to borrow his name.

The 'pure singing note' of the 'charming' poem will not survive translation, and certainly not a translation which attempts to give the exact sense, rather than the rhythm and the song; but my intention here is prosaic: to discuss what the poet tells us about the monastic life of early Ireland, its purpose and its view of the cosmos of being. This is not the *poet's* intention – he sees, rejoices and sings – but he does, in his progress, show us his understanding of his world:

> *Dúthracar, a Maic Dé bí,*
> *a Rí suthain sen,*
> *bothán deirrit díthreba*
> *commad sí mo threb ...*

From the concise musical sense of the Irish, we decline to the lame explanation, re-translated here for this purpose:

> I wish, Son of the Living God,
> eternal, ancient King,
> to have as my dwelling place
> a hidden house in the wild;
>
> a narrow azure water
> there by its side;
> a pure pool for cleansing sin
> by the Holy Spirit's grace;
>
> a beautiful close wood
> around it on every side
> to give a hidden fosterage
> to birds of all voices;
>
> facing south for warming,
> with a stream across the lawn;
> choice fertile soil,
> good for every plant;

a unity of young men there
– I will tell their number –
humble and obedient,
petitioning the King:

four threes, three fours,
fit to do all good;
two sixes in the church,
one north, one south;

six pairs around me
– besides myself –
always at prayer
to the King who drives the sun;

a church sweet with hangings,
where Heaven's God dwells,
and lights shine
on the white clean text;

a household together,
to receive flesh for nurture,
without lust, without weakening,
without thinking evil.

My choice of provision
I make without concealment:
good fragrant leeks, hens,
speckled salmon and bees,

enough cover and food
from the King of sweet glory;
and to sit for a while
praying to God in some place.

David Greene and Frank O'Connor, like others before them, rather oddly give
to this poem the title, 'The Hermitage'. While the first stanza might seem to
refer to a hermitage – the 'hidden house in the wild' – the poem deals with a
monastery, in fact, with the classic early Irish concept of the perfect monastery,
the imitation of Christ and his Apostles – the abbot and twelve brethren.
St Manchán is represented as laying down the criteria for such a monastery.

He wants, in the first place, seclusion – 'a hidden house in the wild'. This
points to a paradox in the monastic institution of the Early Middle Ages. For
monasteries were centres of population in a thinly peopled world of isolated

farmsteads and scattered tiny hamlets. They were also, to judge by all the literature from and about them, places where there was always coming and going. Some acted as chanceries and archival repositories for the rulers of the emerging Christian States; some were centres of organization for far-flung monastic federations; some were places of pilgrimage, catering for crowds of visitors; some were schools or universities receiving students from many parts. Not all monasteries were the same in nature or served the same purposes – and there were true hermitages (although these seem, as a rule, to have been attached to monasteries, in the sense that the hermit moved out from the community with the permission, and under the direction, of the abbot) – but all had in common the original impulse of withdrawal from the world.

The contradiction was never fully resolved; but often the intention of withdrawal is combined with the practical need for accessibility. Island monasteries provided a means for enjoying a sense of seclusion while being provided with the fastest and most effective means of communication of the day – travel by water. Along the Shannon, for example, there was a string of island monasteries – *Inis Cathaigh, Inis Cealtra, Inis Clothrann, Inis Ainghin, Inis Bó Finne*, and others – as well as the great riverside monastery of Clonmacnoise, 'lost in endless bogs', as Françoise Henry graphically described it, but still centrally located on one of the country's main lines of communication. And Iona, on a small island off a larger island, off the coast of Argyll, was the head of a great federation of churches and the hub of a system of seaborne routes.

The seclusion of the early Irish monastery, therefore, was an inward matter of withdrawal in the mind or spirit, rather than a simple function of location. In an almost wholly rural world, the monastery was less, not more, cut off from the hubbub of a busy world than most secular centres. Pastures and tillage were common to both, but the world of untrammeled nature still waited down the road and dominated the environment. The pleasure of the greenwood could be enjoyed just as readily by the dwellers in a village or rath as by the inhabitants of the monks' cells. Or could they? For this too was a matter of the mind.

The *attitude* to nature is what is important here, and it explains much, if we understand it, about early Irish 'nature poetry'. The pre-Christian pagan Irish seem to have feared and revered the forces of nature. They swore their sacred oaths by them, and perhaps, like those Celts encountered in Illyria by Alexander the Great, they feared only that the sky would fall on them, or that the wind or the sun would take revenge for the foresworn oath. The early Christians in Ireland emphasized that these forces did not rule the universe but were subject, like all creation, to God. St Patrick wrote:

> For the sun is that which we see rising daily at His command, but it will never reign, nor will its splendour last forever. And all those who worship it will be subject to grievous punishment. We, however, worship the true sun, Christ, who will never perish. Nor will those who do His bidding, but they will continue forever just as Christ will continue forever,

> He who reigns with God the Father Almighty and with the Holy Spirit
> before time and now and in eternity. Amen.

With the coming of Christianity, nature took on a wholly different aspect; it was
an artefact and manifestation of the creation of the one God, to be enjoyed and
loved by his servants as part of his gift of life. A spirit that, centuries later,
could have been described as Franciscan, embues much of the marvellous lyric
writing of this time, celebrating creation in its wholeness and in its multitudinous detail.

'Manchán's Hymn' is not really a 'nature poem', however. It is a metrical
prayer which asks for the ideal monastic community, one with sufficient
amenity and provision to make possible the central purpose, reiterated in the
text: prayer (... 'petitioning the King ...' '... praying to God in some place').
It is plain in its description of the virtues and delights of the monastery, in
contrast to the famous (Latin) Bangor hymn, *Benchuir bona regula*, which uses
the metaphors of a litany:

> ... Bangor's happy family,
> Founded on sure faith,
> Graced with hope of salvation,
> Completed with love.
>   A ship never shaken,
> However trimmed by the waves;
> And a spouse ever ready
> For wedding the Lord King.
>   A house full of delights
> Built upon a rock;
> And the true vine
> Transported from Egypt ...

The physical description of the monastery is interwoven with its spiritual significance. Water, in a stream, in a pool, a necessary amenity, becomes the mystical water of life, of baptism 'by the Holy Spirit's grace'. The wood is 'close'
(*immocus* – near and enclosing) in both senses of the English word. It defines
the inwardness of the monastery, but it has an outwardness too, for it is nature,
and it nurtures the wild choir of birds of all kinds which, in parallel with the
psalmistry of the monks praising God, offers untutored song in response to the
Creator. Birds in turn, in communication with humanity, were the voice of
God. Angels and spirits are represented in sculptures of the time as birds; the
representation of the Holy Spirit in the form of a bird was familiar, and we
commonly see a bird perched on King David's harp, inspiring the Psalmist.

The desirable monastery faces 'south for warming'. The meaning of this
can perhaps best be appreciated on Sceilg Mhichíl, where the monastery is
situated on a ledge nearly 200 m. above sea level near the peak of the conical

shaped rock, the Great Skellig, in the Atlantic off the Kerry coast. There are six cells, in a row, or street, sheltered by the rise of rock behind them from the prevailing winds, and looking south along the headlands and splintered rocks of the Kerry and Cork coasts. The Skellig too possibly had an abbot and twelve monks; it seems exactly right in scale for it. Spending ten summer days on the rock many years ago while measuring the monastery, I was struck by the shelter and amenity of that seemingly exposed ledge, 'facing south for warming'. The ideal of the poet of 'Manchán's hymn' is practical. He prays not only for a good aspect but for good soil, to grow the plants for the community's sustenance.

He specifies the community in three stanzas in which he makes an inter-lace out of a play on the simple permutations of a numerology of the factors of twelve: four threes, three fours, two sixes, six twos. These alternations, return-ing to the same picture in different patterns, are like the shifting dapples of leaf-shadows cast by a tree on a sunny day with a light breeze. The twelve, however, we are told at the outset, should form a unity. It is stated to be unity of pur-pose – to pray – and it is implied to be unity of spirit. We are shown the twelve. The church lies east and west and the aisle is divided, with six monks on one side, six on the other. It is 'sweet with hangings' – linens on the walls. We are reminded of that remarkable seventh-century description by Cogitosus of the church of Kildare, which was also divided along the nave – but with an addi-tional transverse division for the chancel – and had painted hangings. It had candles too, with their spires of light shining on the text of Gospels and Psalms

The unity was to have a leader: '... six pairs around me – besides myself...'; and we see the ancient structure of the *comitatus*, for which there is much precedent long before Christ and the Apostles, as there are many examples long after. The *comitatus*, as a political and social structure, can be inferred in the European Bronze Age, and is explicit in early medieval legend – as in the tales of King Arthur and the Round Table. It survives into present-day pol-itics, as in the entourages of modern American Presidents, and must for long have seemed the logical design for the governance and leadership of a purpose-ful society. It was the structure of the early monastic community, a band of men led by their 'father' (*abba*), storming heaven. The men are together; the nourishment provided for their flesh is like that provided for their souls, and purifies them of concupiscence, of envy, of backsliding They serve the King – the figure constantly used for God – and the King rules the world of nature about them: he 'drives the sun'. His power is acknowledged, and the sun-chariot is no longer manned by the Sun. A transcendent purpose is at work through the poem.

The practicality returns in the closing stanzas. The desirable community will receive its *tuarasdal* from the King it serves: its grant for service; 'cover and food', the monastic provision: garden herbs, fish from the stream, honey from the apiary (and beekeeping seems to have come, with Christianity, from the Romans). And the purpose is reiterated again: ' ... to sit for a while pray-ing to God in some place'.

The poem, like that which it celebrates and requests, is a unity. It presents us with a microcosm of Irish Christianity of the Early Middle Ages. Everything in it is in the measure of the time and place. God is not imaged as an oriental and remote universal ruler but as a King, powerful but a leader of his people, *primus*, not *inter pares*, certainly, but *inter suous*. For the Irish of the time, the Romans who crucified Christ were not the worst villains of that piece: that part was reserved for those Jews who participated, since Jesus was a Jew, and the Crucifixion was that most heinous of deeds in early Irish eyes, kin-murder. Baptism had made the Christian Irish kin of the Lord, and they celebrated and joined in his governance of the universe and of the wild world about them, which they viewed now with kindly eyes. 'Manchán's Hymn' circles round that simple vision.

30

Domhnall Mór Ua Briain
and the Normans

It is proper to regard the intervention of Henry II in Irish affairs as the beginning of the tangled story of Anglo-Irish political relations, but it is not proper to regard the history of Ireland from 1169 onwards as simply the history of Anglo-Irish relations. The invaders were a new and large, but not an unprecedented, element in Irish politics: for some centuries there had already been sizeable bodies of foreigners playing their part in the country's affairs. They were welcomed or opposed not on nationalistic grounds but according as they fitted the exigencies of dynastic politics. They were absorbed in varying degrees, and a society which had not for long known meaningful centralized rule but which had for long practised an oriental flexibility of response to the pressures and demands of over-kings was possessed of techniques adequate to deal with the demands of the overlordship of distant English kings.

The careers of leading Irish kings of the time of the invasion were largely governed by traditional ambitions and considerations which had little to do with the newly arrived foreigners. They were of course conditioned in varying degree by the activities of the invaders, but were still directed in the main to Irish dynastic ends. The history of Gaelic civilization in Ireland was not terminated by the Anglo-Norman invasion: it had another four and a half centuries to run, and its distant downfall was not foreseen by the twelfth-century kings.

The special interest of Domhnall Mór Ua Briain is bound up with the importance of Munster in Irish history from the eighth century on. In early Ireland Munster was the largest and potentially the most powerful of the over-kingdoms, dominating the southern half of the island and intermittently competing with the Uí Néill kingdoms of the northern half for the tribute of the stubborn Lagin. The Eoghanacht kings of Cashel had been formidable rivals to the Uí Néill kings of Tara. Neither Tara nor Cashel had a single dynastic line: both, through the operation of the Irish succession system, drew their kings in irregular alternation from different branches of the broad dynastic groupings, and both, in their rivalry, were weakened by this lack of continuity and by the

Unpublished. This was given as a Thomas Davis Lecture on RTÉ in 1969.

internal struggles to which it gave rise. However, in the eighth, and again in the ninth, century Cashel was able to challenge Tara on its own ground – in the midlands – and, as Professor Kelleher of Harvard has recently demonstrated, it is probable that in response to this challenge the Uí Néill encouraged the rise of the hitherto subordinate Dál gCais dynasty in Clare, and the division of Munster. Added to this, Munster, again probably as a result of Uí Néill interference, failed to develop the trends which were perceptible in the other major kingdoms, towards dynastic consolidation and the development of a territorial kingdom in place of the old loose federation of over-kings.

The usurpation of Cashel by Dál gCais led, in the subsequent career of Brian Bóroimhe, to the hoisting of the Uí Néill with their own petard. Brian held Tara as well as Cashel, took hostages and tribute throughout Ireland, ratified the primacy of Armagh, possibly even took the first measures towards a reorganization of the Irish church, and acted in many ways with all the freedom from traditional inhibitions of one whose power existed only in despite of the traditional system. But his domination of Ireland was personal and died with him.

However, he left a high precedent and a vigorous line. The descendants of Brian for several generations kept a grip on Munster and aspired to the rule of Ireland, until they were for a time eclipsed in the early twelfth century. Brian himself was killed at Clontarf in 1014, together with his son Murchad, and Murchad's son. Another son of Brian, Donnchad, succeeded to what was left of his father's political heritage, and in the period up to 1051 he steadily built up a base of power in Munster and the midlands. But this was the time which was to be known as that of the 'high kings with opposition'. Donnchad's rise was checked first by a resurgence of the Uí Conchubhair of Connacht, who under their king Áed, in 1051, raided Dál gCais and felled the sacred tree at Mag Adair, the traditional inauguration place of the dynasty – an act of symbolic significance. Then a dynastic struggle broke out within Dál gCais between the sons of Donnchad and the sons of his brother Tadg. The powerful Leinster king, Diarmait mac Máel na mBó was brought into this in 1058. Limerick was burnt, and finally Donnchad departed to Rome, leaving the kingship to his nephew Tairdelbhach. Tairdelbhach was a powerful king who campaigned far into the northern half of Ireland and undoubtedly aspired to the high kingship. On his death in 1089, his kingdom of Munster was divided between his three sons, but within a year one of them, Muirchertach, was in undisputed control.

This was the man who went nearest to repeating the achievements of his great-grandfather, Brian Bóroimhe, a task which had by now become traditional for the Dalcassian kings. He subdued Dublin and Leinster in 1089, invaded Connacht and took its kingship in 1092, received the submission of the king of Tara in 1093, and by the turn of the century seemed well on the way to justify the title by which he was addressed by the archbishop of Canterbury – 'most glorious king of Ireland'. He had dealings with the Normans. He married a daughter to Arnulf de Montgomery and another to Sigurd son of Magnus Bareleg king of Norway, and appears to have been involved in Welsh

and Norman intrigues against Henry I of England. He exerted a powerful a
important influence on church affairs, presiding at the famous synod of 11
when he handed Cashel over to the church, and that of 1111, when the pr
gramme for reform was laid down. His declining years however saw growi
resistance to his pretensions and were overshadowed by the rise of Tairdelbha
Ua Conchubhair of Connacht and by the partial rivival of the ancient Munst
dynasty, the Eoghanachta, now to be represented by the family of M
Carthaigh. Munster, under pressure from the powerful king of Connacht, w
divided: north Munster (Tuadhmhumhain or Thomond) under Ua Briain, a
south Munster (Deasmhumhain or Desmond) under Mac Carthaigh. Aft
Muirchertach's death, Cashel was held by Eoghanacht kings again – Tadg M
Carthaigh in the early 1120s and Cormac MacCarthaigh in 1127. The Ua Bria
domination of Munster was restored in 1139, and three nephews of Muircherta
resumed the effort, which had been more or less continuous since Clontarf,
make the descendants of Brian Bóroimhe dominant in Ireland; but again riv
ries within the Ua Briain dynasty not only prevented the expansion of th
kingdom, but brought in outsiders to divide it. One branch of the fami
headed by Tairdelbhach, son of Diarmait, allied itself with Diarmait M
Murchadha of Leinster; another branch, headed by Tairdelbhach's broth
Tadc, allied itself with Tairdelbhach Ua Conchubhair of Connacht. At the gr
battle of Móin-mhór, Tairdelbhach Ua Briain was defeated and he was su
sequently banished from Munster. Ua Conchubhair then partitioned Muns
again in 1152 between Tadg Ua Briain and Diarmait Mac Carthaigh. The ba
ished Tairdelbhach Ua Briain in the meantime went to the north, where
made an ally of Muirchertach Mac Lochlainn, who in due course interve
successfully on his behalf in Munster.

The detail of these somewhat monotonous dynastic quarrels gives us a p
ture of the political preoccupations of a twelfth-century Irish king, which
must have if we are to see the events of the Anglo-Norman invasion in th
historical context.

In 1168, a year before the invasion took place, Domhnall Mór, son
Tairdelbhach Ua Briain, assumed the kingship of Thomond, after a period
especially bitter warfare within the dynasty. The history, briefly sketched abo
of the fortunes of the Ua Briain kingdom since Brian Bóroimhe would h
been well known to Domhnall. It would have guided his actions much m
than any appreciation of the real meaning of the Norman invasion: as we h
seen, even in dealing with the affairs of Thomond alone, it was common pr
tice to call in outside allies in dynastic disputes, and it was in this capa
that the Anglo-Normans were first brought in. Domhnall was five generati
removed from Brian Bóroimhe. In each of those generations the descendant
Brian had seemed close to repeating his achievement. The Ua Briain visio
the high kingship was to persist in some form into the thirteenth century
must still have been vivid enough in the 1160s. The main lines of policy fo
Ua Briain king were by now traditional, and were clear: to retain domina

in Munster, which implied firm control first of west Munster, south of the Shannon mouth, and the subordination of Desmond; to divide and hold at bay Connacht, which commanded the most direct route into the heart of Thomond; to hold sway over the border territory of Osraige; to hold Dublin and divide Leinster; and then to obtain control of the north midlands. This policy had been balked by the rise of a strong power in Connacht – the most serious threat to it – and it had been countered by the repeated Connacht policy of dividing Munster. Indeed, immediately after the accession of Domhnall, and before he could begin to establish himself, the partition of Munster was confirmed again by Ruaidhri Ua Conchubhair, who marched to Knockany with his ally Ua Ruairc of Bréifne and took the hostages of Munster, a fine being laid on the people of Desmond for complicity in the killing of Domhnall Mór's brother and rival Muirchertach.

Since the time of Brian Bóroimhe, Cashel was no longer the royal seat of Munster. Even before the Rock was handed over to the church in 1101 by Muirchertach Ua Briain, it seems clear from a number of passing references that Limerick was functioning at least as the effective capital of Thomond. A special attachment to Kincora, Béal Bóramha and Killaloe, the ancient centre of the dynasty, upstream a few miles from the Norse city, did not preclude this. It was in the city, among the Norse townfolk, that an Ua Briain king was to be found in times of crisis or when affairs of state were in question. The region at the lower end of Lough Derg was home, where they spent money in patronage, where they retired, where they died: Limerick was the place of business. In this the Ua Briain kings were modernizers in comparison with many of the other provincial kings; as they showed too in other ways. Muirchertach Ua Briain had been the first important royal patron of the church reform at the beginning of the century. The dynasty was involved in marriages and other dealings overseas. They plainly appreciated the value of a port, and it is clear from some references that it was in Limerick that they held their sources of negotiable wealth. They must have been reasonably well informed about the outside world. They were building Romanesque churches in the middle years of the century, with a more French flavour than is to be found elsewhere in the country at this period: one of the earliest of these is the church at Killaloe of St Flannan, who figures in the genealogy of that branch of Dál gCais from which Brian sprang. And the very succession of the dynasty at this period conformed much more closely to the father-and-son succession of feudal Europe than, for example, the Eoghanacht succession did.

Shortly after Domhnall Mór became king, he secured his position in Thomond by blinding his brother Brian of Sliabh Bladhma, who had briefly been king of Ormond, the area east of Limerick. Domhnall however, even with a secure base, was not possessed of the same freedom of action as his predecessors. If he had followed the established pattern he would have marked the opening of his kingship by taking the hostages of west Munster to demonstrate his dominance over Desmond. Two new factors in the situation prevented this taking place immediately. First, Ruaidhri Ua Conchubhair was exploiting the advantage secured by Connacht, which could now intervene more or less at will in Munster affairs and maintain the partition of the province into Thomond and Desmond. Second, Ruaidhri Ua Conchubhair was now faced with a major crisis as the result of the successful return of the banished Diarmaid Mac Murchadha, with foreign assistance, to claim his kingdom of Leinster. Domhnall Mór had a close connexion with Diarmaid: he was married to his daughter.

The crisis did not mature until 1170. In 1168, Domhnall gave his hostages to Ruaidhri at Knockany; in 1169 Diarmaid, while he awaited reinforcements from overseas, gave hostages also to Ruaidhri, including his own son. In 1170, both of the *Leth Mogha* kings abandoned their hostages and turned on Ruaidhri. Domhnall's first activities as king therefore were directed to this external threat rather than to the internal stabilisation of Munster. In this he may, initially at least, have been encouraged by the fact that Desmond – a more formidable power in the previous half century than it had been for a long time before – was now itself threatened by Leinster and Leinster's foreign allies. At any rate, the annals tell us of great warfare between Thomond and Connacht in 1170.

Just as Diarmaid Mac Murchadha had introduced Norman knights and men-at-arms into Leinster, because of their prowess and technical skill as soldiers, to help him regain his kingdom, so through his good offices, his son-in-law Domhnall now introduced them to Thomond. A band led by Robert FizStephen, Meiler FitzHenry and Robert de Barry marched to Limerick and joined Domhnall's forces. Ruaidhri Ua Conchubhair assembled a large fleet on the Shannon and sailed down through Lough Derg to attack Domhnall, while the people of west Connacht invaded Clare and the Uí Mhaine of east Connacht invaded Ormond. The Uí Mhaine reached Killaloe and destroyed the wooden bridge there which had first been built by Tairdelbhach Ua Briain in 1071. The three-pronged invasion was unsuccessful in its main object however: Ruaidhri, who now had other grave matters calling for his attention, withdrew after suffering some reverses, without securing submission from Domhnall. Domhnall's small band of foreign auxiliaries then returned across Ireland again to re-join Diarmaid's forces.

At this stage, Diarmaid Mac Murchadha had, with his allies, control of Leinster, including Osraige, the border territory which was always first claimed by Munster in its periods of expansion. He had agreed with Ruaidhri to send back his foreign auxiliaries when his kingdom should be secure. Instead, he now decided to call in more formidable forces and make a bid for control of Ireland: Strongbow came, took Waterford, married Diarmaid's daughter, and then moved with Diarmaid to take Dublin.

At this point Domhnall Ua Briain's policy appears to have changed. The external threat to his ambitions from Connacht was now overshadowed by a greater threat, so he changed sides and, for a time at least, re-deployed his forces.

He submitted to Ruaidhri Ua Conchubhair in 1171 and gave hostages to him again, and when Ruaidhri, with the aid of Ua Ruairc and Ua Cearbhaill and of the Manx fleet, went to invest Dublin in that year, Domhnall joined him and camped with his forces at Kilmainham outside the city. The siege was undone by a successful sortie, and the investing force was routed. Strongbow, who had been in the city, marched south to restore the situation in south Wexford, where FitzStephen had been over-run in his fortified position on the Slaney. Then he turned north again to deal with Osraige, whose king had refused to accept Strongbow's overlordship and had launched an attack on Éile. He called on, and received, the help of Ua Briain for this expedition: Osraige was of special importance to an ambitious Munster king. Domhnall came with a strong force to join Strongbow in his parley with Domhnall Mac Gilla Phátraic of Osraige, and used the opportunity to plunder the territory. According to the Song of Dermot, Domhnall Ua Briain wished to have the king of Osraige killed although he had come to parley under Maurice de Prendergast's safe-conduct, but de Prendergast succeeded in preventing this in spite of the willingness of the other barons. In the meantime, Diarmaid Mac Carthaigh of Desmond, apparently while Domhnall was away, raided north to Limerick, inflicted a defeat on the Norse of the city, and partly burned their fortress and market.

On 17 October, Henry II landed near Waterford, where Diarmaid Mac Carthaigh submitted to him. Domhnall Ua Briain did likewise on the Suir, probably somewhere near Cashel. Giving fealty to Henry certainly meant no more to Domhnall than acknowledging a powerful but distant over-king, one who in his distance was probably preferable to an over-king like Ua Conchubhair on his borders. Henry, it is true, sent a constable to Limerick, but Limerick was Ua Briain's own ground. However, more seriously, Henry did some years later grant Limerick and Thomond to Philip de Braose, a member of his company of knights, and although this grant was not put into effect immediately, it opened the way for a direct Norman threat to Ua Briain. In the meantime, having proceeded to Dublin and received the submission of other Irish kings, Henry caused a synod to be summoned in the winter of 1171–72 at Cashel, where Domhnall Mór is said to have built a cathedral in 1169. This cathedral is something of a mystery, for while the church built by Cormac Mac Carthaigh is still intact upon the Rock, there is not the faintest vestige of any structure of 1169. If it ever existed, and was not simply an unfulfilled project, it must have been new, or perhaps unfinished, when the synod met.

From this time onwards, whatever ambitions for expansion Domhnall may have had in emulation of his predecessors were checked by the build-up of new forces in the country, and his energies were mainly directed – and on the whole successfully – to the consolidation and defence of Thomond and Limerick, and by extension, of Munster as a whole.

In 1173 the Normans made the first deep freebooting raid into Munster, when Raymond FitzGerald, who had been appointed commander of the Earl's troops, plundered Lismore and the territory around it. Lismore had long enjoyed Mac Carthaigh patronage and was the chief ecclesiastical centre of Desmond. Its sack was also a matter of concern to an Ua Briain. Part of the Cork fleet under the command of Gilbert son of Turgarius attacked ships assembled at Youghal by part of the Norman force for carrying off cattle and other plunder, but the Normans were victorious in the sea battle. On land, Raymond defeated Diarmaid Mac Carthaigh who had come with a force to intercept him, and the Normans returned with a large prey to Waterford. Domhnall Mór intervened indirectly. He descended on a castle Strongbow had built at Kilkenny and plundered and demolished it.

He now apprears to have resumed alliance with Ruaidhri Ua Conchubhair, for when a further expedition was mounted, this time against north Munster, under the command of Hervey de Montmorency, Ruaidhri marched to join Domhnall. Strongbow, who was with the Constable Hervey, learning of this, sent to Dublin for reinforceements, but these were attacked in camp at Thurles by Domhnall and by Ruaidhri's son Conchubhar, and were disastrously defeated. Strongbow retreated in haste to Waterford.

This was the first serious check the Normans had received since the invasion, and Domhnall followed it by taking rapid measures to secure Munster. He killed Gilla Pátraic, son of Domhnall Mac Gilla Phátraic, of Osraige, and the son of An Leithdeirg Ua Conchubhair of Corcu Modruad, and blinded his cousin Diarmaid son of Tadg Ua Briain and his grand-nephew Mathghamhain son of Tairdelbhach. He took the measure which his predecessors had normally taken on entering the kingship of Thomond, and campaigned into west Munster. The effect of the victory of Thurles was that the Norse of Waterford revolted against the Normans, so that Strongbow, who had fallen back on that city, found himself in serious difficulties, and Ruaidhri Ua Conchubhair organised a new alliance in the midlands against the Normans. This was checked by Raymond FitzGerald, who had been in England but now returned to organise countermeasures in Meath. Ua Conchubhair, abandoning any hope of regaining control over the midlands, turned instead to check the resumed vigour of Ua Briain power on his southern borders. He marched into Munster and expelled Domhnall from Thomond, and then apparently encouraged the Normans in Dublin to mount an attack on Limerick with his connivance. Raymond, with a force of 820, marched to Osraige, where Domhnall's enemy Domhnall Mac Gilla Phátraic joined him to guide his forces to Ua Briain's city. The walls were stormed and a large booty taken. Early the following year Raymond was recalled to England by the King, and was on his way when Domhnall Ua Briain returned from the south and laid the city under siege. Raymond turned back, accompanied by Domhnall of Osraige and Muirchertach Mac Murchadha of Leinster, and Domhnall, raising the siege, came to bar their way at Cashel. His force was brushed aside and Raymond entered Limerick a few days later.

Ruaidhri Ua Conchubhair, still at war with Domhnall, had a fleet on Lough Derg. Raymond parleyed with him and with Domhnall: both swore fealty to the English king and gave hostages to Raymond, and Domhnall apparently gave hostages again to Ruaidhri and made peace with him. Raymond then, leaving Limerick garrisoned, marched south to Cork to restore Desmond to Diarmaid Mac Carthaigh whose kingdom had been usurped by his son Cormac. Here he received, secretly, news of the death of Strongbow. He hastened back to Limerick, decided after taking counsel that he could no longer stay so far from Dublin, and finding no one else who could take it over, he committed the city of Limerick to Domhnall's custody on behalf of the king and received new oaths of fealty. No sooner had Raymond left than Domhnall destroyed the bridge and set fire to parts of the island city to cut Limerick off completely from the land beyond the Shannon to the east.

From now on Domhnall Mór held Limerick, and while he lived the Normans did not again penetrate to the centre of his power, although an unsuccessful attempt was made by Philip de Braose, to whom Thomond had been granted by King Henry. In 1177 however there was further Norman intervention in Desmond, arising from dynastic feuds within the Mac Carthaigh family: Miles de Cogan and FitzStephen plundered Cork and then marched on Waterford. De Cogan and FitzStephen had been granted Cork earlier in the year by Henry at Oxford, and de Braose Limerick. Domhnall renewed his attacks on Desmond, and the annals for the year describe bitter warfare and suggest depopulation of some areas. Having secured their fiefs in the south the Normans now turned north to Limerick, but here they were unsuccessful and de Braose retired without his fief. Ua Briain ultimately made peace with Mac Carthaigh at Cashel, and for a time hostilities ceased between Thomond and Desmond.

After this for a number of years – in fact until the arrival of Prince John – the career of Domhnall was relatively peaceful. His policy must, perforce, from now on be on the defensive, for almost every time he had campaigned out of Thomond, he had been attacked in the rear at his Limerick base. Ua Conchubhair and Mac Carthaigh were both seriously weakened: to hold out the Norman power which had crippled them, he must concentrate on keeping a grip on his kingdom at home. These years of relative peace appear to be the period in which he mainly exercised the patronage as builder, founder and restorer which characterised his reign. He built three cathedrals, at Cashel, at Killaloe (where his brother Consaidin was bishop) and at Limerick. He founded the Cistercian abbeys of Kilcooley, Holy Cross and Corcomroe. He also built Suir, Fermoy, Inchicronan, Canon Island, Clare Abbey and Killone. It was almost certainly he who re-edified the churches of Lough Derg and the Lower Shannon, at Holy Island, Tomgraney and elsewhere, since they show work which appears to be of his time. In this he was perhaps following consciously in the footsteps of his great ancestor Brian to whom the original building of a number of these is attributed. He is said to have built a castle at Croom and a castle at Adare, both on the Maigue river. We have evidence for most of these, we must depend on surmise for others, and we cannot name the sixteen abbeys he is credited with founding in Munster. But clearly he was a supporter of the new religious orders – both the Augustinian Canons and the Cistercians – and his foundation charters and land grants show the rudiments of an administration. Some of this work was done in time of war; we may perhaps surmise that most of it was the work of the period of peace.

In 1177 Prince John, at Oxford, was named Lord of Ireland. In 1185 he was knighted and sent to govern his lordship. He arrived at Waterford and succeeded immediately in offending those who came to greet him, including Ua Faeláin of Dési. He built fortifications along the Suir and towards Limerick, alarming many of the Irish, including Domhnall Mór, who moved against him and inflicted a number of reverses on his forces. These however appear to have been relatively inconclusive encounters.

In the meantime Domhnall became involved in Connacht again, in a war within the Ua Conchubhair dynasty, when he plundered, with Norman allies, west Connacht, in reprisal for which Cathal Cearrach plundered and burned Killaloe. In 1188 Domhnall was again involved in Connacht. John de Courcy marched west, and Domhnall joined Conchubhar Ua Conchubhair, king of Connacht, against him. The invaders were deflected northward to cross the Erne into Donegal. De Courcy was headed off from here by a hosting of Cenél gConaill, and as he passed back over the Curlew mountains he was attacked by Domhnall and Conchubhar.

Domhnall's last battles were fought in 1192, when a renewed Norman advance was made into north Munster, along the line of the Suir and towards the Limerick plain, apparently to realise speculative land-grants issued by John. These invaders were driven back by Domhnall, who gained a second victory over Norman forces at the crucial river-crossing at Thurles. In 1194 he died, with his kingdom of Thomond intact.

If we regard Domhnall Mór's career solely from the point of view of the invasion, we must reckon him a rare example of an Irish king who successfully resisted the Normans. Grants of his lands might be made to foreigners, but he contrived to prevent any effective Norman expropriation of his territories. Indeed the failure of the Normans to make any permanent settlement in Thomond throughout the Middle Ages is largely due to his effectiveness in keeping them out in this critical early period. It is doubtful however if he himself or his contemporaries would judge his career by this criterion. The retention of the kingship of Thomond fell far short of the ambition of a twelfth century Ua Briain king. On the other hand, it must be said that it is very doubtful if Domhnall, able and vigorous though he was, could have overcome the power of Connacht even if there had been no Norman invasion, and Connacht was the real impediment to his expansive ambitions. His career appears to follow the pattern set by the policies of his predecessors: he seems at no time to have regarded the Normans as more than a new element in a familiar situation.

31

Crosses and Kings

In 1960, after limited excavation at the monastic site of *Tech Theille* (Tihilly) in Offaly, the Office of Public Works re-erected there a high cross, assembled from large fragments. Of the ancient monastery there remain above ground only the cross, an inscribed grave-slab and some remains of a stone church, within a collapsed cashel enclosure.

In its original state the high cross was an assembly of three separate parts: the finial, which has a tenon for insertion into a mortise on the cross-head; the head-and-shaft; and the base. The finial and the head-and-shaft are in fine-grained sandstone. The base is of a coarser conglomerate, probably carved from an erratic boulder locally obtained. It is massive and is circular on plan. Crowning the cross was the finial, in the form of a simplified gabled roof. The head-and-shaft were carved in relief on all sides, the carvings on each face of the shaft being arranged in four panels, defined by simple mouldings which ran continuously from the head to the base, the mouldings returning on themselves midway across the top and bottom of each panel, breaking the frame at that point. This 'broken frame' is a distinctive feature found on a group of twelve extant high crosses. Within the framing are decorative and figured motifs.

The principal figure-sculpture is on what is taken to have been originally the west face. Here, on the cross-head, is a representation of the Crucifixion. Christ is shown nude, with outstretched and rather elongated arms. His head, beardless, appears to be tonsured, or else with the hair trimmed in a 'page-boy' fashion. Representations of the lance- and sponge-bearers are squeezed in with difficulty under the arms. The sponge-bearer, on Christ's right, is shown with a shaft bearing what appears to be a cup extended up towards the lips of Christ. The lance-bearer is depicted in the act of piercing his side. On the same side of the cross, in the second panel from the top, the Fall is depicted: Adam and Eve, with a stylized tree which forms, as it were, a pair of arched niches for the two figures and also accommodates the Serpent, who is

---

A full discussion of the matters touched on more briefly here, entitled 'The High Crosses of Tech Theille (Thihilly), Kinnitty, and Related Sculpture', was published in E. Rynne, ed., *Figures from the Past: Studies in Figurative Art in Christian Ireland in honour of Helen M. Roe*, Dún Laoghaire (1987), 131–58.

twined around its trunk. There is no other figure carving, but there is on the lowest panel of the west face what appears to be a winged horse, and on the lowest panel on the east face a pair of birds with their necks intertwined and between them what may be an urn. On the east face of the cross-head there is a roundel embellished with six bosses arranged around a central boss, all badly defaced. The other panels have interlacing (including animal-interlace), spirals and frets.

A cross which has many close similarities to this stands in the grounds of Castle Bernard, some distance away to the south-west, on the lower slope of the Slieve Bloom mountains, in the same county of Offaly. It is not in its original position, having been moved from the nearby village of Kinnitty, site of the early monastery of *Cenn Etig*, and re-erected. The upper limb of the cross is missing, as is much of the head. Old photographs show that there once was a finial. Like the cross of Tech Theille, that at Kinnitty was originally carved in three parts: the finial, the head-and-shaft, and a large base.

The finial was in the form of a house or church or tomb, with a steeply pitched roof. It was outlined with mouldings which may have represented posts, beams and barges. The roof was ornamented with a relief pattern copying tiles or shingles. The walls were also ornamented, with what appear to have been tight knotworks of ribbon-interlace. The base is heavy and unevenly squarish on plan. On the south face of the cross (probably originally the west face) the Crucifixion is shown on the cross-head. Christ is depicted nude, his feet bound. His hair flows down over his shoulders as if in two pigtails or plaits. As on the Tech Theille cross, lance- and sponge-bearers are squeezed in, the sponge-bearer lifting a cup on the end of a rod to the lips of Christ. Because of damage to the cross, only the head of the lance-bearer now remains, and the tip of his lance entering Christ's side. The shaft of the cross has four panels on each face, most of them framed, with the 'broken frame' as at Tech Theille. Below the Crucifixion scene, on the second panel, there are depicted the figure of a harpist, seated on a chair with a bird over his head, and, facing him, a standing figure (obviously an ecclesiastic) raising a bell and holding a crozier. On the head, at the north (originally east) face of the cross, there is at the crossing, a roundel bearing six spiral-linked bosses around a central boss, and immediately below that on the cross-head a pair of birds linking their necks. On the shaft, the top panel shows the Fall, which is similar to the equivalent on the cross of Tech Theille.

Otherwise the Kinnitty cross is embellished with spirals and interlaces. It has also, however, inscriptions, on the bottom (unframed) panels on the north and south sides. The late Domhnall Ó Murchadha made careful rubbings of these in August 1983, by a method he had devised, and enabled them to be read:

OR[OIT] DO RIG MAELSECHNAILL M[AC] MAELRUANAID
OROIT AR RIG HERENN
[A prayer for King Maelsechnaill son of Maelruanaid. A prayer for the King of Ireland]

and:

> OR[OIT] DO COLMAN DORRO. IN CROSSA AR RIG HERENN
> OR[OIT] DO RIG HERENN
> [A prayer for Colmán who made the cross for the King of Ireland. A prayer for the king of Ireland.]

These writings leave no doubt of one significance of the monument. Maelsechnaill mac Maelruanaid was king of Tara from AD 846 to 862. His reign is marked by an achievement which is summarized as follows by F.J. Byrne:

> The Uí Néill concept of high-kingship was first converted into political reality by Maelsechnaill mac Maele Ruanaid, styled *rí Érenn uile*, 'king of all Ireland', at his obit in 862.

Maelsechnaill belonged to Clann Cholmáin, the western branch of the southern Uí Néill. His great-grandfather, Domhnall Midi, had been the first of the lineage to be king of Tara. Since then, the kingship had alternated between Clann Cholmáin and Cenél nEógain from the north. The last king of the eastern branch of the southern Uí Néill had been Cinaed, of Síl nÁedo Sláine, who died in 728.

The Tara kingship by this date was the most important in Ireland, but for a quarter of a century before Maelsechnaill came to it, Feidilmid mac Crimhthainn, the king-abbot of Munster, had asserted a counter-claim, even attempting to seize the Tara kingship (with what success is uncertain – if he had any, it was brief). The country was also troubled by the activities of the Vikings, especially in the previous ten years, with the appearance of large fleets and the construction of fortified bases. Maelsechnaill's first noteworty act, in 845, was the capture and drowning of the Viking chieftain Turgesius, who had established himself on the waters of the Shannon and the midland lakes.

As king, Maelsechnaill inflicted some defeats on the Norse, brought their base at Dublin under control, suppressed a revolt by the king of Brega (of the rival Síl nÁedo Sláine) and in due course succeeded in obtaining the submission of most parts of Ireland. In 851 he secured that of the King of Ulaid at an assembly in Armagh. In 854 he marched to Cashel, and in 858 through Desmond to the south coast. He also handled skilfully the newly powerful kingdom of Osraige and its ambitious King, Cerball mac Dúnlainge. In 859 he held an assembly at Rathugh in Westmeath: Osraige was taken from the nominal suzerainty of the King of Cashel and attached to *Leth Cuinn*; Armagh's rule, in ecclesiastical matters, was in effect extended over all Ireland, and a high-kingship was, virtually, established.

The last years of his reign continued to be troubled, particularly by the northern Uí Néill Cenél Eógain dynasty, whose leader Áed (to be Maelsechnaill's immediate successor as King of Tara) called on allies (including Síl nÁedo Sláine) against the high-king.

The reiteration of Maelsechnaill's title 'King of Ireland' on the Kinnitty cross echoes its reiteration in the annals (and incidentally is a reassurance that this is not a retrospective interpolation in the ninth-century records).

He is the first Uí Néill king of whom it is recorded that he raided as far as the south coast. In connection with his first incursion into Munster, when he went as far as Indeoin na nDéisi (near Clonmel) to receive the hostages of the Déisi, it is worth noting that Macalister read the inscription on the cross at Killamery in south Kilkenny as asking a prayer for Maelsechnaill – although the reading remains very doubtful.

The close relationship between the crosses of Tech Theille and Kinnitty has been recognised by scholars, but the reassembly of the cross of Tech Theille makes possible the beginning of a fuller assessment of their place in the general sequence of high-cross sculpture.

There are several ways of approaching this, since there are different kinds of questions that we would wish to ask about monuments like the Irish crosses. What exactly was their function in the monastery, or in society as a whole? Who had them put up, and why? Who were the craftsmen? How and where did they learn their trade? What was their relationship to their clients or patrons? How did they organise their work? With what other works, in what media, and where, were they familiar?

In all this, we are baulked by the fact that the study of Irish society of this period is barely text-aided. We have accounts, often highly stylized or quite fanciful, provided by small and probably atypical groups in their own interests or in the interests of their patrons. We have, for example, extensive law-tracts which tell us about the minds of lawyers and similar professionals, and preserve relics and traces of earlier forms of society, but do not necessarily inform us very well about real life in the eighth or ninth century.

The world of craft, at that date in Ireland, is for us virtually prehistoric. There must, for example, have been large vocabularies in early Irish for the technical processes, products and details of metalworking, sculpture, painting. weaving, building and so on. The great bulk of it is lost to us.

For this reason the normal documenting methods of art history are not available. We must fall back on the methods of archaeology – not wholly suited to this purpose. There is a temptation to resort to dubious, pseudo-art-historical methods; to invent a documentation, largely by rash, even random, analogies and comparisons between different cultures whose actual relationahips with one another may remain very obscure even to the most diligent historical researcher. The temptation is all the more dangerous if we indulge the illusion that Dark-Age Christian culture was, in Church matters at least, one and indivisible like the seamless garment of Christ. On the contrary, in reality every local church had its own culture – even in Church matters – and could turn the small common stock of Christian ideas and images to its own purposes and its own meaning.

The monuments themselves, studied closely and locally, must be the point of beginning. The 'split frame' found on both the crosses described briefly above, is a quirk, an oddity, a fashion or a fad. It is found on a number of other crosses and it establishes a connection; that is to say some form of communication, either directly or through intermediaries, between the sculptors who made those crosses. It is found on the cross of Durrow, the Cross of the Scriptures at Clonmacnoise, the great west cross of Monasterboice, the broken cross at Kells, and the crosses of Termonfechin, Camus, Killary, Armagh, Donaghmore (in Tyrone) and Conor.

The total is twelve. The crosses selected by this single diagnostic feature have some other features in common, but they belong to more than one distinguishable group. Eight of them are fully-figured, or Scripture, crosses, in which at least the two main faces of the shaft are wholly occupied by figured scenes in panels. The cross of Durrow may be added to the eight. It is not quite fully-figured, as defined, but it belongs to one of the most coherently defined sets in the country, in which the combination of a large number of distinctive features compellingly suggests that they are all from one workshop. And the other members of the set, the Cross of the Scriptures at Clonmacnoise, the Market Cross at Kells and Muiredach's Cross at Monasterboice, are all types of the fully developed Scripture Cross. This leaves three crosses with 'split frames' wholly outside the fully-figured groupings – the crosses of Termonfechin, Tech Theille and Kinnitty.

But we can add to this the information that the 'split fame' spans a period of something of the order of twenty years at least. Domhnall Ó Murchadha's rubbing of the inscription there has confirmed that the Clonmacnoise cross was erected under the auspices of Flann Sinna, King of Ireland, who was the son of Maelsechnaill mac Maelruanaid and who reigned from 879 to 916.

We could go on to make the further, more tentative, suggestion that the 'split frame' crosses of the earlier part of this time-span, in the middle years of the ninth century, are the south-westerly ones (Tech Theille, Kinnitty, Durrow) and that the later ones tend towards the north-east midlands and south Ulster. But Termonfechin, on the east coast north of the Boyne, goes with the south-western set. Did Maelsechlainn patronize a local craftsman, or craftsmen, on the far Munster borders of his territory? Or did he send for his sculptors to Kells or Duleek or thereabouts? Or did they come from some such centre as Clonmacnoise. It would seem, on a fine balance of probabilities, that the most likely source is the Boyne area.

The 'split frame' is only one device. If we look at another feature which the crosses of Tech Theille and Kinnitty have in common, we find another, and somewhat different, set of relations. This feature is the disc at the crossing containing six spirals around a central spiral boss. We find similar features on the main cross at Duleek, the south cross at Kells and the crosses at Tynan Abbey and Old Eghish. There is a seven-spiral group of the same character, but not at the crossing, on the Tybroughney fragment (in south Tipperary), and a superficially similar but four-spiral group on a slab from Carrowntemple, County Sligo, and also on the fragmentary cross-head at Drumcullin, in Offaly. Only at Kinnitty and at Kells however is the disc set in a square panel.

This is the Irish distribution. But the device is found in Scotland, at the crossing of crosses and cross-slabs, at Rothesay, Skinnet, Iona, Kilnave, Meigle, St Madoes, Fowlis Wester, Dyce and Aberlemno; and – not at the crossing – at Rosemarl, Shandwick, Nigg, Dunnichen, Aberlemno and Meigle.

This raises the large question of the Scottish relationships of the Irish crosses. We must obviously take into account here the background of the founding of Kells, from Iona, at the beginning of the ninth century. We are told in the *Annals of Ulster* that the monastery of Kells was founded in 804, nine years after the beginning of a series of destructive and deadly raids on the Columban metropolitan monastery of Iona. A great part of the Iona community moved in due course to Ireland, and inland to Kells, bringing with them the important relics of their founder.

Kells, we are told, was given to [the community of] Columba 'without battle'. This is a unique formula, and Françoise Henry suggested an ingenious emendation: 'without payment' (*sine pretio* instead of *sine proelio*). However, it may not be necessary to amend the text. If we consider the significance of Kells on the one hand and Iona on the other in terms of the Irish situation shortly after 800, we can see that 'without battle' may indeed be the correct reading.

Iona by 800 had long been a centre of major political importance as well as being, ecclesiastically, one of the most important powers in the Irish polity. Kells was a hill-fort and, according to historical legend, a royal site of great antiquity, formerly *Dún Chuile Sibhrinne*, later *Ceannanus*, then *Kenlis*, from which the anglicized form 'Kells' derives. *Dún Chuile Sibhrinne* was said to have been built by the mythological 'Golden-Age' king Fiacha Finnailches (whose death in battle, according to the chronologists of myth, occurred in 1209 BC). It is said to have been occupied by the legendary Cormac mac Airt, whose 'heroic biography' (studied by Tomás Ó Cathasaigh) was potent in its significance for the ancestral explanations of eighth- and ninth-century dynasts. (The Ciannachta, for example, who occupied the territory around the lower Boyne, were said to owe their lands to a gift from Cormac to their ancestor Tadhg son of Cian.) More importantly, perhaps, it had been occupied by the redoubtable sixth-century king Diarmait mac Cerbhaill. In the legendary history he figures as an adversary of Columba; but by the late seventh century Columba's successor Adhamhnán, abbot of Iona, reports that Diarmait had been 'ordained by the authority of God as ruler of all Ireland'. Adhamhnán, and the Iona authorities generally, were advocates of the accommodations between church and state that were to produce ordained or anointed kings in Western Europe. The first reliably documented of these is Áedán mac Gabráin, ordained in Scotland by Columba himself. Adhamhnán's description of Diarmait as King of Ireland by divine right must be regarded with skepticism. Diarmait, however, by Adhamhnán's time, had become an important ancestral figure, encrusted with legend. He was a major dynastic founder, having established the 'southern Uí Néill' dynasty in both its main rival lineages, through his sons Colmán Már and Áed Sláine. His own credentials as a 'descendant of Niall' may be spurious, but by 800 they had become part of established dynastic history. His son Áed Sláine, ancestor of Síl nÁedo Sláine, was associated in legend with the Kells hill-fort. And, by 800, Síl nÁedo Sláine, in the north-east midlands, had for three quarters of a century been eclipsed by Clann Cholmáin, in the south-west midlands.

The seventh century, at the end of which Adhamhnán wrote, had been turbulent with ecclesisatical power-struggles, but by its end accommodation was being reached between such important centres as Armagh, Kildare and Clonmacnoise. Armagh emerged to primacy and guided the attempts at church and state centralization. In 737 Cathal mac Finguine, King of Cashel, appears to have proclaimed the 'Law of Patrick' in Munster. He went on to make some sort of attempt at holding Tara as well as Cashel. He was, quite likely, an anointed king. Áed mac Néill, of Ailech, became King of Tara in 797 and was probably the first Uí Néill king to be ecclesiastically anointed (he came to be known as *Áed oirdnide*). This probably happened at the assembly, attended by the abbot of Armagh, at Dún Cuair, in 804, where Áed took the hostages of the Laigin, exempted clergy from military service, and plainly was attempting, hand-in-hand with the Church, to establish a central authority. Such attempts were a grievance to those who were, for the moment, at a disadvantage in the power-structure of the country and did not want to see it fixed by new arrangements – such dynasties as Síl nÁedo Sláine, for example.

In this context we can see that the intrusion of the politically skilled and powerful clerics of Iona into the midland-Ulster borderlands and into the sphere of influence of Armagh in 804 must have required negotiation. We may compare the handing over of Ceannanus to the Church with that dramatic gesture, hundreds of years later, by which Muirchertach ua Briain handed over the ancient Eoghanacht royal centre of Cashel to the Church in 1101. That the grant was made 'without battle' was worth recording. We may associate it with the plans of Áed Oirdnide who was attempting the founding of a new polity, that same year, at Dún Cuair, forty kilometres south of Kells on the border of Laigin. The hill-fort itself, no doubt, like Tara, had long been disused. The local chief at the time of the grant, Cathal son of Fiachra, of Feara-Cúl (the territory around Kells), appears to have had as his centre Raith Airthir, beside Tailtiu.

We are told that 68 persons were killed in a raid on Iona in 806, and the following year the new *civitas* was made at Kells. For the same year, 807, the Four Masters record the destruction of the church of Columcille at Kells – which may reflect some local resentments, although accidental fires were, of course, common. But the main move from Iona probably happened about then.

Áed Oirdnide's policy of centralization was by no means wholly successful – his reign was troubled by both secular and ecclesiastical conflicts – but a beginning had been made.

We have on the site of Kells itself a document of compromise. The south cross bears the inscription PATRICII ET COLUMBAE CRUX. If we bear in mind that, just over a century earlier, when Adhamhnán wrote his *Life of Columba*, the 'holy bishop Patrick' – who receives a passing mention – was quite peripheral to the concerns of Iona, we can appreciate that this inscription registers an agreement, or at least an understanding: Armagh's primacy is acknowledged. (The second colophon in the Book of Durrow may possibly have a similar purpose.) We may take the cross to be a monument erected very soon after the arrival of the Iona community – say, around 810–830.

Those who arrived to make a new ecclesiastical metropolis at Kells in the opening decades of the ninth century came from a cosmopolitan and sophisticated establishment which, for much more than a hundred years, had had far-flung connections and an artistic eclecticism resulting from contact with several different cultures. How much of this they brought with them it is difficult to say. The crosses on Iona display some of the eclecticism, and, if we take into account the wider artistic sphere of Iona, from the Inner Hebrides through Argyll and up the Great Glen to the Moray Firth, we find several distinct cross-forms, on which are combinations of motifs that shift kaleidoscopically.

On Iona, the surviving crosses tend towards the slab-like in their proportions. They have some ornamental motifs in common, but they vary considerably otherwise, and it is clear that different traditions of cross-design are represented. A common feature, however, is the combination of bosses with swarming serpents spiralling out from them that is so common in western Scotland. In its form and proportions (the almost top-heavy open-ringed head) and in the shape and disposition of its rivet-skeuomorphs, St John's Cross on Iona startlingly resembles the two crosses at Ahenny in south Tipperary. Only a little less startlingly, the resemblance may be found on the cross of Kildalton on Islay. Motifs most closely paralleled on the western Ossory group are to be found also on the unringed slab-cross at Kilnave on Islay, as well as on some fragments at Tarbat at the far end of the Great Glen.

These very small groups are characterized by, among other things, spiral patterns related to the classic trumpet-patterns of the earlier manuscript and metalworking traditions. In the classic trumpet-pattern, the strands springing from a spiral diverge until they are stopped at the characteristic lens-shape (the 'trumpet-mouth'), from which other strands converge to spin into a neighbouring spiral. This is found on both crosses at Ahenny and on the Kilkieran cross, but with a flattening of the lens which suggests a certain unhappiness with the motif on the part of the sculptors. The same revealing detail is found on a slab at Gallen in Offaly.

Elsewhere the lens is replaced, either by a ball or boss – as on the east face of the Kildalton cross and on the arms (west face) of the Cross of Patrick and Columba at Kells – or by a device somewhat resembling the scroll-joints often depicted on animal forms. This devolved trumpet-pattern with scroll-joints is found at Tybroughney, Dromiskin, Termonfechin, Drumcliff, Clonmacnoise (the South Cross), Kells (the Market Cross), Kinnitty and Tech Theille. It is a conservative suggestion that the full trumpet-pattern (with lens motif) is not found after 800.

The Cross of Patrick and Columba has three features which link it with Scotland: the seven-bossed roundel on the crossing; the Kildalton-like forms on the west face of the arms; and the inhabited vine motif (the Tree of Life), widespread in Northumbrian art. Otherwise, the cross appears to fit comfortably into the Irish tradition established, it would appear, by 800, in the area bounded by the Suir, the Barrow, the Shannon, and, roughly, the Ulster borderlands.

We must accept that the Irish-Scottish connection in the design and sculpture of high crosses was established, not through the foundation of Kells, but earlier, before 800, somewhere in that large area; that the most important axis for the development of the *shape* of the monuments was that between the Suir valley and the Inner Hebrides; that the diffusion of the iconography of the figure carving is almost certainly a good deal more complex, involving old traditions in different parts of Britain and Ireland, the circulation of manuscripts and small carvings such as ivory book-covers, and the movement of masons and sculptors with their templates and pattern-books.

It is possible that the free-standing ringed cross, of the distinctive Irish type, was evolved on Iona. St John's Cross there is the most thoroughgoing example of a great wooden construction sheeted with metal and elaborately ornamented, all translated into stone. And R.B.K. Stevenson has shown the background of joinery to the Iona crosses and pointed out that:

> The Iona artists, then, were eclectic at least to the extent of sometimes incorporating Northumbrian ideas and sometimes not, and could omit the 'Celtic' ring even when not copying completely the Nortumbrian shape ...

If the form was evolved on Iona, it remained virtually confined – in Scotland – to the immediate vicinity, while giving rise to a somewhat different type of monument – the slab, with a ringed cross in relief (which must obviously be secondary to the free-standing type) found widely in Pictland. But it is also possible that the type evolved on the slopes of Slievenamon in a group of obscure monasteries along the border between south-west Osraige and the northern marches of Déisi Mumhan.

Did stewards or emissaries from the Iona metropolis, on their business in Ireland, some time in the eighth century, come upon the two masterpieces of art at Ahenny and arrange for the craftsmen to come to their own Lhasa of the West? Or did sculptors from Iona, for some now obscure reason, arrive in the Suir valley, to construct monuments for monasteries of which we now know virtually nothing (or for a King of Osraige, aspiring to greatness)?

At any rate, once the form was evolved, it clearly had a stimulating effect on the stonecarvers, who were already skilled in fine work in parts of the country. There was an established school of carving along the lower Shannon, to which witness is borne by the earlier grave-slabs at Clonmacnoise, Gallen, and, perhaps, Inis Cealtra. There may have been a stone-carving tradition on the lower

Boyne and the middle Erne, although for the date in question this is not certain. It is not until about 800 that we can begin to discern clearly several sculptural traditions in parts of the country; and already by then these are interacting.

Bearing all this in mind, we can move forward half-a-century or so to look more closely at the two crosses with which we began. The occurrences and associations of three features common to the two crosses have been looked at: the 'split frame', the seven-bossed disc on the crossing, and the devolved trumpet-pattern. If we take into account all the other features of the two crosses, it soon emerges that there is a close relationship between them and the crosses of the lower Boyne valley – both the fully-figured monuments (very close) and (even closer) the style represented by the crosses of Duleek and Termonfechin. The figured Ulster crosses are somewhat less close. There is a remarkable lack of overall matching with either the Barrow or the west Ossory crosses, while the Clonmacnoise group, spatially so near, seems less close than the crosses of the Boyne. It is reasonably clear that the fully-figured crosses of Ulster, the Boyne area and the Clonmacnoise area, and the minimally-figured monuments at Termonfechin, Duleek, Tech Theille, Kinnitty (and Drumcullin and one or two other fragments might be added) are sub-groups of a fairly large stylistic group.

To develop the relationships within this group further we have available an alternative means of comparison between the Kinnitty Cross and the Cross of the Scriptures at Clonmacnoise – perhaps the most fully-figured of all the fully-figured crosses. The deficiency of the Cross of the Scriptures in abstract or decorative panels makes motif comparison somewhat difficult. But the inscriptions on it and at Kinnitty shed new light on the subject.

The texts on the two monuments may be compared:

Kinnitty: OR[OIT] DO RIG MAELSECH/NAILL M[AC] MAELRUANAID
Clonmacnoise: OR[OIT] DO RIG FLAIND M[AC] MA/... MAELSECHNAILL
Kinnitty: OROIT AR RIG HERENN
Clonmacnoise: O/ROIT DO RIG HERENN
Kinnitty: OR[OIT] DO COLMAN DORRO/... IN CROSSA AR RIG HERENN
Clonmacnoise: OR[OIT] DO COLMAN DORRO/... IN CROSSA AR/... RIG FLAIND
Kinnitty: OR[OIT] DO RIG HERENN
Clonmacnoise: (no equivalent).

We are certainly dealing with two works from the same atelier, and the evidence is persuasive that we are dealing with the same hand. The two crosses were made by Colmán, for two kings, father and son.

The minimum interval between the crosses is 17 years; the maximum is 70, since Maelsechnaill reigned from 846 to 862 and his son from 879 to 916. If the two works are from the same hand, 17 years is not an unreasonable period to allow for; 70 years is.

The value of the inscriptions we have on the crosses (including Muiredach's Cross at Monasterboice) is vitiated by the fact that, at the period, among both laity and clergy there was an abundance of Muiredachs and a superabundance of Colmáns. Not only was there a Colmán who was abbot of Clonmacnoise in the early tenth century, but there was a Colmán of Kinnitty who also died in the early tenth century. So it is just possible that we are dealing with two abbots Colmán. Since the Petrie reading of the Clonmacnoise text was accepted, it was assumed that the Colmán in the inscription was the abbot, who also collaborated with Flann Sinna in the building of the cathedral. But the plain sense of the inscriptions is that it was Colmán who *made* the crosses.

Similarly, with Muiredach's Cross at Monasterboice, we are not necessarily confined to the two known abbots Muiredach in looking for the person who, in this case 'had the cross made'. The other two inscriptions give us the names of kings as the patrons. *Muiredach* was quite a common kingly name, especially in the north, in the ninth century, as a glance through the annals will confirm.

In other words, all three crosses may be royal monuments. The Colmán of Clonmacnoise and Kinnitty was probably, not an abbot, but the artificer who made the crosses. Muiredach, the patron of the Monasterboice cross, may be, not an abbot, but a king. As it happens there is a royal Muiredach who reasonably fills the bill. He is Muiredach son of Cathal, King of Uí Cremthainn, who died, according to the *Annals of Ulster*, in 867. South of the Boyne mouth an ancient people, the Ciannachta, was dominated and absorbed by Síl nÁedo Sláine of the southern Uí Néill. North of the river, however, the Fir Ardda Ciannachta, as they were known (their territory is represented by the barony of Ferrard) retained some independence into the ninth century and had resisted an attempt by the King of Knowth to take them over. But they were inevitably involved in struggles for both secular and ecclesiastical power which in the ninth century engaged Síl nÁedo Sláine, Clann Cholmáin, the Ulaid, two main branches of the Airgialla (the Airthir and Uí Cremthainn), Cenél nEógain of the northern Uí Néill and, in some obscure way, the Vikings. Within the Airgialla, the Airthir, under Cenél nEógain dominance, obtained control of Armagh, ousting the rival Uí Cremthainn; but Uí Cremthainn seem to have gained a grip on some of Armagh's southerly dependencies, including for a time Monasterboice and its territory of Fir Ardda Ciannachta. Muiredach's son Cummascach is described as 'king of the people of Ard Ciannacht' in the *Annals of Ulster* when they record his death at the hands of the Ulaid in 896.

The most likely time for Maelsechnaill to have proclaimed his Kingship of Ireland on the cross he erected at Kinnitty was after his assembly at Rathugh in 859. Kinnitty is just on the frontier of Éile, and astride the route the Osraige were wont to take into Cenél Fiachach and Delbna Bethra in their expansionist raids. Similarly, the most likely moment for Flann to proclaim his kingship on a monument at Clonmacnoise (where his mother was buried in 888) was after he received the submission of the King of Connacht at Athlone in 897. An alternative, of course, would be just after his accession in 879 – which would make better sense of the stylistic evidence of the inscriptions. These questions must remain open for the moment; but the inscriptions give us a datum from which to work and add a political dimension to the study of early Irish sculpture which in turn may help to elucidate the whole subject.

32

Fauves and Peasants

At first sight, *Animals in Art and Thought* might seem a somewhat forced category for a major and comprehensive work. Do animals occupy so special a place in either art or thought as to justify singling them out and separating them from the mainstream of both? Is there sufficient continuity or consistency in the way people have looked at animals, or thought about them, to make a subject-matter – of animals in the human imagination – and to write a history?

It is one of the qualities of Francis Klingender's major, but unfinished, work that an affirmative answer emerges fairly clearly, although it is not a simple affirmation. Part of the reason, perhaps, is the very fact that the work was unfinished when Klingender died in 1955. The history was intended to continue down to the present century, but the notes which the author left on the Renaissance and onwards were so scrappy and incomplete that the editors felt it better to summarize them in a brief epilogue and to end the main text with the Middle Ages.

This gives a unity. Klingender discusses neither extra-European (Asian or African) art to any great extent, nor Greek and Hellenistic art in any depth. What he does is to demonstrate the continuity of barbarian art from early prehistoric times onwards, and its persistence of feeling. We are led through the shifts of meaning and significance from the early hunters' apprehension of the world down to that of medieval European man. It is only at this point, with the Renaissance, that we come to the beginning of a new, sentimental, sensibility which had only marginally affected European art in earlier times.

More important, perhaps, is Klingender's demonstration of the importance of animals in the imagination of so many centuries. That importance has been so much diminished, and so altered in emphasis, since the scientific revolution and the technological conquest of nature, that Klingender, had he continued the work as planned, would probably have found himself dealing with a different and less significant subject-matter. Animals do not play a large part either in the life or in the imagination of most people in our present urban world. We have reduced them to objects of sentimentality or to sources of a much less clearly defined guilt than that which our hunting ancestors knew.

Previously published in *Studio International*, London, March 1972.

The book shows us their ancient importance. At first they were man's equals, or betters, sharing the world with him, doomed with him to the same competitive violence, by which he and they must live, in which one species must prey upon another. We see them through the eyes of Palaeolithic hunters. Many of the cave paintings and engravings seem to modern sensibilities to be superb works of art. So perhaps they are. But closer examination shows us that the animals are seen with eyes which aimed neither at detached observation nor at capturing the beauty or the joy of animal life. They are seen with hunters' eyes. The selection, of angle, of colour, of subject, of mode of representation, shows us that we are looking at diagrams: how to kill; how to work magic to make the game fertile and plentiful; how to placate. Such paintings have a remote resemblance, in purpose, to those pleasant drawings one finds in cookery books and in butchers' shops, in which the body of an ox is shown divided up into areas marked 'rump', 'rib steak', and so on.

Klingender goes on, from an introduction which makes us aware of the over-whelming importance of animals in the early human imagination, to develop his theme in dealing with the complexity of agricultural-pastoral and urban societies. He touches here and there on the well-known lack of interest of settled peasant societies in representational art and their preference for an abstract linear ornament which we find equally in the earliest Neolithic cultures of Europe and in Indian villages of the present day. He shows this linear art being invaded by animal representations or animal ornament (about which he is particularly good), with the emergence of barbarian societies that were not composed of peasants and which established a dynamic and often hostile relationship with the growing urban civilizations of the East. He shows us the changing relationships of men and animals in the societies of the ancient world and the early Middle Ages, and the way in which animals became archetypes and potent symbols in mystical philosophy.

In all this, Klingender handles an enormous mass of material with great skill and accuracy. Had he completed and revised his work, he might have presented it differently, perhaps rearranging parts of it to bring out his main themes more clearly, making it less of a one-damned-thing-after-another kind of history. But the material is very solidly there, and his research was not only wide but refreshingly good at mastering all kinds of special fields.

Unfortunately the lapse of time since 1955 does make a difference. The whole perspective of the prehistoric and ancient world has shifted in these years, as new critical techniques eroded an old synthesis and as a new one slowly began to emerge. The book now seems old-fashioned in its historical approach. It seems old-fashioned in another way. Klingender, who was forty-seven when he died, came just at the end of those one or two generations of Westerners who treated the poetic intuitions of Freud and Marx as Revelation. It is through a familiar (to the point of contempt) and out-moded early-twentieth-century telescope that he looks at man's fate. This is not much more than to say that in reading *Animals in Art and Thought* one is conscious that one is not reading a work of the seventies. And the consciousness is connected with the fact that the book is essentially one of *ideas* – although these are based on a good deal of research. It stands, in character, somewhere between the work of Émile Mâle and that of André Malraux.

33

The Dressing of Stone

There is one technical detail which can often be observed in old buildings, where the stone has not been too much exposed to weathering, which is simple in itself, and which is yet of considerable interest and significance for social change. This is the dressing or tooling with which the wrought stonework is finished. It can be observed where the masonry has been sheltered, shaded or otherwise protected from the effects of rain and frost, as a distinctive pattern of marks left by the mason's implement and by his technique in using it.

For example, in every decorated Irish Romanesque building, without exception, where the tooling can still be discerned, it is of the same variety: diagonal axing, showing as a series of strokes, or surface cuts, each a few centimetres long, whose direction is diagonal in relation to the bedding of the stone. This is not remarkable in itself. It is the common finish for twelfth-century stonework in Western Europe, and indeed it continues as the normal finish to a considerably later date. As an indicator of change and innovation, however, it is of considerable interest in Ireland, since it appears to arrive as a new technique about AD 1100.

Earlier Irish churches, of the type which often have the projections – known as *antae* – of the side walls at the gable end, and also have stone-lintelled doorways with inward-inclined jambs, the normal finish of wrought work is quite different. It is a shallow pocking produced by hammer dressing, and it gives quite a different character to the masonry. Stonework dressed in this way could often be brought to a very fine and precise ashlar finish, and the quality of the work is such that even after a thousand years of weathering the joints often remain very close – they must originally have been all but invisible. There are many good examples of this fine shallow-pocked dressing on churches throughout the country. A particularly good example occurs on the doorway of the little church at Killulta, Co. Limerick, where the wrought masonry is of excellent quality. It may also be seen on stonework other than that of buildings. Querns or millstones seem to have been dressed by the same technique.

This finish is not confined to the primitive churches. It occurs on slightly more elaborate buildings, such as churches consisting of nave-and-chancel,

This appeared in the 'Roots' column in the *Irish Times* on 29 November 1972.

even with round arches, but without Romanesque ornament. In these the voussoirs which make up the chancel arch are commonly plain and square-cut. An example of such a church may be seen at Tully, Co. Dublin. The same pocked finish may be seen on other plain round arches, like the very fine ones which form the ancient gateway to Glendalough.

It would seem then that the use of the mason's axe came to Ireland not with the new developments which involved the addition of small chancels to the formerly simple single-celled little churches, nor with the use of the round arch as such, but with Romanesque ornament. The point is of more than passing interest, for, while a new style or ornament could conceivably be introduced to the country through the medium of sketches or pattern-books from which it might be copied by the native masons, a new tooling techique would seem to imply the arrival of foreign masons or, just possibly, the return of Irish ones who had been apprenticed abroad.

There is one fine series of monuments which appears to span the transition from one type of tooling to the other. Most of the Round Towers, which are sufficiently numerous to provide a good range for the study of such changes, seem to show the earlier, pocked, tooling, but some of them are dressed with the axe.

The towers were studied by Margaret Stokes, who arranged them in a typological series – according to the style of their masonry. Her chronology by masonry style is matched by the chronology as suggested by occasional references in the annals, or by the ornamental features sometimes found associated with these buildings. She distinguished four groups of Round Towers, through which a progression can be discerned from structures rather roughly constructed with unwrought stones (as at Scattery, or Castledermot) to those in which the masonry is of well-wrought, coursed, carefully shaped stones, which are sometimes fitted together with the interlocking joint of the kind called a 'joggle' (as at Ardmore). It is on the last two of her groups that diagonal axed masonry is found; but it does not occur on all towers of these groups. It can be seen however, on the Round Towers of Drumlane and Ardmore, and at St Finghin's at Clonmacnoise, among others.

The earliest building with diagonal tooling for which we have a date is in fact a Round Tower, O'Rourke's Tower at Clonmacnoise, which was finished, according to the annals, in 1124. This is built throughout of axed masonry. The Round Tower at Cashel, on the other hand, which is not very different in the style or quality of its workmanship, has pocked tooling as well as some axed. It may have been put up shortly after Muirchertach O'Brien gave Cashel to the Church in 1101.

With the change in technique there is also a fairly general, although not universal, change in the materials preferred by the masons. Most of the buildings on which the pocked or hammer dressing is used have their wrought features constructed in limestone. Sandstone clearly was preferred by the twelfth-century craftsmen who used the axe. So we have in this single small feature of a large group of Irish buildings – a feature which might well pass unnoticed – an indication of a social and cultural change which must in turn reflect many other social and cultural changes.

Diagonal axed tooling is confined neither to buildings in the Romanesque style nor to the twelfth century. It persists through the early Gothic work of the thirteenth and fourteenth centuries. Slight changes may be observed, however, even within this period of continued employment of the one technique. The width of the cut made by the axe seems to be less at the end of the period than at the beginning, suggesting that some modifications took place in the mason's implements over the span of about two hundred years.

But the technique persisted until and into the period of decining building activity in the fourteenth century. With the revival of architecture in Ireland shortly after about AD 1400, a completely new method of finishing wrought stone appears. And limestone again becomes the favoured medium for the stonecutters. Further changes can be observed down the years, not only in the more obvious decorative motifs and mouldings, but in the finish. It is often possible to place, even if roughly, an unornamented fragment of wrought stone in its context, and to say that it is eighteenth-century, or sixteenth-century, work, even though no trace remains other than the track of the stone-mason's hammer or chisel. And it is quite an interesting pastime to observe the changing modern techniques on well-dated series like the headstones in old country churchyards, and to realise that in small things as well as large an enduring mark can be made.

34

The Battle of Dysert

The visitor to Quin, County Clare, can inspect there the ruins of one of the best preserved of the late medieval friaries of the west of Ireland. It was built, or founded, by the MacNamaras for the Franciscan Friars Minor, and has an intact cloister, a full range of domestic buildings, and the slender tapering bell-tower which is so characteristic of these distinctive western Gothic buildings. It is in fact possible to climb the tower by a winding stair all the way to the corbie-stepped battlements. From here there is a view of a landscape on which the imprint of the later Middle Ages is still strong.

It is a landscape of low rolling hills, studded with the ruins of fortified tower houses; half a dozen may be seen from the friary belfry. The hills impede distant prospects, even from this elevation, but the direction of Limerick, away to the south-east, is revealed by the persistent cloud of smoke from the cement factory, just down-river from the city. A great forest once extended between Quin and Limerick, of which some traces remain around Cratloe. The view due south is towards the Shannon estuary. This is masked by the hills but as like as not an aircraft taking off or landing, over Bunratty, will indicate to the visitor on the tower the general direction of the great waterway. A few miles due west is the tower of Clareabbey; beyond that, a little northward, the town of Ennis, and beyond that again, to the north-west, the road winding up among small lakes towards the grey flags of the Burren.

In the immediate vicinity of the friary there are several items of interest to be observed. The friary tower overshadows another ruin, that of a late medieval parish church, just across a small stream to the west. In the fields around the friary, extending southward towards the modern village of Quin, can be seen the traces and outlines of buildings, fairly regularly arranged: there had once been a more extensive village or town here. And, most interesting of all, it is possible by leaning out between the battlements and peering down on the friary ruins themselves. to see the full outline of a square keepless castle, with four round bastion towers at the angles, on whose foundations and lower courses the Franciscan buildings were constructed. Closer examination of this feature, at ground level, shows that a strong Norman castle, of the distinctive

---

This was published in the *Irish Times* in the series 'Wars and Rumours'.

mid-thirteenth-century type, had been built here, but had then been 'slighted', leaving its massive walls standing only to about the height of a man.

All of this illustrates significant episodes in the history of medieval Clare. Thomond ('North Munster') which, in time, after the Anglo-Norman invasion, was reduced to approximately the extent of the present county of Clare, was the patrimony of the descendants of Brian Bóroimhe, the O'Briens. Their king at the time of the invasion, Domhnall Mór, had contrived in a career of highly opportunistic warfare and diplomacy to hold the country west of the Shannon against permanent Norman intrusion, but after his death things changed, although he was followed by able rulers. Domhnall himself had submitted to Henry II; his successors followed suit. These, in the thirteenth century, were involved, like all their kind, in wars and conflicts, on the one hand with dynastic rivals, on the other with the increasingly pressing Norman claims and attempts which arose from speculative land-grants. In Thomond, such claims and attempts were progressive after the death of Domhnall Mór, affecting initially the country west of Limerick along the north shore of the Shannon estuary. Settlement began here by the end of the twelfth century; Henry III made additional land-grants in the 1240s, and in 1276 Edward I granted all of Thomond to Thomas de Clare, brother of the Earl of Gloucester and descendant of Strongbow. Earlier grants had involved much of the south-eastern part of the modern county, and by the middle of the thirteenth century this region was being extensively settled and fortified by Norman grantees. By the end of the century, the area through which the road from Limerick to Shannon Airport now passes was being 'Normanized', much as south Kilkenny and south Wexford were, with Flemish and Welsh tenants being settled in farms and villages. Quin was taken by de Clare about the time of his grant of Thomond. It was he who built the great square castle; he also re-edified the church across the stream – St Finghin's Church, which was already there when he came in – and he held the town of Quin as a strong point on the road which led to Clonroad (Ennis) and the heart of Thomond. Bunratty, at the mouth of another stream which flowed into the Shannon, was his also; he rebuilt a castle there.

As happened elsewhere in the country, the Norman intrusion was partly impeded, partly assisted, by the political fragmentation of Gaelic Ireland, and by the incessant family feuds and wars arising from the native system of succession. Primogeniture was not practised in this system. Instead, the new ruler was selected from a small kin-group of eligible people. Although the system was being considerably modified by the later Middle Ages, it still led to contests, often bloody, which were literally fratricidal and internecine. Such a feud convulsed the O'Brien dynasty in the second half of the thirteenth century.

Conor O'Brien succeeded his father Donagh Cairbreach in 1242. In the 1250s he made war, successfully, on the Anglo-Normans in the Limerick area, but soon afterwards he was faced with an uprising led by rivals within Thomond. In 1286 he was ambushed and killed while on a punitive expedition, near Bell Harbour in north Clare, and he was buried in Corcomroe Abbey. His successor, Brian Ruadh was challenged by his nephew, Turlough. Brian Ruadh had entered on his rule warring against the Anglo-Normans, but he now welcomed the alliance of de Clare (who had just been granted Thomond) against Turlough. The alliance was not very successful, and de Clare treacherously murdered Brian Ruadh – an act which, even in a time of treachery and murder among the ruling families, was regarded as scandalous. He was seized while a guest of de Clare at Bunratty, dining at his table, and was dragged to death by horses, his head then being cut off and his mangled and mutilated corpse strung up by the heels. To add to the barbarity of the murder itself, the *Annals of Clonmacnoise* report that they had entered into a most solemn bond of alliance, swearing 'all the oaths of Munster, as bells, relics of the saints, and bachalls', mingling their blood in a vessel and dividing the Host between them at Mass.

Brian Ruadh's sons attacked and defeated de Clare at Quin (it was to prevent this happening again that, a year later, he began building his castle there), but Turlough also attacked de Clare and defeated him. Turlough succeeded in making himself King of Thomond, and the sons of Brian followed their father's example and entered again into the alliance with his murderer, de Clare. This led to the fiercest and bloodiest period of the feud, which culminated in the death of Brian Ruadh's son Donagh, by drowning in the Fergus, after a parley he was holding with Turlough broke up in a violent quarrel. Turlough then came to an arrangement with de Clare, whom he allowed to retain, for a yearly rent, the south-east Clare area. Turlough died in 1306, and his arrangement with the Norman broke down under his son and successor Donagh. Richard de Clare in 1311 returned to the alliance with the line of Brian Ruadh, supporting Brian's grandson, who was King of Thomond until 1313.

By 1317, the representative of the line of Brian Ruadh was Donagh son of Dónal. He was supported in his contest for the rule of Thomond by Richard de Clare, whose long-term aim was to secure his father's grant of the kingdom. The representative of the line of Turlough was his son Murtough, who also had Norman supporters – the de Burgos of Connacht and the Butlers. In the meantime, the whole balance in Ireland, such as it was at the beginning of the fourteenth century, had been upset by the large-scale invasion that brought the war of the Scots against Edward II across the Channel to Ireland. Edward Bruce, brother of the King of Scots who had defeated Edward at Bannockburn in 1314, landed at Larne in 1315 with a large army, and began ravaging the English areas of Ireland, in the process sparking off marginal conflicts.

In 1316, in an important battle at Athenry, William de Burgo and Richard de Bermingham defeated Felim O'Conor, King of Connacht. Donagh O'Brien, of the line of Brian Ruadh, supported Felim O'Conor and fought on the losing side. In 1317 he faced Diarmaid, brother of his rival Murtough, in another battle at Corcomroe. Here Donagh was defeated and killed. In the same year, Bruce's army had marched to Dublin, which he did not take, and then to Limerick, turning from there to march back to the north.

Murtough O'Brien, of the line of Turlough, now faced Richard de Clare, and the ensuing conflict concerned the destiny of Thomond, whether it would be another great Norman earldom or whether it would remain an O'Brien kingdom. This issue was decided in 1318.

Richard de Clare marched from Bunratty to Quin, and continued northward; then turned west, north of Ennis. On 10 May he entered the country of the O'Deas, north-west of Ennis, organising his force in three columns, of which he took the centre himself. Near Dysert O'Dea, the Normans came upon a detachment of horse and foot, part of the forces of Conor O'Dea, driving cattle acoss a stream. The Normans increased their pace, to seize the cattle, and O'Dea's people turned to face them, but then fell back, drawing them across two streams. A running fight ensued, and at a fairly early stage Richard de Clare was killed by O'Dea's men. The battle, however, became harder; the other two Norman columns rejoined the centre and pressed hard on O'Dea; but the forces of O'Hehir and of O'Conor of Corcomroe came up at a fast pace from the west to reinforce O'Dea. O'Conor of Corcomroe sought out the son of Richard de Clare and killed him. Murtough O'Brien and his men were some distance away, to the north-east, when the battle began. They made haste and arrived late in the day, crossing the Fergus and charging into the melée. At this the Normans broke.

The account written many years later by Seán MacCraith, *Caithréim Thoirdhealbhaigh*, recounts what happened after the fight:

> As for O'Brien and his people: with cutting down and expeditious slaying of their perpetual enemies, earnestly they follow the rout right into Bunratty of the spacious roads; and (a thing which never had happened) the manner in which he found the town before him was: deserted, empty, wrapped in fire. For upon his wife's and his household's receiving of the tidings that de Clare himself was killed, with one consent they betake them to their fast galleys and shove off on Shannon, taking with them the choicest of the town's wealth and valuable effects, and having at all points set in on fire. From which time to this, never a one of their breed has come back to look after it.

The long contest, culminating in the battle of Dysert, which settled the destiny of Clare for many years, was essentially a dynastic conflict among the O'Briens. It was the involvement of the de Clares in this conflict, together with their great misfortune at Dysert – that both father and son should be killed at a time when the whole country was disturbed and unstable – which led to the failure of the Anglo-Norman settlement in one corner of the island. And no two parts of Ireland have the same history of Norman settlement.

It is that failure that can be viewed, as it were, from the top of the tower of Quin. What difference it made, whether an area in the later Middle Ages was ruled by a Hiberno-Norman family or by an old Gaelic family, is another question. that it made *some* long-term cultural difference is probable, since, although the Norman-ruled areas were, many of them, notoriously Gaelic in language and custom, there was in them a strong admixture of French tradition which enriched and modified the native tradition. The different fortunes of different areas have added to the regional and local diversity of Ireland. For Clare, the decision was completed on 10 May 1318.

Index

There is variation in the forms of personal names in this collection, depending on the date of writing and the period being dealt with. Surnames appear in Ireland in the eleventh and twelfth centuries. Earlier names are indexed with the given name as the heading, e.g., 'Áed ua Conchubhair'. Later names are given with the surname as the heading, e.g., 'Ua Conchubhair, Ruaidhri'. Anglicized forms of Irish names are also employed: 'Mac Carthy' ('Mac Carthaigh'), 'O'Conor' ('Ua Conchubhair'), etc.